# DAILY MEDITATION

# By J. H. JOWETT, D.D.

The Whole Armour of God
  12mo, cloth.....................net $1.35

My Daily Meditation for the Circling Year.  12mo, cloth............net $1.35
  "There is something to think about each day. It is scriptural, spiritual, stimulating."
  —*Herald and Presbyter.*

Things That Matter Most
  Devotional Papers. A Book of Spiritual Uplift and Comfort. 12mo, cloth....net $1.35

The Transfigured Church
  A Portrayal of the Possibilities Within the Church. 12mo, cloth............net $1.35

The High Calling
  Meditations on St. Paul's Letter to the Philippians. 12mo, cloth...........net $1.35

The Silver Lining
  A Message of Hope and Cheer, for the Troubled and Tried. 12mo, cloth.....net $1.15

Our Blessed Dead
  16mo, boards....................net 25c

The Passion for Souls
  Devotional Messages for Christian Workers. 16mo, cloth....................net 60c

The Folly of Unbelief
  And Other Meditations for Quiet Moments. 12mo, cloth....................net 60c

## *SENTENCE PRAYERS for EVERY DAY*

The Daily Altar
  A Prayer for Each Day. Cloth.....net 25c
  Leather.........................net 35c

Yet Another Day
  A Prayer for Each Day. 32mo, cloth, net 25c
  Leather.........................net 35c
  A new large type edition. Cloth....net 75c
  Leather ........................net $1.00

# My Daily Meditation
## for the Circling Year

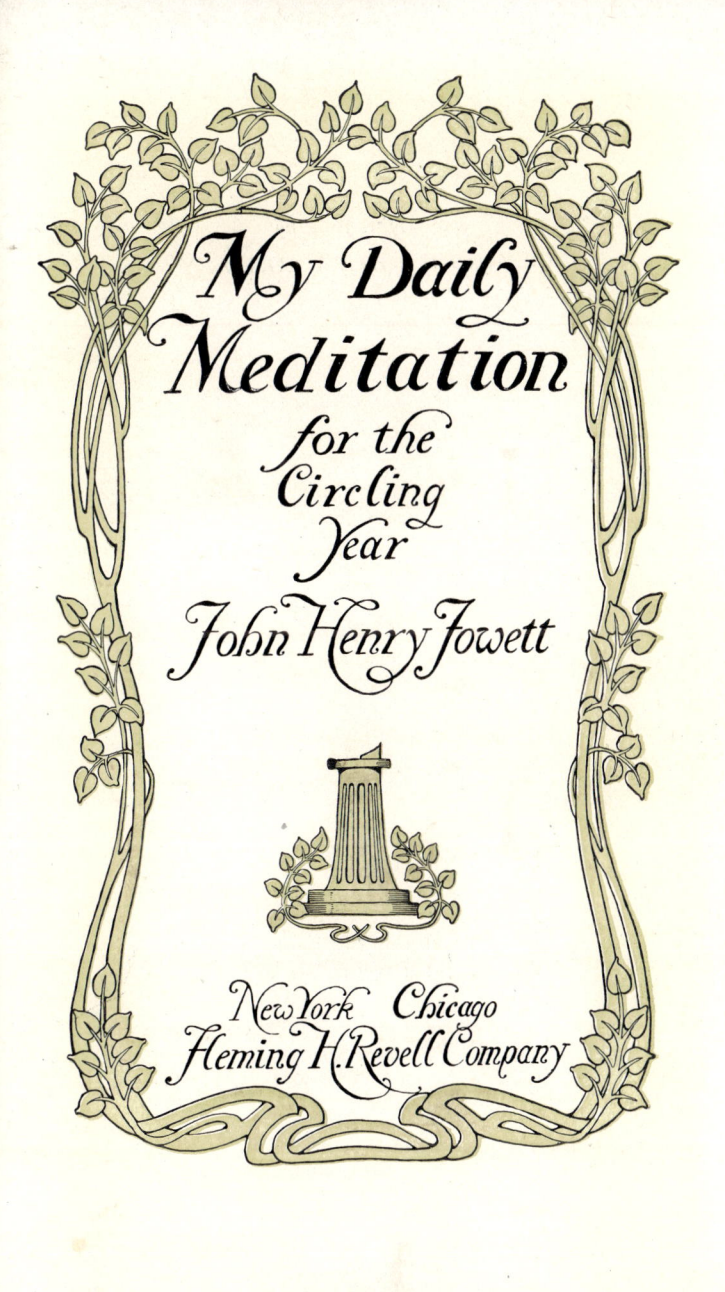

### John Henry Jowett

New York     Chicago
Fleming H. Revell Company

Copyright, 1914, by
FLEMING H. REVELL COMPANY

New York: 158 Fifth Avenue
Chicago: 125 N. Wabash Ave.
Toronto: 25 Richmond St., W.
London: 21 Paternoster Square
Edinburgh: 100 Princes Street

# FOREWORD

THE title of this book sufficiently interprets its purpose. I hope it may lead to such practical meditation upon the Word of God as will supply vision to common tasks, and daily nourishment to the conscience and will. And I trust that it may so engage the thoughts upon the wonders of meditation, as will fortify the soul for its high calling in Jesus Christ our Lord.

J. H. JOWETT.

Fifth Avenue Presbyterian Church,
New York.

# JANUARY The First

## THE UNKNOWN JOURNEY

*" He went out not knowing whither he went."*
—HEBREWS xi. 6-10.

ABRAM began his journey without any knowledge of his ultimate destination. He obeyed a noble impulse without any discernment of its consequences. He took " one step," and he did not " ask to see the distant scene." And that is faith, to do God's will here and now, quietly leaving the results to Him. Faith is not concerned with the entire chain; its devoted attention is fixed upon the immediate link. Faith is not knowledge of a moral process; it is fidelity in a moral act. Faith leaves something to the Lord; it obeys His immediate commandment and leaves to Him direction and destiny.

And so faith is accompanied by serenity. " He that believeth shall not make haste "—or, more literally, " shall not get into a fuss." He shall not get into a panic, neither fetching fears from his yesterdays nor from his to-morrows. Concerning his yesterdays faith says, " Thou hast beset me behind." Concerning his to-morrows faith says, " Thou hast beset me before." Concerning his to-day faith says, " Thou hast laid Thine hand upon me." That is enough, just to feel the pressure of the guiding hand.

## THE LARGER OUTLOOK
### Genesis xv. 5-18.

"AND He brought him forth abroad, and said, Look now toward heaven!" The tent was changed for the sky! Abraham sat moodily in his tent: God brought him forth beneath the stars. And that is always the line of the Divine leading. He brings us forth out of our small imprisonments and He sets our feet in a large place. He desires for us height and breadth of view. For "as the heavens are high above the earth" so are His thoughts higher than our thoughts, and His ways than our ways. He wishes us, I say, to exchange the tent for the sky, and to live and move in great, spacious thoughts of His purposes and will.

How is it with our love? Is it a thing of the tent or of the sky? Does it range over mighty spaces seeking benedictions for a multitude? Or does it dwell in selfish seclusion, imprisoned in merely selfish quest? How is it with our prayers? How big are they? Will a tent contain them, or do they move with the scope and greatness of the heavens? Do they just contain our own families, or is China in them, and India, and "the uttermost parts of the earth"? "Look now towards the heavens!" Such must be our outlook if we are the companions of God.

## JANUARY The Third

### *THE NEVER-FAILING SPRINGS*
#### Genesis xvii. 1-8.

"I WILL establish My covenant." The good promises of God are never revoked. They are like springs which know no shrinking in times of drought. Nay, in time of drought they reveal a richer fulness. The promises are confirmed in the hour of my need, and the greater my need the greater is my bounty. And so it was that the Apostle Paul came to " rejoice in his infirmities," for through his infirmities he discovered the riches of Divine grace. He brought a bigger pitcher to the fountain, and he always carried it away full. "As thy days so shall thy strength be."

So I need never fear that the promise of yesterday will exhaust itself before to-morrow. God's covenant goes with us like the ever-fresh waters of the wilderness. " They drank of that rock which followed them, and that rock was Christ." Every fulfilment of God's promise is the pledge of one to come.

God has no road without its springs. If His path stretches across the waste wilderness the " fountains shall break out in the desert," and " the wilderness shall rejoice and blossom as the rose."

## THE GOD OF THEIR SUCCEEDING RACE

Exodus vi. 2-8.

"I APPEARED unto Abraham... I will be to you a God." The covenant made with the father was renewed to the children. The father's death did not disannul the promise of the Lord. Death has no power in the realms of grace. His moth and his rust can never destroy the ministries of Divine love. Abraham died and was laid to rest, but the river of life flowed on, and the bounties of the Lord never failed. The village well quenches the thirst of many generations: and so is it through the generations with the wells of grace and salvation. The villagers have not to dig a new well when the patriarch dies: "the river of God is full of water."

And thus I am privileged to share the spiritual resources of Abraham, and the still richer resources of the Apostle Paul. Nothing was given to him that is withheld from me. He is like a great mountaineer, and he has climbed to lofty heights; but I need not be dismayed. All the strength that was given to him, in which he reached those lofty places, is mine also. I may share his elevation and his triumph. "For the promise is unto you and your children, and to all that are afar off."

## JANUARY The Fifth

*THE FLOWERS THAT NEVER FADE*
### 1 Peter i. 1-9.

"AN inheritance incorruptible." I am writing these words in the Island of Arran. To-morrow I shall leave the land behind, but I shall take the landscape with me! It will be with me in the coming winter, and I shall gaze upon Goat Fell in the streets of New York. The land is a temporary possession, the landscape abides!

The praise of men often dies with the shout that proclaims it. Another idol appears and the feverish worship is transferred to him. The world's garland begins to fade as soon as it is laid upon the brow. The morning after the coronation I possess a handful of withering leaves. But the garland of God's praise acquires new grace and beauty with the years. It is never so fresh and flourishing as just when everything else is fading away. It is glorious in the hour of death! The soul goes, wearing her garland, into the presence of the gracious Lord who gave it.

We can begin even now to wear the flowers of Paradise. We can begin even now to furnish our minds with lovely thoughts and memories. We can have "the mind of Christ."

## "COUNT YOUR BLESSINGS"

Psalm cv. 1-15.

"COUNT your blessings!" Yes, but over what area shall I look for them? There is my personal life. Let me search in every corner. I have found forget-me-nots on many a rutty road. I have found wild-roses behind a barricade of nettles. Professor Miall has a lecture on "The Botany of a Railway Station." He found something graceful and exquisite in the midst of its soot and grime. So I must look even in the dark patches of life, among my disappointments and defeats, and even there I shall find tokens of the Lord's presence, some flowers of His planting.

And there is my share in the life of the nation. "Ye seed of Abraham His servant, ye children of Jacob His chosen." There are hands that stretch out to me from past days, laden with bequests of privilege and freedom. Our feet "stand in a large place," and the place was cleared by the fidelity and the courage of the men of old. I have countless blessings that were bought with blood. The red marks of sacrifice are over all my daily ways. Let me not take the inheritance and overlook the blood marks, and stride about as though it were nought but common ground. Mercies abound on every hand! "Count your blessings!"

## JANUARY The Seventh

### A JOURNAL OF MERCIES
NEHEMIAH ix. 6-11.

"THOU hast performed Thy words: for Thou art righteous." Frances Ridley Havergal kept a journal of mercies. She had a record book, and she crowded it with her remembrances of God's goodness. She was always on the look-out for tokens of the Lord's grace and bounty, and she found them everywhere. Everywhere she had communion with a covenant-keeping God. The Bible became to her more and more the history of her own life and experience. Promise after promise told the story of her own triumphs. She appropriated the goodness of God, and she set her own seal to the testimony that God is true.

Many a complaining life would be changed into music and song by a journal of mercies. Many a fear can be dispersed by a ready remembrance. Memory can be made the handmaid of hope. Yesterday's blessing can kindle the courage of to-day. That is the purposed ministry of "the days that have been." We are to harness the strength of their experiences to the tasks and burdens of to-day; and in the remembrance of God's providences we shall march through our difficulties with singing.

## JANUARY The Eighth

### *HE IS FAITHFUL!*
1 Kings viii. 54-61.

"THERE hath not failed one word of all His good promise." Supposing one word had failed, how then? If one golden promise had turned out to be counterfeit, how then? If the ground had yielded anywhere we should have been fearful and suspicious at every part of the road. If the bell of God's fidelity had been broken anywhere the music would have been destroyed. But not one word has failed. The road has never given way in time of flood. Every bell of heaven is perfectly sound, and the music is full and glorious. "God is faithful, who also will do it."

"God is love," and "love never faileth." The lamp will not die out at the midnight. The fountain will not fail us in the wilderness. The consolations will not be wanting in the hour of our distresses. Love will have "all things ready." "He has promised, and shall He not do it?" All the powers of heaven are pledged to the fulfilment of the smallest word of grace. We can never be deserted! "God cannot deny Himself." Every word of His will unburden its treasure at the appointed hour, and I shall be rich with the strength of my God.

## JANUARY The Ninth

### THE PERILS OF POSSESSIONS
GENESIS xiii. 1-9.

THERE is nothing more divisive than wealth. As families grow rich their members frequently become alienated. It is rarely, indeed, that love increases with the increase of riches. Luxurious possessions appear to be a forcing-bed in which the seeds of sleeping vices waken into strength. For one thing, selfishness is often quickened with success. Plenty, as well as penury, can "freeze the genial currents of the soul." And with selfishness comes a whole brood of mean and petty dispositions. Envy comes with it, and jealousy, and a morbid sensitiveness which readily leaps into strife.

So do our possessions multiply our temptations. So does the bright day "bring forth the adder." So do we need extra defences when "fortune smiles upon us." But our God can make us proof against "the fiery darts" of success. Abram remained unscathed in "the garish day." The Lord delivered him from "the destruction that wasteth at noonday." His wealth increased, but it was not allowed to force itself between his soul and God. In the midst of all his prosperity, he dwelt in "the secret place of the Most High," and he abode in "the shadow of the Almighty."

## JANUARY The Tenth

### THE LUST OF THE EYE
#### Genesis xiii. 10-18.

LOOK at Lot. He was a man of the world, sharp as a needle, having an eye to the main chance. He boasted to himself that he always "took in the whole situation." He said that what he did not know was not worth knowing. But such "knowing" men have always very imperfect sight. Lot saw "all the well-watered plain of Jordan," but he overlooked the city of Sodom and its exceedingly wicked and sinful people. And the thing he overlooked was the biggest thing in the outlook! It was to prove his undoing, and to bring his presumptuous selfishness to the ground.

Look at Abram. His spirit was cool and thoughtful, unheated by the feverish yearning after increased possessions. He had a "quiet eye," the fruit of his faithful communion with God. He was more intent on peace than plenty. He preferred fraternal fellowship to selfish increase. And so he chose the unselfish way, and along that way he discovered the blessing of God. "The Lord is mindful of His own. He remembereth His children." In the unselfish way we always enjoy the Divine companionship, and in that companionship we are endowed with inconceivable wealth.

## JANUARY The Eleventh

### SELF-MADE OR GOD-MADE
MATTHEW vi. 26-33.

THINK of Lot and then think of a lily of the field! Think of the feverishness of the one and of the serenity of the other, or think of the ugly selfishness of the one, and of the graceful beauty of the other! Look upon avarice at its worst, upon a Shylock, and then gaze upon a lily of the field! How alarming is the contrast! The one is self-made, guided by vicious impulses; the other is the handiwork of God. The one is rooted in self-will; the other is rooted in the power of the Divine grace. God has nothing to do with the one; He has everything to do with the other. So one becomes "big" and ugly; the other grows in strength and beauty.

Now the wonder is this, that we, too, may be rooted in the power from which the lily draws its grace. We may draw into our souls the wealth of the Eternal, even the unsearchable riches of Christ. We may put on "the beauty of holiness." We may become clothed in the graces of the Spirit. When we are in the field of the lilies we may appear unto the Lord as kindred flowers of His own garden.

"He that abideth in Me and I in him the same bringeth forth much fruit." "Rooted in Him," we shall "grow up in all things unto Him."

## JANUARY The Twelfth

### TWO OPPOSITES

"*If any man love the world, the love of the Father is not in him.*"—1 JOHN ii. 13-17.

NO man can love two opposites any more than he can walk in contrary directions at the same time. No man can at once be mean and magnanimous, chivalrous and selfish. We cannot at the same moment dress appropriately for the arctic regions and the tropics. And we cannot wear the habits of the world and the garments of salvation. When we try to do it the result is a wretched and miserable compromise. I have seen a shopkeeper on the Sabbath day put up one shutter, out of presumed respect for the Holy Lord, and behind the shutter continue all the business of the world! That one shutter is typical of all the religion that is left when a man " loves the world " and delights in its prizes and crowns. His religion is a bit of idle ritual which is an offence unto God!

So I must make my choice. Shall I travel north or south? Which of the two opposites shall I love—God or the world? Whichever love I choose will drive out and quench the other. And thus if I choose the love of God it will destroy every worldly passion, and the river of my affections and desires will be like " the river of water of life, clear as crystal."

## JANUARY The Thirteenth

### THE MIRACLE IN A DRY PLACE
Psalm cvii. 33-43.

"HE turneth . . . the dry ground into water-springs." This is one of the miracles of grace. The good Lord makes a dry experience the fountain of blessing. I pass into an apparently waste place and I find riches of consolation. Even in "the valley of the shadow" I come upon "green pastures" and "still waters." I find flowers in the ruts of the hardest roads if I am in "the way of God's commandments." God's providence is the pioneer of every faithful pilgrim. "His blessed feet have gone before." What I shall need is already foreseen, and foresight with the Lord means forethought and provision. Every hour gives the loyal disciples surprises of grace.

Let me therefore not fear when the path of duty turns into the wilderness. The wilderness is as habitable with God as the crowded city, and in His fellowship my bread and water are sure. The Lord has strange manna for the children of disappointment, and He makes water to "gush forth from the rock." Duty can lead me nowhere without Him, and His provision is abundant both in "the thirsty desert and the dewy mead." There will be a spring at the foot of every hill, and I shall find "lilies of peace" in the lonely valley of humiliation.

## JANUARY The Fourteenth

### FORGETTING GOD
Deuteronomy viii. 11-20.

"BEWARE . . . lest when thou hast eaten and art full . . . thine heart be lifted up, and thou forget the Lord thy God." I was in a little cottage near Warwick. I said to the good man who lived in it, "Can you see the castle?" and he replied, "We can see it best in the winter when the leaves are off the trees. In the summer time it is apt to be hid!" The summer bounty hid the castle; the winter barrenness revealed it! And so it is in life. In the season of fulness we are prone to be blind to "the house of many mansions," and we forget the Master of the house, the Lord our God. Our material wealth hides our eternal treasure.

What, then, shall we do in the days of our prosperity, when all our trees are in full leaf? We must pray that material things may never become opaque, that they may be always transparent, so that through the seen we may behold the unseen. This is a gift of the Spirit, and it may be ours. He will anoint our eyes with the eye-salve of grace, and everything will become to us a symbol of something better, so that even in the midst of material plenty our hearts will be with our treasure in heaven. Everything will be to us "as it were transparent glass."

## JANUARY The Fifteenth

### THE MINISTRY OF PRAISE
#### Psalm cxv.

"THE Lord hath been mindful of us: He will bless us." In that joyful assurance there is both retrospect and prospect. There is the trodden pathway of Providence, and there is the star of hope! The eyes are steadied and refreshed in sacred memories, and then they gaze into the future with serene and happy confidence. And so the Ebenezer of the soul becomes both a thanksgiving and a reconsecration.

Now perhaps our hopes are thin because our praises are scanty. Perhaps our expectations are clouded because our memories are dim. There is nothing so quickens hope as a journey among the mercies of our yesterdays. The heart lays aside its fears amid the accumulated blessings of our God. Worries pass away like cloudlets in the warmth of a summer's morning. And the recollections of God's goodness always make summer even in the wintriest day.

Now I see why the New Testatment is so urgent in the matter of praise. Without praise many other virtues and graces cannot be born. Without praise they have no breath of life. Praise quickens a radiant company of heavenly presences, and among them is the shining spirit of hope.

## JANUARY The Sixteenth

### THE DISTINCTION OF BEING RECOGNIZED

JOHN x. 1-18.

THE Good Shepherd knows His sheep, and knows them by name. And that is what I am tempted to forget. I think of myself as one of an innumerable multitude, no one of whom receives personal attention. "My way is overlooked by my God." But here is the evangel—the Saviour would miss me, even me!

At a great orchestral rehearsal, which Sir Michael Costa was conducting, the man who played the piccolo stayed his fingers for a moment, thinking that his trifling contribution would never be missed. At once Sir Michael raised his hand, and said: "Stop! Where's the piccolo?" He missed the individual note. And my Lord needs the note of my life to make the music of His Kingdom, and if the note be absent He will miss it, and the glorious music will be broken and incomplete.

There is a common vice of self-conceit, but there is also a common vice of excessive self-depreciation. "My Lord can do nothing with me!" Yes, my Lord knows thee and needs thee! And by the power of His grace thou canst accomplish wonders!

## JANUARY The Seventeenth

### SPIRITUAL DISCERNMENT
*"My sheep hear My voice!"*—JOHN x. 19-30.

THIS is spiritual discernment. We may test our growth in grace by our expertness in detecting the voice of our Lord. It is the skill of the saint to catch "the still small voice" amid all the selfish clamours of the day, and amid the far more subtle callings of the heart. It needs a good ear to catch the voice of the Lord in our sorrows. I think it requires a better ear to discern the voice amid our joys! The twilight helps me to be serious; the noonday glare tends to make me heedless.

*"And they follow Me!"* Discernment is succeeded by obedience. That is the one condition of becoming a saint—to follow the immediate call of the Lord. And it is the one condition of becoming an expert listener. Every time I hear the voice, and follow, I sharpen my sense of hearing, and the next time the voice will sound more clear.

*"And I give unto them eternal life."* Yes, life is found in the ways of a listening obedience. Every faculty and function will be vitalized when I follow the Lord of life and glory. "In Christ shall all be made alive."

My Saviour, graciously give me the listening ear! Give me the obedient heart.

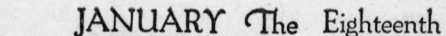

## *FALSE SHEPHERDS*
### Ezekiel xxxiv. 1-10.

THIS word of the Lord puts before me the unlovely lineaments of the false shepherds.

They are self-seeking. They "*feed themselves,*" but they "*feed not the flock.*" They take up religion for what they can make out of it! It is a carnal ambition, not a holy service. It is used for getting, not for giving, for self-glorification and not for self-sacrifice. It is selfishness masquerading as holiness, the thief in the garb of the shepherd.

And, therefore, the false shepherds are devoid of sympathy. "*The diseased have ye not strengthened, neither have ye healed that which was sick.*" Selfishness always tends to benumbment. Humaneness is fostered by sacrifice. Our sympathetic chords are kept refined by chivalrous deeds. Drop the deeds and all our refinements begin to coarsen, and we make no response to our brother's cries of need and pain.

And because there is no sympathy there is no quest. "*My sheep wandered . . . and none did seek after them.*" How can we seek them if we have never missed them, if we have no sense that they are lost? Our Lord came in travail of soul to "seek that which was lost." And I must share His travail if I would share in the search.

## JANUARY The Nineteenth

### THE LOST SHEEP
#### Ezekiel xxxiv. 11-19.

AND now, again, I am bidden to contemplate the gracious ministries of the Good Shepherd.

The Good Shepherd searches the "far country" for His lost sheep. *"I will bring them . . . out of all places where they have been scattered."* He goes into the hard wilderness of cold indifference, and wasteful pride, and desolating sin, searching "high and low" for His foolish sheep. And no place is unvisited by the Great Seeker! Every perilous ravine, where a sheep can be lost, knows the footprints of the Shepherd. And He knows my far-country, and He is seeking me!

And the Good Shepherd brings His wandering sheep back home. *"I will bring them . . . to their own land."* We return from the land of pride to the home of lowliness, from hard indifference to gracious sympathy, from the barrenness of sin to the beauty of holiness. We come back to God's beautiful "lily-land" of eternal light and peace.

And what nutriment the Good Shepherd provides for the home-coming sheep! *"I will feed them in a good pasture."* Our wasted powers shall be renewed and strengthened by the fattening diet of grace. Love shall be both host and meat! "He will satisfy thy mouth with good things."

## THE PASSING OF THE BEAST
### Ezekiel xxxiv. 23-31.

WHEN the Good Shepherd has charge of His flock *"the wild beasts will cease out of the land."* All beastly passions shall be destroyed. The fair gardens of our souls shall no longer be ravaged by sleek pride, or fierce appetite, or ravenous lust. "Thou shalt tread upon the lion and the adder, the young lion and the dragon shalt thou trample under feet."

And the forces of nature shall be in friendly co-operation. *"I will cause the shower to come down in his season."* We are to have mystic allies in sky and field. Nature sides with the man who sides with God. Our very garden becomes our helpmeet when we are cultivating the fruits of the Spirit. The heavens assume a friendly aspect when we are "marching to beautiful Zion." But when we are against the Lord all these forces appear to be hostile. "The stars in their courses fought against Sisera."

And we are to have a joyful assurance of the companionship of our God. *"This shall they know, that I, the Lord their God, am with them."* And in that precious assurance every other treasure is found! Only be sure of that, and we shall walk about as kings and queens!

## THE VALUE OF ONE SOUL
### Matthew xviii. 7-14.

WHAT an infinite value the Lord attaches to one soul! "And *one of them* be gone astray!" I thought He might never have missed the one! And yet the Eastern shepherd says that out of his great flock he can miss the individual face. A face is missing, as though a child were absent from the family circle. When a soul is wandering in the far country there is an awful gap in the Father's house! Is thy place empty? Is mine?

And mark the pangs of the Shepherd's quest. He *"goeth into the mountain and seeketh!"* The Eastern shepherd goes out in tempest, and in rocky ravine, or in thorny scrub that tears the hands and feet, he seeks and finds his sheep. And my Lord sought me, in stony and thorny places, in the darkness of Gethsemane, and in the awful desolations of The Hill.

And the Shepherd found His sheep, and He returns across the hills singing the song of the triumph of grace—

"And up from the mountains, thunder-riven,
  And up from the rocky steep,
A cry arose to the gates of heaven,
  'Rejoice! I have found My sheep!'
And the angels echo around the throne,
  'Rejoice! for the Lord brings back His own!'"

## JANUARY The Twenty-second

### MY OWN SHEPHERD
#### Psalm xxiii.

HOW shall we touch this lovely psalm and not bruise it? It is exquisite as "a violet by a mossy stone!" Exposition is almost an impertinence, its grace is so simple and winsome.

There is the ministry of rest. "*He maketh me to lie down in green pastures.*" The Good Shepherd knows when my spirit needs relaxation. He will not have me always "on the stretch." The bow of the best violin sometimes requires to have its strings "let down." And so my Lord gives me rest.

And there is the discipline of change. "*He leadeth me in the paths of righteousness.*" Those strange roads in life, unknown roads, by which I pass into changed circumstances and surroundings! But the discipline of the change is only to bring me into new pastures, that I may gain fresh nutriment for my soul. "Because they have no changes they fear not God."

And there is "*the valley of the shadow,*" cold and bare! What matter? He is there! "I will fear no evil." What if I see "no pastures green"? "Thy rod and Thy staff they comfort me!" The Lord, who is leading, will see after my food. "Thou preparest a table before me in the presence of mine enemies." I have a quiet feast while my foes are looking on!

## JANUARY The Twenty-third

### *THE GIVER'S HAND*
#### Genesis iv. 3-15.

CAIN and Abel both brought an offering unto the Lord, but one was accepted and the other rejected. It is the giver who determines the worth or the worthlessness of the gift. God looks not at the gift, but at the hand that brings it. "Your hands are full of blood!" "Your hands are unclean!" The Lord demands "clean hands." He will not have our compliments if there is defilement behind them. Our courtesies are rejected if iniquity attends them. The shining gloss on the linen is an offence if the dirt looks through! Who cares for food if presented by unclean hands? "Be ye clean, ye that bear the vessels of the Lord!"

Every gift is welcome to the Lord if offered with clean hands. A mite, or a cup of cold water, or our daily labour, or the first-fruits of garden or field—all receive the blessing of our God if the hands that bring them are free from defilement. So is it with everything we offer to the Lord. A song of praise makes sweet music in the hearing of our God if it come from pure lips! Purity, as Thomas a' Kempis says, gives the wings which carry everything into the Father's presence.

## THE VOICE OF THE DEAD
### Hebrews xi. 1-6.

WITH what voice shall we speak when we are dead? What will men hear when they turn their thoughts toward us? What part of us will remain alive, singing or jarring in men's remembrance? It is the biggest part of us that retains its voice. In some it is wealth, in others it is goodness; some go on speaking in their cruelty, others in their gentleness. Cain still speaks in his jealous passion. Abel speaks in his faith. Dorcas speaks in her "good works and alms-deeds which she did"; Judas Iscariot speaks in his betrayal. Yes, something goes on speaking. What shall it be?

But these biggest things not only continue to speak in the ears of memory, they persist as actual forces in the common life of men. Our faith is not buried with our bones, nor is our avarice or pride. Our characters do not die when our hearts cease to beat. "The evil that men do lives after them," and so does the good. But deeper than our deeds, our dominant dispositions persist and mingle as friends or enemies in the lives of others. By them we, being dead, still speak, and we speak in subtle forces which aid or hinder other pilgrims who are fighting their way to God and heaven.

## JANUARY The Twenty-fifth

### FIRST, MY BROTHER!
#### Matthew v. 17-24.

"FIRST be reconciled to thy brother." We are to put first things first. When we bring a gift unto the Lord He looks at the hand that brings it. If the hand is defiled the gift is rejected. "Wash you, make you clean." "First be reconciled to thy brother, and then come and offer thy gift."

All this tells us why some resplendent gifts are rejected, and why some commonplace gifts are received amid heavenly song. This is why the widow's mite goes shining through the years. The hand that offered it was hallowed and purified with sacrifice. Shall we say that in that palm there was something akin to the pierced hands of the Lord? The mite had intimate associations with the Cross.

And it also tells me why so much of our public worship is offensive to our Lord. We come to the church from a broken friendship. Some holy thing has been broken on the way. Someone's estate has been invaded, and his treasure spoiled. Someone has been wronged, and God will not touch our gift. "Leave there thy gift; first be reconciled to thy brother."

## JANUARY The Twenty-sixth

### THE FIRE OF ENVY

*"Where envying and strife is, there is confusion and every evil work."*—JAMES iii. 13-18.

IN Milton's "Comus" we read of a certain potion which has the power to pervert all the senses of everyone who drinks it. Nothing is apprehended truly. Sight and hearing and taste are all disordered, and the victim is all unconscious of the confusion. The deadly draught is the minister of deceptive chaos.

And envy is like that potion when it is drunk by the spirit. It perverts every moral and spiritual sense. The envious is more fatally stricken than the blind. He gazes upon untruth and thinks it true. He looks upon confusion and thinks it order. Envy is colour-blind. It is like jealousy, of which it is a blood-relation. It never sees anything in its natural hues. It misinterprets everything.

No one can quench the unholy fire of envy but the mighty God Himself. It is like a prairie fire: once kindled it is beyond our power to stamp it out. But God's coolness is more than a match for all our feverish heat. His quenchings are transformations. He converts the perverted and changes envy into goodwill. The bitter pool is made sweet. For confusion He gives order, for ashes He gives beauty, and in the face of an old enemy we see the countenance of a friend.

## THE CONFESSION OF SIN

*"I acknowledge my transgressions; and my sin is ever before me."*—PSALM li. 1-12.

SIN that is unconfessed shuts out the energies of grace. Confession makes the soul receptive of the bountiful waters of life. We open the door to God as soon as we name our sin. Guilt that is penitently confessed is already in the "consuming fire" of God's love. When I "acknowledge my sin" I begin to enter into the knowledge of "pardon, joy, and peace." But if I hide my sin I also hide myself from "the unsearchable riches of Christ." "If we confess our sins He is faithful and just to forgive us our sins and to cleanse us from all unrighteousness."

I must then make confession of sin in my daily exercises in the presence of the Lord. I am taking the way to recovered victory when I tell the Lord the story of my defeat. Satan strengthens his awful chains when he can induce me to keep silence concerning my sin. All his plans are thrown into confusion as soon as I "pour out my soul before the Lord." When I fall let me not add to my guilt the further sin of secrecy. Unconfessed sin breeds in its lurking-place and multiplies its hateful offspring. The soul that makes confession is washed through and through, and the seeds of iniquity are driven out of my soul.

## CLEAN AND UNCLEAN ANGER
### Ephesians iv. 25-32.

"LET all anger be put away from you." And yet only a moment ago the Apostle had written the words, "Be ye angry and sin not." My power of anger is not to be destroyed, it is to be transformed and purified. Anger can be like an unclean bonfire; it can also be like "a sea of glass mingled with fire." There can be more smoke than light in it, more selfish passion than holy purpose. The fuel that feeds it may be envy, and jealousy, and spite, and not a big desire for the good of men and the glory of God. Worldly anger "is set on fire of hell"; holy anger borrows flame from the altar-fires of God.

Our anger reveals our character. What is the quality of our anger? What kindles it? Is it incited by our own wrongs or by the wrongs of another? Is it set on fire by self-indulgence or by a noble sympathy? Here is a sentence which describes the anger of the Apostle Paul: "Who is made to stumble and I burn not?" Paul's holy anger was made to burn by oppression, by the cruelty inflicted upon his fellow-men. His fire had nothing unclean in it; it was pure as the flame of oxygen.

This is the anger we must cherish. We cannot "work ourselves up" into it. We must seek to be "baptized with the Holy Ghost *and with fire.*"

## JANUARY The Twenty-ninth

### NOBLE REVENGE

*"I have delivered him that without cause is mine enemy."*—PSALM vii. 4.

THAT is the noblest revenge, and in those moments David had intimate knowledge of the spirit of his Lord. "If thine enemy hunger, feed him!"

*Evil for good is devil-like.* To receive a favour and to return a blow! To obtain the gift of language, and then to use one's speech to curse the giver! To use a sacred sword is unholy warfare! All this is devil-like.

*Evil for evil is beast-like.* Yes, the dog bites back when it is bitten. The dog returns snarl for snarl, venom for venom. And if, when I have been injured, I "pay a man back in his own coin," if I "give him as good as he gave," I am living on the plane of the beast.

*Good for good is man-like.* When I requite a man's kindness by kindness! When I send presents to one who loads me with benefits! This is a true and manly thing to do, and lifts us far above the beast.

*Good for evil is God-like.* Yes, that lifts me into "the heavenly places in Christ Jesus." Then I have "the mind of Christ." Then do I unto others as my Saviour has done unto me.

## JANUARY The Thirtieth

### IRRESISTIBLE ARTILLERY

*"When I cry unto Thee, then shall mine enemies turn back."*—PSALM lvi.

BUT it must be a real "cry"! It must not be an idle recitation which sheds no blood. It must be a cry like the cry of the drowning, a cry which cleaves the air like a bullet. Said a man to me some while ago, "Assault the heavens with cries for me!" That is the cry which takes the kingdom by storm.

When such a cry rends the heavens, "my enemies turn back." A secret and irresistible artillery begins to play upon them, and their strength fails. Yes, believing prayer calls these invisible allies into the field. "The mountains are full of horses and chariots of fire round about!" And the enemy flies!

*"This I know."* The psalmist is building upon experience. The miracle has happened a hundred times. Many a morning has he seen the enemy vaingloriously tramping the field, and he has cried unto the Lord, and before nightfall there has been a perfect rout. Blessed is the man who has had such heartening dealings with the Lord that he can now face a hostile host in unclouded faith and assurance!

# JANUARY The Thirty-first

## UNDER HIS WINGS

*"In the shadow of Thy wings will I make my refuge."*—PSALM lvii.

COULD anything be more tenderly gracious than this figure of hiding under the shadow of God's wings? It speaks of bosom-warmth, and bosom-shelter, and bosom-rest. "Let me to Thy bosom fly!"

And what strong wings they are! Under those wings I am secure even from the lions. My animal passions shall not hurt me when I am "hiding in God." The fiercest onslaughts of the devil are powerless to break those mighty wings. The tenderest little chick, "one of these little ones," nestling behind this soft and gentle shelter, shall be perfectly secure; "none of its bones shall be broken."

I do not wonder that this sheltering psalmist begins to sing! *"I will sing and give praise!"* I have often listened to the sheltering chicks, hiding behind the mother's wings, and I have heard that quaint, comfortable, contented sound for which our language has no name. It is a sound of incipient song, the musical murmur of satisfaction. "I will sing unto Thee . . . for Thy mercy is great."

## FEBRUARY The First

### THE SOUL IN PRISON

*"Bring my soul out of prison!"*—PSALM cxlii.

I TOO, have my prison-house, and only the Lord can deliver me.

There is *the prison-house of sin*. It is a dark and suffocating hole, without friendly light or morning air. And it is haunted by such affrighting shapes, as though my iniquities had incarnated themselves in ugly and repulsive forms. None but the Lord can bring me out.

And there is *the prison-house of sorrow*. My griefs sometimes wrap me about like cold confining walls, which have neither windows nor doors. It seems as though a fluid sorrow can congeal into a cold, hard temperament, and hold me in its icy embrace. And none but the Lord can bring me out.

And there is *the prison-house of death*. I must perforce pass through the gate of death. Shall I find it a castle of gloom, or is there another gate through which I shall emerge into the fair, sweet paradise of God? My Master is Lord of the road! And He tells me that death shall not be a castle of captivity, but only a thoroughfare through which I shall pass into the realm of eternal day.

## FEBRUARY The Second

### HOW TO APPROACH A CRISIS
*"It shall be given you in that same hour."*—
MATTHEW x. 16-28.

AND so I am not to worry about the coming crisis! "God never is before His time, and never is behind!" When the hour is come, I shall find that the great Host hath made "all things ready."

When the crisis comes *He will tell me how to rest*. It is a great matter to know just how to rest—how to be quiet when "all without tumultuous seems." We irritate and excite our souls about the coming emergency, and we approach it with worn and feverish spirits, and so mar our Master's purpose and work.

When the crisis comes *He will tell me what to do*. The orders are not given until the appointed day. Why should I fume and fret and worry as to what the sealed envelope contains? "It is enough that He knows all," and when the hour strikes the secrets shall be revealed.

And when the crisis comes *He will tell me what to say*. I need not begin to prepare my retorts and my responses. What shall I say when death comes, to me or to my loved one? Never mind, He will tell thee. And what when sorrow or persecution comes? Never mind, He will tell thee.

## FEBRUARY The Third

### TRANSFORMING THE HARD HEART

*The Lord " turned the flint into a fountain of waters."*—PSALM cxiv.

WHAT a violent conjunction, the flint becoming the birthplace of a spring! And yet this is happening every day. Men who are as "hard as flint," whose hearts are "like the nether millstone," become springs of gentleness and fountains of exquisite compassion. Beautiful graces, like lovely ferns, grow in the home of severities, and transform the grim, stern soul into a garden of fragrant friendships. This is what Zacchæus was like when his flint became a fountain. It is what Matthew the publican was like when the Lord changed his hard heart into a land of springs.

No one is "too far gone." No hardness is beyond the love and pity of God. The well of eternal life can gush forth even in a desert waste, and "where sin abounds grace doth much more abound." Let us bring our hardness to the Lord. Let us see what He can make of our flint. When we are dry and "feelingless," and desire is dead, let us bring this Sahara to the great Restorer, and "the desert shall rejoice and blossom like the rose."

## FEBRUARY The Fourth

### SPIRITUAL BUOYANCY

*"When thou passeth through the waters they shall not overflow thee."*—ISAIAH xliii. 1-7.

WHEN Mrs. Booth, the mother of the Salvation Army, was dying, she quietly said, " The waters are rising but I am not sinking." But then she had been saying that all through her life. Other floods besides the waters of death had gathered about her soul. Often had the floods been out and the roads were deep in affliction. But she had never sunk! The good Lord made her buoyant, and she rode upon the storm! This, then, is the promise of the Lord, not that the waters of trouble shall never gather about the believer, but that he shall never be overwhelmed. He shall " keep his head above them." Yes, to him shall be given the grace of " aboveness." He shall never be under, always above! It is the precious gift of spiritual buoyancy, sanctified good spirits, the power of the Christian hope. When we are in Christ Jesus circumstances shall never be our master. One is our Master, and " we are more than conquerors in Him that loved us, and washed us from our sins in His own blood."

## FEBRUARY The Fifth

### EVERYWHERE THE GATE OF HEAVEN

*"Surely the Lord is in this place, and I knew it not."*—GENESIS xxviii. 10-22.

THAT is the first time for many a day that Jacob had named the name of God. In all the dark story of his wicked intrigue the name of God is never mentioned. Jacob wanted to forget God! God would be a disturbing presence! But here he encounters Him in a dream, and in the most unlikely place. "And he was afraid, and said, How dreadful is this place!"

Jacob had yet to learn that there is everywhere "a ladder set up on the earth and the top of it reaches to heaven." There was a ladder from the very tent in which he wore his deceptive skin. There was a ladder from the secret place where he and his mother wove their mischievous plot. There is no corner of earth which is cut away from the Divine vigilance. God gets at us everywhere.

But there is a merciful side to all this. If the ladder be everywhere, and God can get at us, then also everywhere we can get at God. There are "ascending angels" who will carry our confessions, our prayers, our sighs and mournings, to the very heart of the eternally gracious God.

## FEBRUARY The Sixth

### *THE HOME-BIRD*
Psalm xci. 1-12.

I READ a sentence the other day in which a very powerful modern writer describes a certain woman as "having God on her visiting list." We may recoil from the phrase, but it very vitally describes a very awful commonplace. Countless thousands have God on their visiting lists. They pay Him courtesy-calls, and between the calls He is forgotten. Perhaps the call is paid once a week in the social function of worship. Perhaps it is paid more rarely, like calls between comparative strangers. How great the contrast between a caller and one who dwells in the secret place! It is the difference between a flirt and a "home-bird," between one who flits about on a score of fancies, and one who settles down in the solid satisfaction of a supreme affection.

"*Shall abide under the shadow of the Almighty.*" Such is the reward of the "home-bird," the settled friend of the Lord. The shadow of the Lord shall rest upon him continually. I sometimes read of our monarchs being "shadowed" by protective police. In an infinitely more real and intimate sense the soul that dwells in "the secret place" is shadowed by the sleepless grace and love of God.

## LEAVING ITS MARK

*"Fear not, thou worm Jacob, I will make thee a threshing instrument with teeth."*—Isaiah xli. 8-14.

COULD any two things be in greater contrast than a worm and an instrument with teeth? The worm is delicate, bruised by a stone, crushed beneath a passing wheel; an instrument with teeth can break and not be broken, it can grave its mark upon the rock. And the mighty God can convert the one into the other. He can take a man or a nation, who has all the impotence of the worm, and by the invigoration of His own Spirit He can endow them with strength by which they will leave a noble mark upon the history of their time.

And so the "worm" may take heart. The mighty God can make us stronger than our circumstances. We can bend them all to our good. In God's strength we can make them all pay tribute to our souls. We can even take hold of a black disappointment, break it open, and extract some jewel of grace. When God gives us wills like iron we can drive through difficulties as the iron share cuts through the toughest soil. "I will make thee," saith the Lord, "and shall He not do it?"

## FEBRUARY The Eighth

### REVISITING OLD ALTARS

"*I will make there an altar unto God, who answered me in the day of my distress.*"—GENESIS xxxv. 1-7.

IT is a blessed thing to revisit our early altars. It is good to return to the haunts of early vision. Places and things have their sanctifying influences, and can recall us to lost experiences. I know a man to whom the scent of a white, wild rose is always a call to prayer. I know another to whom Grasmere is always the window of holy vision. Sometimes a particular pew in a particular church can throw the heavens open, and we see the Son of God. The old Sunday-school has sometimes taken an old man back to his childhood and back to his God. So I do not wonder that God led Jacob back to Bethel, and that in the old place of blessing he reconsecrated himself to the Lord.

It is a revelation of the loving-kindness of God that we have all these helps to the recovery of past experiences. Let us use them with reverence. And in our early days let us make them. Let us build altars of communion which in later life we shall love to revisit. Let us make our early home "the house of God and the gate of heaven." Let us multiply deeds of service which will make countless places fragrant for all our after years.

## THE ROCK AND THE BOWING WALL
### Psalm lxii.

HERE are two symbols by which the psalmist describes the confidence of the righteous. "*He only is my rock.*" Only yesterday I had the shelter of a great rock on a storm-swept mountain side. The wind tore along the heights, driving the rain like hail, but in the opening of the rock our shelter was complete.

And the second symbol is this: "*He is my high place.*" The high place is the home of the chamois, out of reach of the arrow. "Flee as a bird to your mountain!" Get beyond the hunter's range! Our security is found in loftiness. It is our unutterable privilege to live in the heavenly places in Christ Jesus. Such is the confidence of the righteous.

In this psalm there is also another pair of symbols describing the futility of the wicked. The wicked is "*as a bowing wall.*" The wall is out of perpendicular, out of conformity with the truth of the plumb-line, and it will assuredly topple into ruin. So is it with the wicked: he is building awry, and he will fall into moral disaster. He is also "*as a tottering fence.*" The wind and the rain dislodge the fence, it rots at its foundations, and one day it lies prone upon the ground.

## FEBRUARY The Tenth

### REGISTERING A VERDICT

*"The Lord our God will we serve, and His voice will we obey."*—JOSHUA xxiv. 22-28.

HERE was a definite decision. Our peril is that we spend our life in wavering and we never decide. We are like a jury which is always hearing evidence and never gives a verdict. We do much thinking, but we never make up our minds. We let our eyes wander over many things, but we make no choice. Life has no crisis, no culmination.

Now people who never decide spend their days in hoping to do so. But this kind of life becomes a vagrancy and not a noble and illumined crusade. We drift through our days, we do not steer, and we never arrive at any rich and stately haven.

It is therefore vitally wise to "make a vow unto the Lord." It is good to pull our loose thinkings together and to "gird up the loins of the mind." Let a man, at some definite place, and at some definite moment, make the supreme choice of his life.

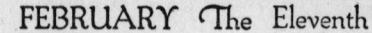

## THE HILL COUNTRY OF THE SOUL

Psalm cxxi.

THERE should be a hill country in every life, some great up-towering peaks which dominate the common plain. There should be an upland district, where springs are born, and where rivers of inspiration have their birth. "I will lift up mine eyes unto the hills."

The soul that knows no hills is sure to be oppressed with the monotony of the road. The inspiration to do little things comes from the presence of big things. It is amazing what dull trifles we can get through when a radiant love is near. A noble companionship glorifies the dingiest road. And what if that Companion be God? Then, surely, "the common round and daily task" have a light thrown upon them from "the beauty of His countenance."

The "heavenlies" are our salvation and our defence. "His righteousness is like the great mountains." "The mountains bring forth peace unto His people."

## FEBRUARY The Twelfth

### THE BULB AND THE SOIL

*" He that hath My commandments, and keepeth them, he it is that loveth Me."*—JOHN xiv. 15-24.

YES, but how can I keep them? Some one sent me a bulb which requires a certain kind of soil, but he also sent me the soil in which to grow it. He sent instructions, but he also sent power. And when I am bidden to keep a commandment I feel as though I have received the bulb but not the soil! But is this God's way of dealing with His people? I will read on if perchance I may find the gift of the soil.

" He that abideth in Me . . . the same bringeth forth much fruit." That is the gift I seek. For the keeping of His commandments the Lord provides Himself. I am not called upon to raise fruits out of the soil of my own will, out of my own infirmity of aspiration or desire. I can rest everything in God! I can " abide in Him," and I may have the holy energies of the Godhead to produce in me the fruits of a holy and obedient life. The good Lord provides both the bulb and the soil.

It is the tragedy of life that we forget this, and seek to make a soil-bed of our own. And thus do we suffer the calamity of fruitless labour, the heavy drudgery of tasks beyond our strength. " Come unto Me, all ye that labour and are heavy laden, and I will give you rest."

## GRUDGES

*"Thou shalt not bear any grudge."*—LEVITICUS xix. 11-18.

HOW searching is that demand upon the soul! My forgiveness of my brother is to be complete. No sullenness is to remain, no sulky temper which so easily gives birth to thunder and lightning. There is to be no painful aloofness, no assumption of a superiority which rains contempt upon the offender. When I forgive, I am not to carry any powder forward on the journey. I am to empty out all my explosives, all my ammunition of anger and revenge. I am not to "bear any grudge."

I cannot meet this demand. It is altogether beyond me. I might utter words of forgiveness, but I cannot reveal a clear, bright, blue sky without a touch of storm brewing anywhere. But the Lord of grace can do it for me. He can change my weather. He can create a new climate. He can "renew a right spirit within me," and in that holy atmosphere nothing shall live which seeks to poison and destroy. Grudges shall die "like cloud-spots in the dawn." Revenge, that awful creation of the unclean, feverish soul, shall give place to good-will, the strong genial presence which makes its home in the new heart.

## IMPERFECT CONSECRATION
### MATTHEW xix. 16-22.

THE rich young ruler consecrated a part, but was unwilling to consecrate the whole. He hallowed the inch but not the mile. He would go part of the way, but not to the end. And the peril is upon us all. We give ourselves to the Lord, but we reserve some liberties. We offer Him our house, but we mark some rooms "Private." And that word "Private," denying the Lord admission, crucifies Him afresh. He has no joy in the house so long as any rooms are withheld.

Dr. F. B. Meyer has told us how his early Christian life was marred and his ministry paralyzed just because he had kept back one key from the bunch of keys he had given to the Lord. Every key save one! The key of one room kept for personal use, and the Lord shut out. And the effects of the incomplete consecration were found in lack of power, lack of assurance, lack of joy and peace.

The "joy of the Lord" begins when we hand over the last key. We sit with Christ on His throne as soon as we have surrendered all our crowns, and made Him sole and only ruler of our life and its possessions.

## FEBRUARY The Fifteenth

### THE WITNESS OF YESTERDAY
Psalm lxxviii. 1-8.

OUR yesterdays are to be the teachers of our children. We are to take them over our road, and show them the pitfalls where we stumbled and the snares that lured us away. And we are to show them how we found the springs of grace, and how the Lord made Himself known to us in daily providence and care. We are to relate His exploits, "His wonderful dealings with the children of men." We must make our life witness of God to our children, and when their minds roam over our road they must see it radiant with the grace and mercy of the Lord.

The best inheritance I can give my child is a steadfast witness of my knowledge of God. The testimony of a light that never failed may give him the needful wisdom when his own way becomes troubled with clouds and darkness. And what a story it is, this story of the deeds of our gracious God. It is full of quickening for weary and desponding souls. It is a perfect reservoir of inspiration for those whose desire has failed, and in whose lives the wells of impulse have become dry. Let us bring forward yesterday's wealth to enrich the life of to-day. "Do ye not remember the miracle of the loaves?"

## FEBRUARY The Sixteenth

### CROWDING OUT GOD
*"Lest thou forget."*—DEUTERONOMY iv. 5-13.

THAT is surely the worst affront we can put upon anybody. We may oppose a man and hinder him in his work, or we may directly injure him, or we may ignore him, and treat him as nothing. Or we may forget him! Opposition, injury, contempt, neglect, forgetfulness! Surely this is a descending scale, and the last is the worst. And yet we can forget the Lord God. We can forget all His benefits. We can easily put Him out of mind. We can live as though He were dead. "My children have forgotten Me."

What shall we do to escape this great disaster? *"Take heed to thyself!"* To take heed is to be at the helm and not asleep in the cabin. It is to steer and not to drift. It is to keep our eyes on the compass and our hands on the wheel. It is to know where we are going. We never deliberately forget our Lord; we carelessly drift into it. "Take heed."

*"And keep thy soul diligently."* Gardens run to seed, and ill weeds grow apace. The fair things are crowded out, and the weed reigns everywhere. It is ever so with my soul. If I neglect it, the flowers of holy desire and devotion will be choked by weeds of worldliness. God will be crowded out, and the garden of the soul will become a wilderness of neglect and sin.

## FEBRUARY The Seventeenth

### BLESSINGS AND CURSINGS

*"He read all the words of the law, the blessings and the cursings."*—JOSHUA viii. 30-35.

WE are inclined to read only what pleases us, to hug the blessings and to ignore the warnings. We bask in the light, we close our eyes to the lightning. We recount the promises, we shut our ears to the rebukes. We love the passages which speak of our Master's gentleness, we turn away from those which reveal His severity. And all this is unwise, and therefore unhealthy. We become spiritually soft and anæmic. We lack moral stamina. We are incapable of noble hatred and of holy scorn. We are invertebrate, and on the evil day we are not able to stand.

We must read "all the words of the law, the blessings and the cursings." We must let the Lord brace us with His severities. We must gaze steadily upon the appalling fearfulness of sin, and upon its terrific issues. At all costs we must get rid of the spurious gentleness that holds compromise with uncleanness, that effeminate affection which is destitute of holy fire. We must seek the love which burns everlastingly against all sin; we must seek the gentleness which can fiercely grip a poisonous growth and tear it out to its last hidden root. We must seek that holy love which is as a "consuming fire."

## THE SUBTLETY OF TEMPTATION
### James i. 12-20.

EVIL enticements always come to us in borrowed attire. In the Boer War ammunition was carried out in piano cases, and military advices were transmitted in the skins of melons. And that is the way of the enemy of our souls. He makes us think we are receiving music when he is sending explosives; he promises life, but his gift is laden with the seeds of death. He offers us liberty, and he hides his chains in dazzling flowers. "Things are not what they seem."

And so our enemy uses mirages, and will-o'-the-wisps and tinselled crowns. He lights friendly fires on perilous coasts to snare us to our ruin. And therefore we need clear, sure eyes. We need a refined moral sense which can discriminate between the true and the false, and which can discern the enemy even when he comes as "an angel of light." And we may have this wisdom from "the God of all wisdom." By His grace we may be kept morally sensitive, and we shall know our foe even when he is a long way off.

# FEBRUARY The Nineteenth

## THE THOUGHT AFAR OFF
### Psalm cxxxix. 1-12.

"THOU knowest my thought afar off." That fills me with awe. I cannot find a hiding-place where I can sin in secrecy. I cannot build an apparent sanctuary and conceal evil within its walls. I cannot with a sheep's skin hide the wolf. I cannot wrap my jealousy up in flattery and keep it unknown. "Thou God seest me." He knows the bottom thought that creeps in the basement of my being. Nothing surprises God! He sees all my sin. So am I filled with awe.

"Thou knowest my thought afar off." This fills me also with hope and joy. He sees the faintest, weakest desire, aspiring after goodness. He sees the smallest fire of affection burning uncertainly in my soul. He sees every movement of penitence which looks toward home. He sees every little triumph, and every altar I build along life's way. Nothing is overlooked. My God is not like a policeman, only looking for crimes; He is the God of grace, looking for graces, searching for jewels to adorn His crown. So am I filled with hope and joy.

## FEBRUARY The Twentieth

### TAMPERING WITH THE LABEL

1 JOHN iii. 4-10.

SIN is transgression. It is the deliberate climbing of the fence. We see the trespass-board, and in spite of the warning we stride into the forbidden field. Sin is not ignorance, it is intention. We sin when we are wide-awake! There are teachers abroad who would soften words like these. They offer us terms which appear to lessen the harshness of our actions; they give our sin an aspect of innocence. But to alter the label on the bottle does not change the character of the contents. Poison is poison give it what name we please. "Sin is the transgression of the law."

Let us be on our guard against the men whose pockets are filled with deceptive labels. Let us vigilantly resist all teachings which would chloroform the conscience. Let us prefer true terms to merely nice ones. Let us call sin by its right name, and let us tolerate no moral conjuring either with ourselves or with others. The first essential in all moral reformation is to call sin "sin." "If we confess our sin He is faithful and just to forgive us our sin."

## FEBRUARY The Twenty-first

### GRACE REIGNS!
#### ROMANS v. 12-21.

WHEN old Mr. Honest came to the river, and he entered the cold waters of death, the last words he was heard to utter by those who stood on the shore were these:—" Grace reigns!" All through his pilgrimage old Mr. Honest had been in Emmanuel's land where grace reigned night and day. It was through grace that he had found the way of life. It was through grace that he had been delivered from the beasts and pitfalls of the road. It was grace that had given him lilies of peace, and springs of refreshment, and the fine air that inspired him in difficult tasks. And in death he still found "grace abounding," and the Lord of the changing road was also Lord of the dark waters through which he passed into the radiant glories of the cloudless day.

In every yard of a faithful pilgrimage we shall find the decrees of sovereign love. We are never in alien country. "Grace reigns" in every hill and valley, through every green pasture and over every rugged road, in every moment of "the day of life," and in the last sharp passage through the transient night of death.

## FEBRUARY The Twenty-second

### THE THREE GARDENS
REVELATION xxii. 1-14.

THE Bible opens with a garden. It closes with a garden. The first is the Paradise that was lost. The last is Paradise regained. And between the two there is a third garden, the garden of Gethsemane. And it is through the unspeakable bitterness and desolation of Gethsemane that we find again the glorious garden through which flows " the river of water of life." Without Gethsemane no New Jerusalem! Without its mysterious and unfathomable night no blessed sunrise of eternal hope! " We were reconciled to God by the death of His Son."

We are always in dire peril of regarding our redemption lightly. We hold it cheaply. Privileges easily come to be esteemed as rights. And even grace itself can lose the strength of heavenly favour and can be received and used as our due. " Gethsemane can I forget?" Yes, I can; and in the forgetfulness I lose the sacred awe of my redemption, and I miss the real glory of " Paradise regained." " Ye are not your own; ye are bought with a price." That is the remembrance that keeps the spirit lowly, and that fills the heart with love for Him " whose I am," and whom I ought to serve.

## FEBRUARY The Twenty-third

### THE PROCESS AND THE END

*"Ye have seen the end of the Lord: that the Lord is very pitiful, and of tender mercy."*—
JAMES v. 7-11.

AND so we are bidden to be patient. "We must wait to the end of the Lord." The Lord's ends are attained through very mysterious means. Sometimes the means are in contrast to the ends. He works toward the harvest through winter's frost and snow. The maker of chaste and delicate porcelain reaches his lovely ends through an awful mortar, where the raw material of bone and clay is pounded into a cream. In that mortar-chamber we have no hint of the finished ware. But be patient, even in this chamber of affliction the ware is on the way to glory!

And so it is with the ministries of our Lord. He leads us through discords into harmonies, through opposition into union, through adversities into peace. His means of grace are processes, sometimes gentle, sometimes severe; and our folly is to assume that we have reached His ends when we are only on the way to them. "The end of the Lord is very pitiful, and of tender mercy." "Be patient, therefore," until it shall be spoken of thee and me, "And God saw that it was good."

## FEBRUARY The Twenty-fourth

### MOVING TOWARDS DAYBREAK

*"He hath brought me into darkness, but not into light."*—LAMENTATIONS iii. 1-9.

BUT a man may be in darkness, and yet in motion toward the light. I was in the darkness of the subway, and it was close and oppressive, but I was moving toward the light and fragrance of the open country. I entered into a tunnel in the Black Country in England, but the motion was continued, and we emerged amid fields of loveliness. And therefore the great thing to remember is that God's darknesses are not His goals; His tunnels are means to get somewhere else. Yes, His darknesses are appointed ways to His light. In God's keeping we are always moving, and we are moving towards Emmanuel's land, where the sun shines, and the birds sing night and day.

There is no stagnancy for the God-directed soul. He is ever guiding us, sometimes with the delicacy of a glance, sometimes with the firmer ministry of a grip, and He moves with us always, even through "the valley of the shadow of death." Therefore, be patient, my soul! The darkness is not thy bourn, the tunnel is not thy abiding home! He will bring thee out into a large place where thou shalt know "the liberty of the glory of the children of God."

## THE FRESH EYE

*" His compassions fail not: they are new every morning."*—LAMENTATIONS iii. 22-33.

WE have not to live on yesterday's manna; we can gather it fresh to-day. Compassion becomes stale when it becomes thoughtless. It is new thought that keeps our pity strong. If our perception of need can remain vivid, as vivid as though we had never seen it before, our sympathies will never fail. The fresh eye insures the sensitive heart. And our God's compassions are so new because He never becomes accustomed to our need. He always sees it with an eye that is never dulled by the commonplace; He never becomes blind with much seeing! We can look at a thing so often that we cease to see it. God always sees a thing as though He were seeing it for the first time. "Thou, God, seest me," and "His compassions fail not."

And if my compassions are to be like a river that never knows drought, I must cultivate a freshness of sight. The horrible can lose its horrors. The daily tragedy can become the daily commonplace. My neighbour's needs can become as familiar as my furniture, and I may never see either the one or the other. And therefore must I ask the Lord for the daily gift of discerning eyes. "Lord, that I may receive my sight." And with an always newly-awakened interest may I reveal "the compassions of the Lord!"

## FEBRUARY The Twenty-sixth

### THE CELLARS OF AFFLICTION
#### Psalm xxxiv. 9-22.

SAMUEL RUTHERFORD used to say that whenever he found himself in the cellars of afflictions he used to look about for the King's wine. He would look for the wine-bottles of the promises and drink rich draughts of vitalizing grace. And surely that is the best deliverance in all affliction, to be made so spiritually exhilarant that we can rise above it. I might be taken out of affliction, and emerge a poor slave and weakling. I might remain in affliction, and yet be king in the seeming servitude, "more than conqueror" in Christ Jesus. It is a great thing to be led through green pastures and by still waters; I think it is a greater thing to have a "table prepared before me *in the presence of mine enemies.*" It is good to be able to sing in the sunny noon; it is better still to be able to sing "songs in the night."

And this deliverance may always be ours in Christ Jesus. The Lord may not smooth out our circumstances, but we may have the regal right of peace. He may not save us from the sorrows of a newly-cut grave, but we may have the glorious strength of the immortal hope. God will enable us to be masters of all our circumstances, and none shall have a deadly hold upon us.

## THE MIGHT OF FRAILTY
### Psalm cv. 23-36.

THAT is the wonder of wonders, that the Almighty God will use frail humanity as the vehicles of His power, and will make Moses and Aaron shine with reflected glory. Man can send an electric current into a fragile carbon film and make it incandescent. He can send his voice across a continent, and make it speak on a distant shore. And the Lord God can do wonders compared with which these are only as the dimmest dreams. He can send His holy power into human speech, and the words can wake the dead. He can send His virtue into the human will, and its strength can shake the thrones of iniquity. He can send His love into the human heart, and the power of its affection can capture the bitterest foe.

And so the word "impossible" becomes itself impossible when the soul of man is in fellowship with the Lord of Hosts. The pliant will becomes an iron pillar. The weak heart becomes "as a defended city" when it is the home of God. Dumb lips become the thrones of mysterious eloquence when touched with divine inspiration.

## FEBRUARY The Twenty-eighth

### THE TEST OF FULNESS
DEUTERONOMY viii. 1-10.

"AND thou shalt eat and be full, and thou shalt bless the Lord thy God." Fulness is surely a more searching test than want. Fulness induces sleep and forgetfulness. Many a man fights a good fight with Apollyon in the narrow way, who lapses into sleepy indifference on the Enchanted Ground. Men often sit down to a full table without "grace." Pain cries out to God, while boisterous health strides along in heedlessness. Yes, it is our fulness that constitutes our direst peril. "This was the iniquity of Sodom, *fulness* of bread and abundance of idleness."

And so our tests may come on the sunny day. A nation's supreme tests may come in its prosperity. The sunshine may do more damage than the lightning. The soul may falter even in Beulah land, where "the sun shines night and day."

Prayer must not, therefore, tarry until sickness and adversity come. We must "pray without ceasing" in the cloudless noon, lest we are stricken with "the arrow that flieth by day." We must seek the eternal strength when no apparent enemy crouches at our gate, and when our easy road is lined with luxuriant flowers and fruit.

## INVINCIBLE RELIANCE
### Hebrews xi. 17-22.

"ACCOUNTING that God was able." That is the faith that makes moral heroes. That is the faith that prompts mighty ventures and crusades. It is faith in God's willingness and ability to redeem His promises. It is faith that if I do my part He will most assuredly do His. It is faith that He cannot possibly fail. It is faith that when He makes a promise the money is already in the bank. It is faith that when He sends me into the wilderness the secret harvest is already ripe from which He will give me "daily bread." It is faith that "all things are now ready," and in that faith I will face the apparently impossible task.

And thus the "impossible" leads me to the "prepared." The desert leads me to "fields white already." The hard call to sacrifice leads me to the "lamb in the thicket." "God is able," and He is never behind the time. The critical need unveils His grace.

Faith goes out on this invincible reliance. It is "the assurance of things hoped for." And by faith it inherits these things and is rich and strong in their possession.

## MARCH The First

### OVERCHARGING THE HEART
#### LUKE xxi. 25-36.

HERE is a great peril. Our hearts may be "*overcharged with surfeiting, and drunkenness, and cares of this life, and so that day come upon you unawares.*" Our mode of living may send our spirits to sleep. Yes, we may so ill-use our bodies that the watchman sleeps at his post! We can over-eat, and dim our moral sight. A man's daily meals have vital relationship with his vision of the Lord. If I would have a clear spirit I must not overburden the flesh.

And therefore am I bidden to "*take heed*" to myself. I must exercise common sense, the most important of all the senses. I must put a bridle upon my appetite, and hold it in subjection to my Lord.

And I must "*watch!*" The devil is surpassingly cunning, and, if he can, he will mix an opiate even with the sacramental wine. He will lure me among the winsome poppies, and put me into a perilous sleep.

And I must "*pray!*" I have a great and glorious Defender! Let me humbly yet confidently use Him, and I shall be delivered from the snares of appetite, and from the benumbing influence of all excess.

## MARCH The Second

### THE POWER OF THE CROSS
#### JOHN x. 11-18.

"I LAY down my life." In that supreme sacrifice all other sacrifices turn pale. In the power of that sacrifice the blackest guilt finds forgiveness. Its energies seek out the ruined and desolate life with glorious offer of renewal. When the Lord laid down His life the entire race found a new beginning. Our hope is born at the Cross. It is there that "the burden of our sin rolls away." In His night we find daybreak. When He said, "It is finished," our soul could sing, "Life is begun."

And so pilgrims gather at the Cross. Songs are heard there, the "sweetest ever sung by mortal tongues." And the power of the Cross never wanes. Its glorious grace reaches the soul to-day as in the earliest days. It inspires the despairing heart. It transforms the mind. It remakes the tissues of the will. There is no shattered power that the power of the Cross cannot restore. "We are complete in Him."

"In the Cross of Christ I glory,
    Towering o'er the wrecks of time;
All the light of sacred story
    Gathers round its head sublime."

## PREPARING FOR THE BRIDE
### JOHN xiv. 1-14.

OUR Lord has prepared a place. It is the Bridegroom "getting the house ready" for the bride. And, therefore, the preparations are not made grudgingly and with slow reluctance. Everything is of the best, and done with the swift delight of love. "Come, for all things are now ready."

And our Lord will fetch His bride to the prepared place. "I am the way." We become so wrapt up in Him that nothing else counts. I once travelled through the Black Country with a fascinating friend, and I never saw it! And we can become so absorbed in our glorious Bridegroom that we shall be almost oblivious of adverse circumstances which may beset us. Yes, even this is possible: "He that believeth in Me shall never see death!"

"I will receive you unto Myself." The last obscuring veil is to be rent, and we are to see Him "face to face." And that will be home, for that will be satisfaction and peace. The deepest hunger of the soul will be gratified in a glorious contentment, and we shall find that "the half hath not been told."

## THE GREAT COMPANION
### John xiv. 15-31.

AND so even the road is to have the home-feeling in it. "*I will not leave you orphans.*" Yes; there is to be something of home even in the way to it. I find something of Devonshire even in Dorsetshire; Shropshire gives me a taste of Wales. My Lord will not leave me comfortless. Heaven runs over, and I find its bounty before I arrive at its gate. The "Valley of Baca" becomes "a well."

And there are to be wonderful visions to speed the pilgrim's feet. "*I will manifest Myself unto him.*" At unexpected corners the glory will break! We shall be assuming that we have picked up a common traveller, and suddenly we shall discover it is the Lord, for He will be made known to us "in the breaking of bread." And at many "risings" of the road, where the climbing is stiff and burdensome, we shall be inspired with many a glorious view, and we shall see "the land that is very far off."

The one condition is, that I keep His word. If I am obedient, He will appear unto me, and the humdrum road will shine with miracles of grace.

## MARCH The Fifth

### THE TENT AND THE BUILDING
2 CORINTHIANS v. 1-9.

AT present we live in a tent—"*the earthly house of this tabernacle.*" And often the tent is very rickety. There are rents through which the rain enters, and it trembles ominously in the great storm. Some tents are frail from the very beginning, half-rotten when they are put up, and they have no defence even against the breeze. But even the strongest tent becomes weather-worn and threadbare, and in the long run it "falls in a heap!" And what then?

We shall exchange the frail tent for the solid house! *"If the earthly house of this tabernacle be dissolved, we have a building of God, a house not made with hands, eternal in the heavens."* When we are unclothed we shall find ourselves clothed with our house which is from heaven. The glory of this transition can only be confessed by "the saints in light." To awake, and discover that the creaking, breaking cords are left behind, that all the leakages are over, that we are no longer exposed to the cutting wind, that pain is passed, and sickness, and death—this must be a wonder of inconceivable ecstasy!

And "absent from the body" we shall be "present with the Lord."

## HOME-LIFE IN GOD
### JOHN xvii. 20-26.

THE home-life in God is to be a life of perfect union—"*I in them, and Thou in Me.*" Home is only another name for union. It is the perfect fusion of life with life, the harmonizing of differences as many different notes combine to form the mystery of choral song. And so will it be in the home-land! Our manifold individualities will be retained, but we shall "fit into one another," and in the perfect harmony we shall hear the "new song" of heaven.

And we are to prepare that union by the contemplation of the glory of the Lord. "*That they may behold My glory.*" Yes, and we can begin to do that now. We can lift our eyes away from the ugly compromises of men and fix them upon the radiant holiness of the Lord. We can look away from the dirty Alpine village and gaze upon the virgin snow of the uplifted heights. "Looking unto Jesus!"

And in that contemplation we shall most assuredly become transformed. "*I have given unto them the glory which Thou gavest Me.*" That is our wonderful possibility. For thee and me is this prize offered, we can "awake in His likeness."

## MARCH The Seventh

### THINGS MISSING IN HEAVEN
#### REVELATION xxi. 1-7.

WHAT a number of "conspicuous absences" there are to be in "the home-land!"

No more sea! John was in Patmos, and the sea rolled between him and his kinsmen. The sea was a minister of estrangement. But in the home-country every cause of separation is to be done away, and the family life is to be one of inconceivable intimacy. No more sea!

And no more pain! Its work is done, and therefore the worker is put away. When the building is completed the scaffolding may be removed. When the patient is in good health the medicine bottles can be dispensed with. And so shall it be with pain and all its attendants. "The inhabitant never says: 'I am sick!'"

And no more death! "The last enemy that shall be destroyed is Death." "Yes, he, too, shall drop his scythe, and his lax hand shall destroy no more for ever. Death himself shall die! And all things that have shared his work shall die with him. "The former things have passed away." The wedding-peal which welcomes the Lamb's bride will ring the funeral knell of Death and all his sable company.

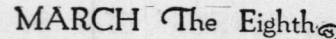

## THE CITIZENS OF THE HOME-LAND
### Revelation vii. 9-17.

THE citizen of "the home-land" wears white robes. His habits are perfectly clean. And the purity which he wears is a Divine gift and not a human accomplishment. It cannot be attained by self-sacrifice; it is ours through the sacrifice of our Lord. "They have washed their robes and made them white in the blood of the Lamb."

And every citizen of the home-land bears a palm in his hand. It is the emblem of conquest and sovereignty. By the grace of Christ they have been lifted above self and sin, and the devil, and death, and "made to sit with Him" on His throne. The palm is the heavenly symbol that all their spiritual enemies are under their feet.

And every citizen of the home-land takes part in the new song. The home-folk are therefore one in purity, one in self-conquest, and one in praise. "Salvation unto our God which sitteth upon the throne!" In that melody of thankfulness their union is deepened and enriched.

And we, too, can begin now to wear the white robe! And even now can we carry the palm! And even now we can join in the song of ceaseless praise.

## MARCH The Ninth

### NEARING HOME!
2 Timothy iv. 1-8.

HERE is a most valiant pilgrim nearing home! By the mercy of Christ he can look back upon a brave day, and there's a fine hopeful light in the evening sky.

He has fought well! *"I have fought a good fight."* And his has been a hard field. The enemy has ever regarded him as a leader in the army of the Lord and against him has the fiercest fight been waged. But he has never lost or stained his flag.

And he has run well! *"I have finished my course."* There was no melancholy turning back when the feverish start had cooled. There was no shrinking when the biting wind of malice and persecution swept across his track. On and on he ran, with increasing speed and ardour, until he reached the goal.

And well had he guarded his treasure! *"I have kept the faith."* He was the custodian of "unsearchable riches," and he watched, day and night, lest any infernal burglar should despoil him of his wealth. He guarded his gospel, his liberty, his hope, as the sentinels guard the crown jewels in the Tower.

And now the hard day is nearly over. "Henceforth there is laid up for me a crown of righteousness which the Lord will give me at that day."

## EXALTATION BY SEPARATION

2 CORINTHIANS vi. 11-18.

WHEN we turn away from the world, and leave it, we ourselves are not left to desolation and orphanhood. When we "come out from among them" the Lord receives us! He is waiting for us. The new companionship is ours the moment the old companionship is ended. "I will not leave you comfortless." What we have lost is compensated by infinite and eternal gain. We have lost "the whole world" and gained "the unsearchable riches of Christ."

And therefore separation is exaltation. We leave the muddy pleasures of Sodom and we "drink of the river of His pleasures." We leave "the garish day," and all the feverish life of Vanity Fair, and He maketh us "to lie down in green pastures," "He leadeth us beside the still waters." We leave a transient sensation, we receive the bread of eternity. We forfeit fireworks, we gain the stars!

What fools we are, and blind! We prefer the scorched desert of Sodom to the garden of Eden. We prefer a loud reputation to noble character. We prefer delirium to joy. We prefer human applause to the praise of God. We prefer a fading garland to the crown of life. Lord, that we may receive our sight!

## MARCH The Eleventh

### GOOD AND BAD ROADS

Psalm i.

THERE is nothing breaks up more speedily than a badly-made road. Every season is its enemy and works for its destruction. Fierce heat and intensest cold both strive for its undoing. And "the way of the ungodly" is an appallingly bad road. There is rottenness in its foundations, and there is built into it "wood, and hay, and stubble." How can it stand? "The Spirit of the Lord breatheth upon it," and it is surely brought to nought. All the forces of holiness are pledged to its destruction, and they shall pick it to pieces, and shall scatter its elements to the winds.

"I am the way!" That road remains sound "in all generations." Changing circumstances cannot affect its stability. It is proof against every tempest, and against the most violent heat. It is a road in which little children can walk in happiness and in which old people can walk in peace. It is firm in the day of life, and it is absolutely sure in the hour of death. It never yields! "Thou hast set my feet upon a rock and hast established my goings." "This is the way, walk ye in it."

## THE COMING OF THE LORD
### Luke xvii. 22-32.

IN a certain very real way the Lord is coming every moment. And the great art of Christian living is to be able to discern Him when He arrives. He may appear as the village carpenter; or we may "suppose Him to be one of the gardeners," and we may mistake His appearing! He may meet us in some lowly duty, or in some seemingly unpleasant task. He may shine in the cheeriness of some triumph, or whisper to us in a message of good news. "I come again." And if our eyes are open we shall see Him coming continually. It is by this perception that the value of our life is measured and weighed.

But He will also come again "suddenly," when the soul will be translated into unknown climes. He will come again in the sable robes of death. Shall we know Him? Will our eyes be so keen and true that we shall be able to pierce the dark veil and say "It is the Lord!" This has been the joyful experience of countless multitudes. When the summons came their souls went forth, not as victims to encounter death, but as the bride "to meet the bridegroom!" They had intimacy with Him in life; they had glorious fellowship with Him in death!

# MARCH The Thirteenth

## SICKNESS AMONG CHRIST'S FRIENDS
### JOHN xi. 1-16.

AND so sickness can enter the circle of the friends of the Lord. *"He whom Thou lovest is sick."* My sicknesses do not mean that I have lost His favour. The shadow is His, as well as the sunshine. When He removes me from the glare of boisterous health it may be because of some spiritual fern which needs the ministry of the shade. *"This sickness is . . . for the glory of God."* Something beautiful will spring out of the shadowed seclusion, something which shall spread abroad the name and fame of God.

And, therefore, I do not wonder at the Lord's delay. He did not hasten away to the sick friend: *"He abode two days still in the same place where He was."* Shall I put it like this: the awaking bulbs were not yet ready for the brighter light—just a little more shade! We are impatient to get healthy; the Lord desires that we become holy. Our physical sickness is continued in order that we may put on spiritual strength.

And there are others besides sick Lazarus concerned in the sickness: "I am glad *for your sakes* I was not there." The disciples were included in the divine scheme. Their spiritual welfare was to be affected by it. Let me ever remember that the circle affected by sickness is always wider than the patient's bed. And may God be glorified in all!

## MARCH The Fourteenth

### "EVEN NOW!"
#### JOHN xi. 17-31.

LET me consider this marvellous confession of Martha's faith. "I know that *even now*, whatsoever Thou wilt ask of God, God will give it Thee!" Mark the "even now"! Lazarus was dead, and it was midnight in the desolate home. But "even now"! Beautiful it is when a soul's most awful crises are the seasons of its most radiant faith! Beautiful it is when our lamp shines steadily in the tempest, and when our spiritual confidence remains unshaken like a gloriously rooted tree. Beautiful it is when in our midnight men can hear the strains of the "even now"!

And let me consider the wonder of the Divine response. "*I am the resurrection and the life.*" A faith like Martha's will always win the Saviour's best. And here is an overwhelming best before which we can only bow in silent homage and awe. He is the Fountain in whom the stagnant brook shall find currency again. He is the Life in whom the fallen dead shall rise to their feet again.

And what is this? "Whosoever liveth and believeth in Me *shall never die!*" We shall go to sleep, but we shall never taste the bitterness of death. In the very act of closing our material eyes we shall open our spiritual eyes, and find ourselves at home!

## MARCH The Fifteenth

### JESUS AT A GRAVE
#### John xi. 32-45.

HERE is Jesus weeping. "Jesus wept." Why did He weep? Perhaps He wept out of sheer sympathy with the tears of others. And perhaps, too, He wept because some of our tears were needless. If we were better men we should know more of the love and purpose of our Lord, and perhaps many of our tears would be dried. Still, here is the sweet and heartening evangel. He sympathizes with my grief! Never a bitter tear is shed without my Lord sharing the tang and the pang.

Here is Jesus praying! "Father, I thank Thee that Thou hast heard Me." Then it is not so much a prayer as a thanksgiving. He gives thanks for what He is "about to receive." Is this my way? Perhaps I do it before I take a meal. Do I do it before I begin to live the day? In the morning do I thank my God for what I am about to receive? Can I confidently give thanks before I receive the gifts of God, before the dish-covers are removed? Can I trust Him?

And here is Jesus commanding, clothed in sovereign power: "Lazarus, come forth!" That is the same voice which "in the beginning created the heavens and the earth."

## THE NEMESIS OF BIGOTRY
JOHN xi. 46-57.

A FEARFUL nemesis waits upon the spirit of bigotry. Oliver Wendell Holmes has said that bigotry is like the pupil of the eye, the more light you pour into it the more it contracts. The scribes and Pharisees became smaller men the more the Lord revealed His glory. In the raising of Lazarus they saw nothing of the glory of the resurrection life, nothing of the joy of the reunited family, nothing of the gracious ministry of the Lord! "Darkness had blinded their eyes."

And it is also the nemesis of bigotry to be bitter, cruel, and violent. They sought to kill the Giver of life!

It is the ministry of light to ripen and sweeten the dispositions. "The fruit of the light is in all goodness." It is the ministry of the darkness to make men sour and unsympathetic, and revengeful, and to so pervert the heart as to make it a minister of poison and death.

And yet, how powerless is bigotry in the long run! It can no more stay the progress of the Kingdom than King Canute could check the flowing tide! Bigotry slew the Lord, and He rose again! And so it ever is. "Truth crushed to earth shall rise again; the eternal years of God are hers."

## MARCH The Seventeenth

### THE COMMONPLACE OF DEATH
#### LUKE vii. 11-18.

DEATH is never a commonplace. We never become so accustomed to funerals as not to see them. Everybody sees the mournful procession go along the street. A momentary awe steals over the flippant thought, and for one brief season the superficial opens into the infinite abyss.

And yet, while a thousand are arrested, only a few are compassionate. There can be awe without pity; there can be interest without service. When this humble funeral train trudged out of the city of Nain our Lord halted, and His heart melted! There was an "aching void," and He longed to fill it. There was a bleeding, broken heart, and He yearned to stand and heal it. He found His own joy in removing another's tears, His own satisfaction in another's peace.

*"The Lord hath visited His people!"* That is what the people said, and I do not wonder at the saying! And let me, too, be a humble visitor in the troubled ways of men! Let my heart be a well of sweet compassion to all the sons and daughters of grief! Like Barnabas, let me be "a son of consolation."

## MARCH The Eighteenth

### SERENITY IN THE TEMPEST
#### Job xix. 23-27.

PERHAPS I am akin to Job in having experienced the pressure of calamity. I have felt the shock of adverse circumstances, and the house of my life has trembled in the convulsion. Or death has been to my door and has returned again and again, and every time he has left me weeping! All God's billows have gone over me! Verily, I can take my place by the patriarch Job.

But can I share his witness, *"I know that my Redeemer liveth"*? Have I a calm assurance that my ruler is not caprice, and that my comings and goings are not determined by unfeeling chance? When death knocked at my door, did I know that the King had sent him? When some cherished scheme toppled into ruin, had I any thought that the Lord's hand was concerned in the shaking? Even when my circumstances are dubious, and I cannot trace a gracious purpose, do I know that my Vindicator liveth, and that some day He will justify all the happenings of the troubled road?

I will pray for this gracious confidence. I would have a firm step even among disappointments; yea, I would " sing songs in the night! "

## MARCH The Nineteenth

### DEATH AS MY SERVANT
#### REVELATION xx. 1-6.

EVEN now I would rise from the dead. Even now I would know "the power of His resurrection." Even now I would taste the rapture of the deathless life. And this is my glorious prerogative in grace. Yes, even now I can be "risen with Christ," and "death shall no more have dominion over me!"

And yet I must die! Yes, but the old enemy shall now be my friend. He will not be my master, but my servant. He shall just be the porter, to open the door into my Father's house, into the home of unspeakable blessedness and glory. Death shall not hurt me!

I have seen a little child fall asleep while out in the streets of the city, and the kind nurse has taken charge of the sleeper, and when the little one awaked she was at home, and she opened her eyes upon her mother's face.

So shall it be with all who are alive in Christ, and who have risen from a spiritual grave. They shall just fall into a brief sweet sleep, and gentle death shall usher them into the glory of the endless day.

## THE LORD IS AT HAND!

*"Ye know not what hour your Lord doth come."*—MATTHEW xxiv. 42-51.

THEN let me always live as though my Lord were at the gate! Let me arrange my affairs on the assumption that the next to lift the latch will be the King. When I am out with my friend, walking and talking, let me assume that just round the corner I may meet the Lord.

And so let me practise meeting Him! Said a mother to me one day concerning her long-absent boy: "I lay a place for him at every meal! His seat is always ready!" May I not do this for my Lord? May I not make a place for Him in all my affairs—my choices, my pleasures, my times of business, my season of rest? He may come just now; let His place be ready!

If He delay, I must not become careless. If He give me further liberty, I must not take liberties with it. Here is the golden principle, ever to live, ever to think, ever to work as though the Lord had already arrived. For indeed, He has, and when the veil is rent I shall find Him at my side.

## MARCH The Twenty-first

### IN THE GOLDEN CITY
#### Isaiah lii. 1-12.

AND so these are the glories of the golden city. There is *wakefulness*. "Awake! awake!" In the golden city none will be asleep. Everybody will be bright-eyed, clear-minded, looking upon all beautiful things with fresh and ready receptiveness. "The eyes of them that see shall not be dim."

There is *strength*. "Put on thy strength!" There will be no broken wills in the golden city, and no broken hearts. No one will walk with a limp! Everybody will go with a brave stride as to the strains of a band. And no one will tire of living, and the inhabitant never says, "I am sick."

And there is *beauty*. "Put on thy beautiful garments." Bare strength might not be attractive. But strength clothed in beauty is a very gracious thing. The tender mosses on the granite make it winsome. Strength is companionable when it is united with grace. In the golden city there will be tender sentiment as well as rigid conviction.

And these glories will be our defence. A positive virtue is our best rampart against vice. A robust health is the best protection against the epidemic. "The prince of this world cometh, and he hath nothing in me."

## COUNSEL AND MIGHT
### Psalm cxix. 33-40.

THE psalmist prays for *an illumined understanding.* "Teach me, O Lord, the way of Thy statutes." We are so prone to be children of the twilight, and to see things out of their true proportions. Therefore do we need to be daily taught. I must go into the school of the Lord, and in docility of spirit I must sit at His feet. "O, teach me, Lord, teach even me!"

And the psalmist prays for *rectified inclinations.* "Incline my heart unto Thy testimonies." We so often have the wrong bias, the fatal taste, and our desires are all against the will of the Lord. If only my leanings were toward the Lord how swift my progress would be! I strive to walk after holiness, while my inclinations are in the realm of sin. And so I need a clean mouth, with an appetite for the beautiful and the true. "Blessed are they that hunger after righteousness."

And the psalmist prays for *a strenuous will.* "Make me to go in the path of Thy commandments." He is praying for "go," for moral persistence, for power to crash through all obstacles which may impede his heavenly progress. And such is my need. Good Lord, endow me with a will like "an iron pillar," and help me to "stand in the evil day."

## MARCH The Twenty-third

### THE DARK BETRAYAL
#### JOHN xviii. 1-14.

OUR Master was betrayed by a disciple, "one of the twelve." The blow came from one of "His own household." The world employed a "friend" to execute its dark design. And so our intimacy with Christ may be our peril; our very association may be made our temptation. The devil would rather gain *one* belonging to the inner circle than a thousand who stand confessed as the friends of the world. What am I doing in the kingdom? Can I be trusted? Or am I in the pay of the evil one?

And our Master was betrayed in the garden of prayer. In the most hallowed place the betrayer gave the most unholy kiss. He brought his defilement into the most awe-inspiring sanctuary the world has ever known. And so may it be with me. I can kindle the unclean fire in the church. I can stab my Lord when I am on my knees. While I am in apparent devotion I can be in league with the powers of darkness.

And this "dark betrayal" was for money! The Lord of Glory was bartered for thirty pieces of silver! And the difference between Judas and many men is that they often sell their Lord for less! From the power of Mammon, and from the blindness which falls upon his victims, good Lord, deliver me!

## IN GETHSEMANE
### Luke xxii. 39-46.

SURELY this is the very Holy of Holies! It were well for us to fall on our knees and "be silent unto the Lord." I would quietly listen to the awful words, "Remove this cup from Me!" and I would listen again and again until never again do I hold a cheap religion. It is in this garden that we learn the real values of things, and come to know the price at which our redemption was bought. No one can remain in Gethsemane and retain a frivolous and flippant spirit.

"*And there appeared unto Him an angel from heaven, strengthening Him.*" I know that angel! He has been to me. He has brought me angel's food, even heavenly manna. Always and everywhere, when my soul has surrendered itself to the Divine will, the angel comes, and my soul is refreshed. The laying down of self is the taking up of God. When I lose my will I gain the Infinite. The moment of surrender is also the moment of conquest. When I consecrate my weakness I put on strength and majesty like a robe.

"*And when He rose up from His prayer*"—what then? Just this, He was quietly ready for anything, ready for the betraying kiss, ready for crucifixion. "Arise, let us be going."

## MARCH The Twenty-fifth

### THE FEAR OF MAN
JOHN xviii. 15-27.

AND this is the disciple who had been surnamed "The Rock"! Our Lord looked into the morrow, and He saw Simon's character, compacted by grace and discipline into a texture tough and firm as granite. But there is not much granite here! Peter is yet loose and yielding; more like a bending reed than an unshakable rock. A servant girl whispers, and his timid heart flings a lie to his lips and he denies his Lord.

Peter denied the Master, not because he coveted money, but because he feared men. He was not seeking crowns, but escaping frowns. He was not clutching at a garland, but avoiding a sword. It was not avarice but cowardice which determined his ways. He shrank from crucifixion! He saw a possible cross, and with a great lie he passed by on the other side.

But the Lord has not done with Peter. He is still "in the making." Some day he will justify his new name. Some day we shall find it written: "When they saw the boldness of Peter, they marvelled"! Once a maid could make him tremble. Now he can stand in high places, "steadfast and unmovable"!

From the spirit of cowardice and from all temporising, and from the unholy fear of man, deliver me, good Lord!

## MARCH The Twenty-sixth

### THE KING OF KINGS
#### JOHN xviii. 28-38.

WHAT a strange King our Lord appears, claiming mystic sovereignty, and yet betrayed by a false friend!

And yet, even in His apparent subjection His majestic kingliness stands revealed. When I watch the demeanours of Pilate and Jesus, I can see very clearly who it is who is on the throne; Pilate wears the outer trappings of royalty, but my Lord's is "the power and the glory." Pilate fusses about in a little "brief authority," but my Lord stands possessed of a serene dominion. Even at Pilate's judgment bar Jesus is the King.

But His kingdom is "*not of this world.*" And therefore this King is unlike every other King. He seeks His possessions not by fighting, but by "lighting"; not by coercion, but by constraint. His servants do not go forth with swords, but with lamps; not to drive the peoples, but to lead them. His visible throne is a cross, and His conquests are made in the power of sacrifice.

And so His armaments are the Truth, and the Truth alone. "*For this cause came I into the world, that I should bear witness unto the Truth.*" When the Truth wins and wooes, the triumph is lasting. Garlands won by the sword perish before the evening. To be one of the King's subjects is to share His nature. "Everyone that **is** of the truth heareth My voice."

## MARCH The Twenty-seventh

### THE SILENCE OF JESUS
*"He answered him nothing!"*—LUKE xxiii. 1-12.

AND yet, "Ask, and it shall be given you!" Yes, but everything depends upon the asking. Even in the realm of music there is a rudeness of approach which leaves true music silent. Whether the genius of music is to answer us or not depends upon our "touch." Herod's "touch" was wrong, and there was no response. Herod was flippant, and the Eternal was dumb. And I, too, may question a silent Lord. In the spiritual realm an idle curiosity is never permitted to see the crown jewels. Frivolousness never goes away from the royal Presence rich with surprises of grace. "Thy touch has still its ancient power!" So it has, but the healing touch is the gracious response to the touch of faith. "She touched Him, and . . . !"

"*And Herod . . . mocked Him.*" That was the real spirit behind the eager curiosity. And I, too, may mock my Lord! I may bow before Him, and array Him in apparent royalty, while all the time my spirit is full of flippancy and jeers. I may lustily sing: "Crown Him Lord of all," while I will not recognize His rights on a single square foot of the soil of my inheritance. And this it is to be the kinsman of Herod. And this, too, will be the issue; the heavens will be as brass, and the Lord will answer us nothing.

## THE CHOICE OF BARABBAS
### Luke xxiii. 13-24.

BARABBAS rather than Christ! The destroyer of life rather than the Giver of life! This was the choice of the people; and it is a choice which has often stained and defiled my own life.

When I choose revenge rather than forgiveness, I am preferring Barabbas to Christ. For revenge is a murderer, while forgiveness is a healer and saviour of men. But how often I have sent the sweet healer to the cross, and welcomed the murderer within my gate!

When I choose carnal passion before holiness, I am preferring Barabbas to Christ. For is there any murderer so destructive as carnality? And holiness stands waiting, ready to make me beautiful with the wondrous garments of grace. But I spurn the angel, and open my door to the beast.

The devil is always soliciting my service, and the devil "is a murderer from the beginning." Have I never preferred him, and sent my Lord to be "crucified afresh," and "put Him to an open shame"?

Again let me pray—for all my unholy and unwholesome choices, for all my preference of the murderer, forgive me, good Lord!

## MARCH The Twenty-ninth

### MYSTIC ALARM-BELLS
MATTHEW xxvii. 19-25.

PILATE was warned. Pilate's wife had a dream, and in the dream she had glimpses of reality, and when she awoke her soul was troubled. "Have thou nothing to do with that just man!"

And I, too, have mysterious warnings when I am treading perilous ways. Sometimes the warning comes from a friend. Sometimes "the angel of the Lord stands in the way for an adversary." My conscience rings loudly like an alarm-bell in the dead of night. Yes, the warnings are clear and pertinent, but . . . !

Pilate ignored the warning, and handed the Lord to the revengeful will of the priests. Pilate defiled his heart, and then he washed his hands! What a petty attempt to escape the certain issues! And yet we have shared in the small evasion. We have crucified the Lord, and then we wear a crucifix. We violate the spirit, and then we do reverence to the letter. We hand the Lord over to be crucified, and then we practise the postures and gait of the saints. Yes, we have all sought an escape in outer ceremony from the nemesis of our shameful deeds.

My soul, attend thou to the mystic warnings, and "play the man"!

## MARCH The Thirtieth

### THE VICTORY OF MEEKNESS
1 PETER ii. 17-25.

THEN I may be not only the betrayer, but the betrayed. In my inner circle there may be a friend who will play me false, and hand me over to the wolves. What then? Just this—I must imitate the grace of my Lord, and "consider Him."

There must be no violent retaliation. *"When He was reviled, He reviled not again."* The fire of revenge may singe or even scorch my enemy, but it will do far more damage to the furniture of my own soul. After every indulgence in vengeful passion some precious personal possession has been destroyed. The fact of the matter is, this fire cannot be kept burning without making fuel of the priceless furnishings of the soul. "Heat not a furnace for your foe so hot that it do singe yourself."

There must be a serene committal of the soul to the strong keeping of the Eternal God. *"He committed Himself to Him that judgeth righteously."* This is the way of peace, as this is the way of victory. If ever the enemy is to be conquered this must be the mode of the conquest. When men persecute us, let us rest more implicitly in our God.

## MARCH The Thirty-first

### *AT THE CROSS!*
MATTHEW xxvii. 38-50.

LET me listen to the ribald jeers which were flung upon my Lord. And let me listen, not as a judge, but as one who has been in the company of the callous crowd. For I, too, have mocked Him! I have said: "Hail, King!" and I have bowed before Him, but it has been mock and empty homage! I have sung: "Crown Him Lord of all!" but there has been no real recognition of His sovereignty; mine has been a mock coronation. From the seat of the mocker, deliver me, good Lord!

And let me stand near the cross while that awful voice of desolation rends the heavens. *"My God, My God, why hast Thou forsaken Me?"* In that agonizing cry I am led to the real heart of the atonement. My Saviour was standing where His believers will never stand. That was the real death, the death of an inconceivable abandonment. And "He died for me!" He so died in order that I may never taste death. "He that liveth and believeth in Me shall never die."

Every believer will go to sleep, and through a short sleep he will wake in the glory of the Eternal Presence. But he will never die: no, never die!

## THE SHADOW OF THE CROSS
### Luke xxiii. 33-47.

LOOK at our Lord in relation to His foes. *"Father, forgive them; for they know not what they do!"* Their bitterness has not embittered Him. The "milk of human kindness" was still sweet. Nothing could sour our Lord, and convert His goodwill into malice, His serene beneficence into wild revenge. And how is it with me? Are my foes able to maim my spirit as well as my body? Do they win their end by making me a smaller man? Or am I magnanimous even on the cross?

And look at our Lord in relation to the penitent thief. *"To-day shalt thou be with Me in Paradise."* There was no self-centredness in our Saviour's grief. He was the good Physician, even when His body was mangled on the cross. He healed a broken heart even in the very pangs of death. When "there was darkness over all the earth," He let the light of the morning into the heart of a desolate thief. And, good Lord, graciously help me to do likewise!

And all this amazing graciousness is explained in our Lord's relation to His Father. *"Father, into Thy hands I commend My spirit!"* Yes, everything is there! When I and My Father are one, my spirit will remain sweet as the violet and pure as the dew.

## APRIL The Second

### "ON HIM!"

*"The Lord hath laid on Him the iniquity of us all."*—ISAIAH liii.

LET me tell a dream which was given by night to one of my dearest friends. He beheld a stupendous range of glorious sun-lit mountains, with their lower slopes enfolded in white mist. "Lord," he cried, "I pray that I may dwell upon those heights!" "Thou must first descend into the vale," a voice replied.

Into the vale he went. And down there he found himself surrounded with all manner of fierce, ugly, loathsome things. As he looked upon them he saw that they were the incarnations of his own sins! There they were, sins long ago committed, showing their threatening teeth before him!

Then he heard some One approaching, and instinctively he knew it was the Lord! And he felt so ashamed that he drew a cloak over his face, and stood in silence. And the Presence came nearer and nearer, until He, too, stood silent. After a while my friend mastered sufficient courage to lift the corner of his cloak and look out upon the Presence: and lo! all the loathsome things were *on Him!*

"The Lord had laid on Him the iniquity of us all."

## APRIL The Third

## THE STONE ROLLED AWAY
### MARK xvi. 1-8.

I AM always wondering who will roll away the stone! There is a great obstacle in the way, and my frailty is incompetent to its removal. And lo! when I arrive at the place I find that the angel has been before me, and the obstacle is gone! And I would that I might learn wisdom to-day from the miracle of yesterday. Let me not be confounded about a new stone when I know that my fears about the old one had no foundation.

And then the young man at the sepulchre! He is a type of eternal youth, and he is sitting serenely in a routed grave. He represents the un-withering in the very home of corruption. And this, too, is my hope! It is mine in Christ to put on incorruption, and through a brief sleep to become clothed with immortal youth. "There everlasting spring abides, and never withering flowers!"

And I may have the assurance of the coming glory even now. Even now may I taste the heavenly feast, and wear some of the unfading flowers of the glorified. Yes, even now my leaf need not wither, and my hopes may remain unshaken through all my troubled years.

## APRIL The Fourth

### THE RESURRECTION MORNING
#### Matthew xxviii. 1-15.

LET me reverently mark the happenings of this most wonderful morn.

"*It began to dawn.*" Yes, that was the first significance of the resurrection. It was a new day for the world. Everything was to be seen in a new light. Everything was to wear a new face—God, and heaven, and life, and duty, and death! "All things are become new."

"*And there was a great earthquake.*" Yes, and this was significant of the tremendous upheaval implied in the resurrection. The kingdom of the devil was upheaved from its foundations. All the boasted pomp of his showy empire was turned upside down. "I beheld Satan falling!"

"*And the angel rolled away the stone.*" And that, too, is significant of the resurrection. The awful barrier was rolled away, and the grave became a thoroughfare! "This is the Lord's doing; it is marvellous in our eyes."

And there was "*fear and great joy.*" And mingled awe and gladness, a reverential delight.

## APRIL The Fifth

### THE EMPTY TOMB
#### LUKE xxiv. 1-12.

THAT empty tomb means the conquest of death. The Captive proved mightier than the captor. He emerged from the prison as the Lord of the prison, and death reeled at His going. In the risen Saviour death is dethroned; he takes his place at the footstool to do the bidding of his sovereign Lord and King. And that empty tomb means the conquest of sin. Sin had done its worst, and had failed. All the forces of hell had been rallied against the Lord, and above them all He rose triumphant and glorified. A little while ago I discovered a spring. I tried to choke it. I heaped sand and gravel upon it; I piled stones above it! And through them all it emerged, noiselessly and irresistibly, a radiant resurrection!

And so the empty tomb becomes the symbol of a thoroughfare between life in time and life in the unshadowed Presence of our God. Death is now like a short tunnel which is near my home; I can look through it and see the other side! In the risen Lord death becomes transparent. "O death, where is thy sting? O grave, where is thy victory?"

## APRIL The Sixth

### FIRST-HAND KNOWLEDGE OF CHRIST

"*Last of all He was seen of me also.*"—1 CORINTHIANS xv. 1-11.

AND by that vision Saul of Tarsus was transformed. And so, by the ministry of a risen Lord we have received the gift of a transfigured Paul. The resurrection glory fell upon him, and he was glorified. In that superlative light he discovered his sin, his error, his need, but he also found the dynamic of the immortal hope.

"Seen of me also!" Can I, too, calmly and confidently claim the experience? Or am I altogether depending upon another man's sight, and are my own eyes unillumined? In these realms the witness of "hear-says" counts for nothing; he only speaks with arresting power who has "seen for himself." "Sayest thou this thing of thyself, or did others tell it thee of Me?" That is the question which is asked, not only by the Master, but by all who hear us tell the story of the risen Lord. "Has He been seen of thee also?"

My Saviour, I humbly pray Thee to give me first-hand knowledge of Thee. Let me be a witness who can say, "I know that my Redeemer liveth!" Before all the doubts and hesitancies of man enable me to answer, "Have I not seen Jesus Christ our Lord?"

## IF CHRIST WERE DEAD!
### 1 Corinthians xv. 12-26.

"*IF Christ be not risen!*" That is the most appalling "if" which can be flung into the human mind. If it obtains lodging and entertainment, all the fairest hopes of the soul wither away like tender buds which have been nipped by sharp frost! See how they fade!

"*Your faith is vain.*" It has no more strength and permanency than Jonah's gourd. Nay, it has really never been a living thing! It has been a pathetic delusion, beautiful, but empty as a bubble, and collapsing at Joseph's tomb.

"*Ye are yet in your sins.*" The hope of forgiveness and reconciliation is stricken, and there is nothing left but "a certain fearful looking-for of judgment." Nemesis has only been hiding behind a screen of decorated falsehoods, and she will pursue us to the bitter end.

"*We are of all men the most miserable.*" Joy would fall and die like a fatally wounded lark. The song would cease from our souls. The holy place would become a tomb.

"But now *is* Christ risen from the dead!" Yes, let me finish on that word. That gives me morning, and melody, and holy merriment that knows no end.

## APRIL The Eighth

### MY INHERITANCE IN THE RISEN LORD
1 PETER i. 1-9.

IN my risen Lord I am born into "a living hope," a hope not only vital, but vitalizing, sending its mystic, vivifying influences through every highway and by-way of my soul.

In my risen Lord mine is "*an inheritance incorruptible.*" It is not exposed to the gnawing tooth of time. Moth and rust can not impair the treasure. It will not grow less as I grow old. Its glories are as invulnerable as my Lord.

In my risen Lord mine is "an inheritance . . . *undefiled.*" There is no alloy in the fine gold. The King will give me of His best. "Bring forth the best robe, and put it on him." The holiest ideal proclaims my possibility, and foretells my ultimate attainment. Heaven's wine is not to be mixed with water. I am to awake "in His likeness."

And mine is "an inheritance . . . that *fadeth not away.*" It shall not be as the garlands offered by men—green to-day and to-morrow sere and yellow. "Its leaf also shall not wither." It shall always retain its freshness, and shall offer me a continually fresh delight. And these are all mine in Him!

"Thou, O Christ, art all I want."

## THE EVER-LIVING LORD
### REVELATION i. 9-18.

LET me take the simple words, and quietly gaze into the wonderful depths of their fathomless simplicity. An old villager used to tell me it would strengthen my eyes if I looked long into deep wells. And it will assuredly strengthen the eyes of my soul to gaze into wells like these.

"*I am He that liveth.*" What a marvellous transformation it worked upon Dr. Dale, when one day, in his study, it flashed upon him, as never before, that Jesus Christ is alive! "Christ is alive!" he repeated again and again, until the clarion music filled all the rooms in his soul. "Christ is alive!"

"*And was dead.*" Yes, the Lord has gone right through that dark place. There are footprints, and they are the footprints of the Conqueror, all along the road. "Christ leads me through no darker room than He went through before."

"*And, behold, I am alive for ever more.*" "Jesus has conquered death and all its powers." Never more will it sit on a transient throne. Its power is broken, its "sting" has lost its poison, there isn't a boast left in its apparently omnivorous mouth! "Where's thy victory, O grave?" And here is the gospel for me—"Because I live **ye** shall live also."

## APRIL The Tenth

### RESURRECTION-LIGHT

*"If we believe that Jesus died and rose again. . . ."*—1 Thessalonians iv. 13-18.

THAT is the eastern light which fills the valley of time with wonderful beams of glory. It is the great dawn in which we find the promise of our own day. Everything wears a new face in the light of our Lord's resurrection. I once watched the dawn on the East Coast of England. Before there was a grey streak in the sky everything was held in grimmest gloom. The toil of the two fishing-boats seemed very sombre. The sleeping houses on the shore looked the abodes of death. Then came grey light, and then the sun, and everything was transfigured! Every window in every cottage caught the reflected glory, and the fishing-boats glittered in morning radiance.

And everything is transfigured in the Risen Christ. Everything is lit up when "the Sun of Righteousness arises with healing in His wings." Life is lit up, and so is death, and so are sorrow and daily labour and human friendships! Everything catches the gleam and is changed. "We are no longer of the night, but of the day." "Walk as children of light." "Awake, thou that sleepest, arise from the dead, and Christ shall shine upon thee."

## APRIL The Eleventh

### *THROUGH DEATH TO LIFE*
Romans v. 1-11.

THE Lord went through death to make a path to life. He descended into shame and suffering, and appalling desolation in order that He might "open the Kingdom of Heaven to all believers." And the way is now open!

Therefore, "*let us have peace with God.*" Let us reverently and willingly tread the heavenly road, and seek the King's presence, and gratefully accept "the everlasting covenant." Let us go, as once rebel soldiers, and let us surrender our arms, and at His bidding take them again, to fight in His service.

And let us "*glory in tribulation.*" If we are in the King's road, at peace with the King, every stormy circumstance will be made to do us service. Yes, all our troubles will be compelled to minister to us, to robe us, and to adorn us, and to make us more like the sons and daughters of a royal house. "Out of the eater will come forth meat, and out of the strong will come forth sweetness."

And, therefore, let us "*joy in God.*" Don't let us be "the King's own," and yet march in the sulks! Let us march to the music of grateful song and praise.

"Children of the heavenly King,
As ye journey, sweetly sing."

## APRIL The Twelfth

### THE LAMB ON THE THRONE

*"In the midst of the throne stood a Lamb as it had been slain!"*—REVELATION v. 6-14.

NOW strange and unexpected is the figure! A lamb—the supreme type of gentleness! A throne, the supreme symbol of power! And the one is in the very midst of the other. The sacrificial has become the sovereign: the Cross is the principal part of the throne. "I, if I be lifted up, will draw all men unto Me."

Yes, this sovereign sacrificial Lord is to receive universal homage and worship. "*Every creature which is in heaven and on the earth*" is to pay tribute at His feet. And this, not by a terrible coercion, but by a gracious constraint. We are not to be driven, we are to be drawn; we are to move by love—compulsion: the Lamb in God is to win the wills of men.

And I, too, may take my harp and make melodious praise before my King. And I, too, may fill the "golden vials" with my grateful intercession, and heaven shall be the sweeter for the odour of my prayers. And I, too, may sound my loud "Amen," the note of gladsome resignation to the sovereign will of God. Yes, even now I may be one of "the multitude whom no man can number," who, in a new song, ascribe all worthiness to "the Lamb that was slain."

## APRIL The Thirteenth

### PURE GOLD

*"Thou shalt overlay it with pure gold. . . . And there I will meet with thee."*—EXODUS xxv. 10-22.

I MUST put my best into my preparations, and then the Lord will honour my work. My part is to be of "pure gold" if my God is to dwell within it. I must not satisfy myself with cheap flimsy and then assume that the Lord will be satisfied with it. He demands my very best as a condition of His enriching Presence.

My prayers must be of "pure gold" if He is to meet me there. There must be nothing vulgar about them, nothing shoddy, nothing hastily constructed, nothing thrown up anyhow. They must be chaste and sincere, and overlaid with pure gold.

My home must be of "pure gold" if He is to meet me there. No unclean passion must dwell there, no carnal appetite, no defiling conversation, no immoderateness in eating and drinking. How can the Lord sit down at such a table, or make One at such a fireside?

Let me present to Him pure gold. Let me offer Him nothing cheap. Let me ever make the ark of my best, and the Lord will meet me there.

# APRIL The Fourteenth

## RELIGION AS MERE MAGIC

*"And when the ark of the covenant of the Lord came into the camp, all Israel shouted with a great shout."*—1 SAMUEL iv. 1-11.

THEY were making more of the ark than of the Lord. Their religion was degenerating into superstition. I become superstitious whenever the means of worship are permitted to eclipse the Object of worship. I then possess a magic instrument, and I forget the holy Lord.

It can be so with prayer. I may use prayer as a magic minister to protect me from invasive ills. I do not pray because I desire fellowship with the Father, but because I should not feel safe without it. The ark is more than the Lord.

It can be so with a crucifix. A crucifix may become a mere talisman, and so supplant the Lord. I may wear the thing and have no fellowship with the Person. And so may it be with the Lord's Supper. I may come to regard it as a magic feast, which makes me immune from punishment, but not immune from sin. It may be a minister of safety, but not of holiness.

So let mine eyes be ever unto the Lord! Let me not be satisfied with the ark, but let me seek Him whose name is holy and whose nature is love.

## DEGRADING HOLY THINGS
### 1 Samuel vi. 1-15.

I MUST remember that a holy thing can be the minister of a plague. Things that were purposed to be benedictions can be changed into blights. The very ark of God must be in its appointed place or it becomes the means of sickness and destruction. So it is with all the holy things of God; if I dethrone them they will uncrown me.

It is even so with music. Unless I give it its holy sovereignty it will become a minister of the passions, and the angel within me is mastered by a beast. Let me read again Tennyson's "Palace of Sin," and let me heedfully note how music becomes the instrument of ignoble sensationalism, and aids in man's degradation. "But exalt her, and she shall exalt thee."

It is even so with art. It is purposed to be the holy dwelling-place of God, but I can so abuse it as to make it the agent of degradation. Instead of hallowing the life it will debase and impoverish it.

I will therefore remember that, if I infringe the Divine order, I can turn the sacramental cup into a vehicle of moral poison and spiritual blight. "They must be holy who bear the vessels of the Lord."

## APRIL The Sixteenth

### PRIORS OF THE LORD

*"None ought to carry the ark of God but the Levites."*—1 Chronicles xv. 1-3, 11-15.

THERE are prepared people for prepared offices. The Lord will fit the man to the function, the anointed and consecrated priest for the consecrated and consecrating ministry.

But now, in the larger purpose of the Lord, and in "the exceeding riches of His grace," everybody may be a priest of the Lord. "He hath made us to be priests and kings unto God." And He will prepare us to carry our ark, and to "minister in holy things."

I can be His priest in the home. He will anoint me as one who is to engage in holy ministries, and I shall be serving at the altar even while engaged in the lowly duties of the house. The humble meal will be sacramental, and common work will be heavenly sacrifice.

I can be His priest in my class. The Lord will clothe me in "linen clean and white," and in my consecrated spirit my scholars shall discern the incense of sacrifice. And woe is me if I attempt to fill the godly office without my God.

And I can be His priest in my workshop. Yes, in the carpenter's shop I may wear the radiant robe of the sanctified. And I, too, as one of the priests of the Lord, can "bear the sin of many, and make intercession for the transgressor."

## GREAT PRAISE

### 1 Chronicles xvi. 7-36.

"GREAT is the Lord!" So many people have such a little God! There is nothing about Him august and sublime. And so He is not greatly praised. The worship is thin, the thanksgivings are scanty, the supplications are indifferent.

All great saints have a great God. He fills their universe. Therefore do they move about in a fruitful awe, and everywhere there is only a thin veil between them and His appearing. Everywhere they discern His holy presence, as the face of a bride is dimly seen beneath her bridal veil. And so even the common scrub of the wilderness is aflame with sacred fire: the humble "primrose on the rock" becomes "the court of Deity": and the "strength of the hills is His also"!

Yes, a great God inspires great praise, and in great praise small cares and small meannesses are utterly consumed away. When praise is mean, anxieties multiply. Therefore let me contemplate the greatness of God in nature and in providence, in His power, and His holiness, and His love. Let me "stand in awe" before His glory: and in the fruitful reverence the soul will be moved in acceptable praise.

## APRIL The Eighteenth

### MECHANICAL PIETY
PHILEMON 10-18.

THE Apostle Paul declares that benefits may be given in one of two ways—"*of necessity*" and "*willingly.*" One is mechanical, the other is spontaneous. I once saw a little table-fountain playing in a drawing-room, but I heard the click of its machinery, and the charm was gone! It had to be wound up before it would play, and at frequent periods it "ran down." A little later I saw another fountain playing on a green lawn, and it was fed from the deep secret resources of the hills!

There is a generosity which is like the drawing-room fountain. If you listen you can hear the mechanical click, and a sound of friction, arising from murmuring and complaint. And there is a generosity which is like the fountain that is the child of the hills. It is clear, and sweet, and musical, and flows on through every season! One is "of necessity"; the other is "willingly." And "God loveth a cheerful giver."

And prayer can be of the same two contrary orders. One prayer is mechanical, it is hard, formal, metallic. The other is spontaneous, forceful, and irresistible. Listen to the Pharisee—"Lord, I thank Thee that I am not as other men are." It is the click of the machine! Listen to the publican—"God be merciful to me, a sinner!" It is the voice of the deeps.

## APRIL The Nineteenth

### UNION IN HARMONY
*"Be ye all of one mind."*—1 PETER iii. 8-17.

BUT this is not unison: it is harmony. When an orchestra produces some great musical masterpiece, the instruments are all of one mind, but each makes its own individual contribution. There is variety with concordance: each one serves every other, and the result is glorious harmony. "By love serve one another." It is love that converts membership into fraternity: it is love that binds sons and daughters into a family.

Look at a field of wild-flowers. What a harmony of colour! And yet what a variety of colours! Nothing out of place, but no sameness! All drawing resource from the same soil, and breathing the vitalizing substance from the same air!

"And ye, being rooted and grounded in love," will grow up, a holy family in the Lord. If love be the common ground the varieties in God's family may be infinite!

And so the unity which the apostle seeks is a unity of mood and disposition. It is not a unity which repeats the exact syllables of a common creed, but a unity which is built of common trust, and love, and hope. It is not sameness upon the outer lips, but fellowship in the secret place.

## APRIL The Twentieth

### THE JOY OF THE LOVER
ROMANS xii. 9-18.

LOVE finds her joy in seeing others crowned. Envy darkens when she sees the garland given to another. Jealousy has no festival except when she is "Queen of the May." But love thrills to another's exaltation. She feels the glow of another's triumph. When another basks in favour her own "time of singing of birds is come!"

And all this is because love has wonderful chords which vibrate to the secret things in the souls of others. Indeed, the gift of love is just the gift of delicate correspondence, the power of exquisite fellow-feeling, the ability to "rejoice with them that do rejoice, and to weep with them that weep." When, therefore, the soul of another is exultant, and the wedding-bells are ringing, love's kindred bells ring a merry peal. When the soul of another is depressed, and a funeral dirge is wailing, love's kindred chords wail in sad communion. So love can enter another's state as though it were her own.

Our Master spake condemningly of those who have lost this exquisite gift. They have lost their power of response. "We have piped with you, and ye have not danced; we have mourned with you, and ye have not lamented." They lived in selfish and loveless isolation. They have lost all power of tender communion.

## APRIL The Twenty-first

### LOVE AS THE GREAT MAGICIAN
1 John ii. 1-11.

A NEW commandment! And yet it is an old one with a new meaning. It is the old water-pot, but its water has been changed into wine. It is the old letter with a new spirit. It is the old body with a new soul. Love makes all things new! It changes duty into delight, and statutes into songs.

What a magic difference love makes to a face. It at once becomes a face illumined. Love makes the plainest face winsome and attractive. It adds the light of heaven, and the earthly is transfigured. No cosmetics are needed when love is in possession. She will do her own beautifying work, and everybody will know her sign.

What a magic difference love makes in service! The hireling goes about his work with heavy and reluctant feet: the lover sings and dances at his toil. The hireling scamps his work: the lover is always adding another touch, and is never satisfied. Just one more touch! And just another! And so on until the good God shall say that loving "patience has had her perfect work."

Love lights up everything, for she is the light of life. Let her dwell in the soul, and every room in the life shall be filled with the glory of the Lord.

## APRIL The Twenty-second

### SPEECH AS A SYMPTOM OF HEALTH

"*The tongue of the wise is health.*"—
PROVERBS xii. 13-22.

OUR doctors often test our physical condition by the state of our tongue. With another and deeper significance the tongue is also the register of our condition. Our words are a perfect index of our moral and spiritual health. If our words are unclean and untrue, our souls are assuredly sickly and diseased. A perverse tongue is never allied with a sanctified heart. And, therefore, everyone may apply a clinical test to his own life: "What is the character of my speech? What do my words indicate? What do they suggest as to the depths and background of the soul?" "By thy words thou shalt be justified, and by thy words thou shalt be condemned."

God delighteth in truthful lips. Right words are fruit from the tree of life. The Lord turns away from falsehood as we turn away from material corruption, only with an infinitely intenser loathing and disgust.

It is only the lips that have been purified with flame from the holy altar of God that can offer words that are pleasing unto Him.

"Take my lips and let them be
　Filled with messages from Thee."

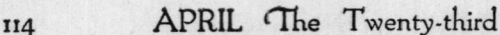

## MASCULINE FORGIVENESS
### COLOSSIANS iii. 12-17.

TRUE forgiveness is a very strong and clean and masculine virtue. There is a counterfeit forgiveness which is unworthy of the name. It is full of "buts," and "ifs," and "maybes," and "peradventures." It moves with reluctance, it offers with averted face, it takes back with one hand what it gives with the other. It forgives, but it "cannot forget." It forgives, but it "can never trust again." It forgives, but "things can never be the same as they were." What kind of forgiveness is this? It is the mercy of the police-court. It is the remission of penalty, not the glorious "abandon" of grace! It is a cold "Don't do it again," not the weeping and compassionate goodwill of the Lord.

"*Even as Christ forgave you, so also do ye.*" That is to be our motive, and that is to be our measure. We are to forgive *because* Christ forgave us. The glorious memory of His grace is to make us gracious. His tender, healing words to us are to redeem our speech from all harshness. In the contemplation of His cross we are to become "partakers of His sufferings," and by the shedding of our own blood help to close and heal the alienation of the world.

And we are to forgive *as* Christ forgave us. Resentment is to be changed into frank goodwill, and filled with the grace of the Lord.

## APRIL The Twenty-fourth

### LIMITED FORGIVENESS
#### Luke xvii. 3-10.

WE are always inclined to set a limit to our moral obligations. We wish, as we say, "to draw a line somewhere." We want to appoint a definite place where obligation ceases, and where the moral strain may be released. The Apostle Peter wished his Master to draw such a line in the matter of forgiveness. "Lord, how oft shall I forgive? Till seven times?" He wanted a tiny moral rule which he could apply to his brother's conduct.

Not so the Lord. Our Master tells His disciple that in those spiritual realms relations are not governed by arithmetic. We cannot, by counting, measure off our obligations. Our repeated acts of forgiveness never bring us nearer to the freedom of revenge. No amount of sweetness will ever permit us to be bitter. We cannot, by being good, obtain a license to be evil. The fact of the matter is, if our goodness is of genuine quality, every act will more strongly dispose us to further goodness. It is the counterfeit element in our goodness that inclines us to the opposite camp. It is when our forgiveness is tainted that we anticipate the "sweetness" of revenge.

## THE HIDDEN FOES
MATTHEW v. 21-26.

OUR Lord always leads us to the secret, innermost roots of things. He does not concern Himself with symptoms, but with causes. He does not begin with the molten lava flowing down the fair mountain slope and destroying the vineyards. He begins with the central fires in which the lava is born. He does not begin with uncleanness. He begins with the thoughts which produce it. He does not begin with murder, but with the anger which causes it. He pierces to the secret fires!

Now, all anger is not of sin. The Apostle Paul enjoins his readers to "be angry, and sin not." To be altogether incapable of anger would be to offer no antagonism to the wrongs and oppressions of the world. "Who is made to stumble, and I burn not?" cries the Apostle Paul. If wrong stalked abroad with heedless feet he burned with holy passion. There is anger which is like clean flame, clear and pure, as "the sea of glass mingled with fire." And there is anger which is like a smoky bonfire, and it pollutes while it destroys.

It is the unclean anger which is of sin. It seeks revenge, not righteousness. It seeks "to get its own back," not to get the wrong-doer back to God. It follows wrong with further wrong. It spreads the devil's fire.

## APRIL The Twenty-sixth

### GOLIATH VERSUS GOD!
1 Samuel xvii. 1-11.

GOLIATH seemed to have everything on his side *except* God. And the things in which he boasted were just the things in which men are prone to boast to-day.

He had physical strength. "His height was six cubits and a span." Athletics had done all they could for him, and he was a fine type of animal perfection.

He had splendid military equipment. "A helmet of brass," and "a coat of mail," and "a spear like a weaver's beam!" Surely, if fine material equipment determines combats, the shepherd-lad from the hills of Bethlehem will be annihilated.

And he enjoyed the enthusiastic confidence of the Philistines. He was his nation's pride and glory! He strode out amid their shouts, and the cheers were like iron in his blood.

But all this counted for nothing, because God was against him. Men and nations may attain to a fine animalism, their warlike equipment may satisfy the most exacting standard, and yet, with God against them, they shall be as structures woven out of mists, and they shall collapse at the touch of apparent weakness. The issue was not Goliath versus David, but Goliath versus God!

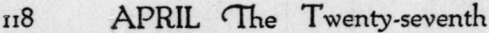

## OBSCURE BIRTHPLACES
### 1 Samuel xvii. 12-27.

GOD'S champion is at present feeding sheep! Who would have expected that Goliath's antagonist would emerge from the quiet pastures? "Genius hatches her offspring in strange places." Very humble homes are the birthplaces of mighty emancipations.

There was a little farm at St. Ives, and the farmer lived a quiet and unsensational life. But the affairs of the nation became more and more confused and threatening. Monarchical power despoiled the people's liberties, and tyranny became rampant. And out from the little farm strode Oliver Cromwell, the ordained of God, to emancipate his country.

There was an obscure rectory at Epworth. The doings in the little rectory were just the quiet practices of similar homes in countless parts of England. And England was becoming brutalized, because its religious life was demoralized. The Church was asleep, and the devil was wide awake! And forth from the humble rectory strode John Wesley, the appointed champion of the Lord to enthuse, to purify, and to sweeten the life of the people.

On what quiet farm is the coming deliverer now labouring? Who knows?

## APRIL The Twenty-eighth

### PREPARING FOR GREAT ENCOUNTERS
#### 1 Samuel xvii. 28-37.

THIS young champion of the Lord had won many victories before he faced Goliath. Everything depends on how I approach my supreme conflicts. If I have been careless in smaller combats I shall fail in the larger. If I come, wearing the garlands of triumph won in the shade, the shout of victory is already in the air! Let me look at David's trophies before he removed Goliath's head.

He had conquered his temper. Read Eliab's irritating taunt in the twenty-eighth verse, and mark the fine self-possession of the young champion's reply! That conquest of temper helped him when he took aim at Goliath! There is nothing like passion for disturbing the accuracy of the eye and the steadiness of the hand.

He had conquered fear. *"Let no man's heart fail because of him."* There was no panic, there was no feverish and wasteful excitement. There was no shouting "to keep the spirits up!" He was perfectly calm.

And he had conquered unbelief. He had a rich history of the providential dealings of God with him, and his confidence was now unclouded and serene. He had known the Lord's power when he faced the bear and the lion. Now for Goliath!

## THE MOOD OF TRIUMPH

"*I come to thee in the name of the Lord of Hosts.*"—1 SAMUEL xvii. 38-54.

THE man who comes up to his foes with this assurance will fight and win. Reasonable confidence is one of the most important weapons in the warrior's armoury. Fear is always wasteful. The man who calmly expects to win has already begun to conquer. Our mood has so much to do with our might. And therefore does the Word of God counsel us to attend to our dispositions, lest, having carefully collected our material implements, we have no strength to use them.

And the man who comes up to his foes with holy assurance will fight with consummate skill. He will be quite "collected." All his powers will wait upon one another, and they will move together as one. He is as self-possessed upon the battlefield as upon parade, as undisturbed before Goliath as before a flock of sheep! And therefore do I say that, fighting with perfect composure, he fights with superlative skill. The right moment is seized, the right stone is chosen, the right aim is taken, and great Goliath is brought low.

## APRIL The Thirtieth

### THE TEST OF VICTORY

"*David behaveth himself wisely.*"—1 SAMUEL xvii. 55—xviii. 5.

THE hour of victory is a more severe moral test than the hour of defeat. Many a man can brave the perils of adversity who succumbs to the seductions of prosperity. He can stand the cold better than the heat! He is enriched by failure, but "spoilt by success." To test the real quality of a man, let us regard him just when he has slain Goliath! "David behaved himself wisely"!

He was not "eaten up with pride." He developed no "side." He went among his friends as though no Goliath had ever crossed his way. He was not for ever recounting the triumph, and fishing for the compliments of his audience. He "behaved wisely." So many of us tarnish our victories by the manner in which we display them. We put them into the shop-window, and they become "soiled goods."

And in this hour of triumph David made a noble friend. In his noonday he found Jonathan, and their hearts were knit to each other in deep and intimate love. It is beautiful when our victories are so nobly borne that they introduce us into higher fellowships, and the friends of heaven become our friends.

## MAY The First

### THE CONDITIONS OF SERENITY
#### Psalm cxxiv.

IF I would be like the Psalmist, I must *clearly recognize my perils*. He sees the "waters," the "proud waters." He beholds the "enemy," and his "wrath," and his "teeth." He sees "the fowler" with his snare! I must not shut my eyes, and "make my judgment blind." One of the gifts of grace is the spirit of discernment, the eyes which not only detect hidden treasure, but hidden foes. The devil is an expert in mimicry; he can make himself look like an angel of light. And so must I be able to discover his snares, even when they appear as the most seductive food.

And if I would be like the Psalmist, I must *clearly recognize my great Ally*. "If it has not been the Lord, who was on our side!" To see the Ally on the perilous field, and to see Him on my side, gives birth to holy confidence and song. "The Lord is on my side, whom shall I fear?" I must make sure of the Ally, and "victory is secure."

And if I would be like the Psalmist, I must not omit the doxology of praise. When the prayer is answered, I am apt to forget the praise. My thanksgivings are not so ready as my requests. And so the apparently conquered enemy steals in again at the door of an ungrateful heart.

## MAY The Second

### THE HAPPY WARRIOR
EPHESIANS vi. 10-18.

HERE is a portrait of the happy warrior! Let me first look at the warrior, and then at the implements with which he fights.

"You cannot fight the French merely with red uniforms; there must be men inside them!" So said Thomas Carlyle. Well, look at this man. *"Strengthened in the Lord, and in the power of His might."* There is a secret communion with the Almighty, and he draws his resources from the Infinite. The water in my home comes from the Welsh hills; every drop was gathered on those grand and expansive uplands. And this man's soldierly strength is drawn from the hills of God; every ounce of his fighting blood comes from the veins of the Lord.

And mark the nature of his armoury. His weapons are dispositions. He fights with "truth," and "righteousness," and "peace," and "faith," and "prayer"! There are no implements like these. A sword will fail where a courtesy will prevail. We can kill our enemies by kindness. And as for the devil himself there is nothing like a grace-filled disposition for putting him to flight! A prayerful disposition can drive him off any field, at any hour of the day or night. "Put on the whole armour of God,"

## OTHER GODS!

*"Thou shalt have no other gods before Me."*
—EXODUS XX. 1-11.

IF we kept that commandment all the other commandments would be obeyed. If we secure this queen-bee we are given the swarm. To put nothing "before" God! What is left in the circle of obedience? God first, always and everywhere. Nothing allowed to usurp His throne for an hour! I was once allowed to sit on an earthly throne for a few seconds, but even that is not to be allowed with the throne of God. Nothing is to share His sovereignty, even for a moment. His dominion is to be unconditional and unbroken. "Thou shalt have no other gods beside Me."

But we have many gods we set upon His throne. We put money there, and fame, and pleasure, and ease. Yes, we sometimes usurp God's throne, and we ourselves dare to sit there for days, and weeks, and years, at a time. Self is the idol, and we enthrone it, and we fall down and worship it. But no peace comes from such sovereignty, and no deep and vital joy. For the real King is not dead, and He is out and about, and our poor little monarchy is as the reign of the midge on a summer's night. Our real kingship is in the acknowledgment of the King of kings. When we worship Him, and Him only, He will ask us to sit on His throne.

## A HEALTHY PALATE

"*How sweet are Thy words unto my taste.*"—
PSALM cxix. 97-104.

SOME people like one thing, and some another. Some people appreciate the bitter olive; others feel it to be nauseous. Some delight in the sweetest grapes; others feel the sweetness to be sickly. It is all a matter of palate. Some people love the Word of the Lord; to others the reading of it is a dreary task. To some the Bible is like a vineyard; to others it is like a dry and tasteless meal. One takes the word of the Master, and it is "as honey to the mouth"; to another the same word is as unwelcome as a bitter drug. It is all a matter of palate.

But what is a man to do who has got a perverted palate, and who calls sweet things bitter and bitter things sweet? He must get a new mouth! And where is he to get it? Not by any ministry of his own creation; his own endeavours will be impotent. A healthy moral palate depends upon the purity of the heart. Our spiritual discernments are all determined by the state of the soul. If the heart be pure, the mouth will be clean, and we shall love God's law. If the soul-appetite be healthy, God's words will be sweet unto our taste. And so does the good Lord give us new palates by giving us new hearts. "Create within us clean hearts, O God, and renew right spirits within us."

## MAY The Fifth

### HEALTHY LISTENING

"*Be ye doers of the word and not hearers only.*"—JAMES i. 21-27.

WHEN we hear the word, but do not do it, there has been a defect in our hearing. We may listen to the word for mere entertainment. Or we may attach a virtue to the mere act of listening to the word. We may assume that some magical efficacy belongs to the mere reading of the word. And all this is perverse and delusive. No listening is healthy which is not mentally referred to obedience. We are to listen *with a view to obedience,* with our eyes upon the very road where the obedient feet will travel. That is to say, we are to listen with purpose, as though we were Ambassadors receiving instructions from the King concerning some momentous mission. Yes, we must listen with an eye on the road.

"Doing" makes a new thing of "hearing." The statute obeyed becomes a song. The commandment is found to be a beatitude. The decree discloses riches of grace. The hidden things of God are not discovered until we are treading the path of obedience. "And it came to pass that as he went he received his sight." In the way of obedience the blind man found a new world. God has wonderful treasures for the dutiful. The faithful discover the "hidden manna."

## MAY The Sixth

### THE PERFECTING OF LOVE
"*Herein is our love made perfect.*"—1 JOHN iv. 11-21.

HOW? By dwelling in God and God in us. Love is not a manufacture; it is a fruit. It is not born of certain works; it springs out of certain relations. It does not come from doing something; it comes from living with Somebody. "Abide in Me." That is how love is born, for "love is of God, and God is love."

How many people are striving who are not abiding. They live in a manufactory, they do not live in a home. They are trying to make something instead of to know Somebody. "This is life, to know Thee." When I am related to the Lord Jesus, when I dwell with Him, love is as surely born as beauty and fragrance are born when my garden and the springtime dwell together. If we would only wisely cultivate the fellowship of Jesus, everything else would follow in its train—all that gracious succession of beautiful things which are called "the fruits of the Spirit."

And "herein is our love made perfect." It is always growing richer, because it is always drawing riches from the inexhaustible love of God. How could it be otherwise? Endless resource must mean endless growth. "Our life is hid with Christ in God," and hence our love will "grow in all wisdom and discernment."

## MAY The Seventh

### IN THE WAYS OF OBEDIENCE
PSALM xix. 7-14.

LET me listen to the exquisite chimes of this wonderful psalm as they ring out the blessedness of the man whose delight is in the law of the Lord. What shall he find in the ways of obedience?

He shall find restoration. "Restoring the soul." He shall find new stores of food along the way. In every emergency he shall find fresh provision; every new need shall discover new supplies. When one store is spent, another shall take its place. "Thou re-storest my soul." In the ways of righteousness the good Lord has appointed ample stores for the provision of all His faithful pilgrims.

He shall find joy. "Rejoicing the heart." In the way of obedience there shall be springs of delight as well as stores of provision. "With joy shall ye draw waters out of the wells of salvation." Fountains of delicious satisfaction rise in the realm of duty, the satisfaction of being right with God, and in union with the eternal will. There is no day without its spring, and "the joy of the Lord is our strength."

He shall find vision. "Enlightening the eyes." The eyes of the obedient are anointed with the eye-salve of grace, and wondrous panoramas break upon the sight. Visions of grace! Visions of love! Visions of glory!

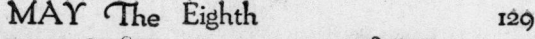

## HOW NOT TO FORGET
DEUTERONOMY xi. 18-25.

IF we wish to retain "the word of the Lord" everything depends upon where we keep it. If we just keep it in the mind, a leaky memory may waste the treasure. A Chinese convert declared that he found the best way to remember the word was to do it! The engraved word became character, written upon the fleshy tables of the heart. He incarnated the word, and it became a vital part of his own personality. He lived it and it lived in him. The word became flesh. This is the only really vital "way of remembrance," to convert the word into the primary stuff of the life.

There is a secondary way by which we may help our apprehension of God's word. "Ye shall teach them." Our hold upon a truth is increased while we impart it to others. The gospel becomes more vivid as we proclaim it to our fellow-men. We see it while we explain it. It grips us the more firmly as we use it to grip our children. This is a great law in life. In these matters it is literally true that memory best retains what she gives away. A truth that is never shared is never really possessed. The word that we teach becomes rooted in our own mind.

## MAY The Ninth

### LOVING THE LORD
#### LUKE x. 21-28.

THE secret of life is to love the Lord our God, and our neighbours as ourselves. But how are we to love the Lord? We cannot manufacture love. We cannot love to order. We cannot by an act of will command its appearing. No, not in these ways is love created. Love is not a work, it is a fruit. It grows in suitable soils, and it is our part to prepare the soils. When the conditions are congenial, love appears, just as the crocus and the snowdrop appear in the congenial air of the spring.

What, then, can we do? We can seek the Lord's society. We can think about Him. We can read about Him. We can fill our imaginations with the grace of His life and service. We can be much with Him, talking to Him in prayer, singing to Him in praise, telling Him our yearnings and confessing to Him our defeats. And love will be quietly born. For this is how love is born between heart and heart. Two people are "much together," and love is born! And when we are much with the Lord, we are with One who already loves us with an everlasting love. We are with One who yearns for our love and who seeks in every way to win it. "We love Him because He first loved us." And when we truly love God, every other kind of holy love will follow. Given the fountain, the rivers are sure.

## MAY The Tenth

### GOD'S USE OF MEN

*"I have surely seen the affliction of My people . . . come now, therefore, I will send thee."*
—Exodus iii. 1-14.

DOES that seem a weak ending to a powerful beginning? The Lord God looks upon terrible affliction and He sends a weak man to deal with it. Could He not have sent fire from heaven? Could He not have rent the heavens and sent His ministers of calamity and disasters? Why choose a man when the archangel Gabriel stands ready at obedience?

This is the way of the Lord. He uses human means to divine ends. He works through man to the emancipation of men. He pours His strength into a worm, and it becomes "an instrument with teeth." He stiffens a frail reed and it becomes as an iron pillar.

And this mighty God will use thee and me. On every side there are Egypts where affliction abounds, there are homes where ignorance breeds, there are workshops where tyranny reigns, there are lands where oppression is rampant. "Come now, therefore, I will send thee." Thus saith the Lord, and He who gives the command will also give the equipment.

## MAY The Eleventh

### BUT——!

*"And Moses answered and said, But——"*—
EXODUS iv. 1-9.

WE know that "but." God has heard it from our lips a thousand times. It is the response of unbelief to the divine call. It is the reply of fear to the divine command. It is the suggestion that the resources are inadequate. It is a hint that God may not have looked all round. He has overlooked something which our own eyes have seen. The human "buts" in the Scriptural stories make an appalling record.

"Lord, I will follow Thee, but——" There is something else to be attended to before discipleship can begin. Obedience is not primary: it must wait for something else. And so our obedience is not a straight line: it is crooked and circuitous; it takes the way of by-path meadow instead of the highway of the Lord. We do not wait upon the Lord's pleasure; we make Him wait upon ours.

There need be no "buts" in our relationship to the King's will. Everything has been foreseen. Nothing will take the Lord by surprise. The entire field has been surveyed, and the preparations are complete. When the Lord says to thee or me, "I will send thee," every provision has been made for the appointed task. "I will not fail thee."

# MAY The Twelfth

## MOUTH AND MATTER

*"Now therefore go, and I will be with thy mouth."*—EXODUS iv. 10-17.

AND what a promise that is for anyone who is commissioned to proclaim the King's decrees. Here can teachers and preachers find their strength. God will be with their mouths. He will control their speech, and order their words like troops. He does not promise to make us eloquent, but to endow our words with the " demonstration of power."

*"And I will teach thee what thou shalt say."* The Lord will not only be with our mouths, but with our minds. He will guide our thoughts as well as our words. He will be as sentinel at the lips. He will be our guide in our processes of meditation and judgment, and He will bring us to enlightened ends. All of which is just this: He will give us mouth and matter.

This does not put a premium upon idleness. The Lord guides when men are honestly groping. He gives us fire when we have built the altar. He works His miracle when we have provided the five loaves. He sends His light through diligent thinking. The divine power is given through the consecrated strength.

## COMMONPLACE FIDELITIES
EXODUS ii. 11-25.

GOD prepares us for the greater crusades by more commonplace fidelities. Through the practice of common kindnesses God leads us to chivalrous tasks. Little courtesies feed nobler reverences. No man can despise smaller duties and do the larger duties well. Our strength is sapped by small disobediences. Our discourtesies to one another impair our worship of God. The neglect of the "pointing" of a house may lead to dampness and fatal disease.

And thus the only way to live is by filling every moment with fidelity. We are ready for anything when we have been faithful in everything. "Because thou hast been faithful in that which is least!" That is the order in moral and spiritual progress, and that is the road by which we climb to the seats of the mighty. When every stone in life is "well and truly laid" we are sure of a solid, holy temple in which the Lord will delight to dwell. The quality of our greatness depends upon what we do with "that which is least."

## MAY The Fourteenth

### CALAMITY AS REVEALER

"*In the year that King Uzziah died I saw the Lord.*"—ISAIAH vi. 1-8.

HE lost a hero, and he found the Lord. He feared because a great pillar had fallen: and he found the Pillar of the universe. He thought everything would topple into disaster, and lo! he felt the strength of the everlasting arms. When Uzziah lived Isaiah had forgotten his Lord. He so depended on the earthly that he had overlooked the heavenly. Uzziah concealed his Lord as a thick veil can hide a face. And when Uzziah died, when the earthly king passed away, the eternal King was revealed; as when by the passing of an earth-born cloud the moon reigns radiant in the open sky.

And thus it is that apparent calamity is often the minister of revelation. The great storm clears the air, and luminous vistas come into view. The howling wind of adversity drives away the earthborn clouds and we see the face of God. Our sorrows prove the occasion of our visions. We see new panoramas through our tears. Bereavement gives us spiritual surprises, and death becomes the servant of life. And so it happens that days which began in gloom end in revelation, and we keep their recurring anniversary with deepening praise.

## GOD IS WIDE-AWAKE

*"Jeremiah, what seest thou? And I said, I see a rod of an almond tree."*—JEREMIAH i. 7-19.

AND through the almond tree the Lord gave the trembling young prophet the strength of assurance. The almond tree is the first to awake from its wintry sleep. When all other trees are held in frozen slumber the almond blossoms are looking out on the barren world. And God is like that, awake and vigilant. Nobody anticipates Him. Wherever Jeremiah was sent on his prophetic mission the Lord would be there before him. Before the prophet's enemies could get to work the Lord was on the field. In the wintriest circumstances of a prophet's life God is wide awake: "He that keepeth Israel shall neither slumber nor sleep."

And still the almond tree has its heartening significance for thee and me. Our God is wide-awake. He looks out upon our wintry circumstances, and nothing is hid from His sight. There is no unrecognized and uncounted factor which may steal in furtively and take Him by surprise. Everything is open. He is wide-awake on the far-off field where the isolated missionary is ploughing his lonely furrow. He is wide-awake on the field of common labour where some young disciple finds it hard to keep clean hands while he earns his daily bread.

## MAY The Sixteenth

### THE DETAILS OF PROVIDENCE

"*The very hairs of your head are all numbered.*"—MATTHEW x. 24-31.

PROVIDENCE goes into details. Sometimes, in our human intercourse, we cannot see the trees for the wood. We cannot see the individual sheep for the flock. We cannot see the personal soul for the masses. We are blinded by the bigness of things; we cannot see the individual blades of grass because of the field.

Now God's vision is not general, it is particular. There are no "masses" to the Infinite. "He calleth His own sheep *by name.*" The single one is seen as though he alone possessed the earth. When God looks at the wood He sees every tree. When He looks at the race He sees every man.

And, therefore, I need not fear that "my way is overlooked by my God." He knows every turning. He knows just where the strain begins at the hill. He knows the perils of every descent. He knows every happening along the road. He knows every letter that came to me by this morning's post. He knows every visitor who knocks at the door of my life, whether the visitor come at the high noon or at the midnight. "There is nothing hid." "The very hairs of your head are all numbered."

## MAY The Seventeenth

### MY BODILY INFIRMITIES
#### John ix. 1-12.

AN infirmity becomes doubly burdensome when we give it a false interpretation. The weight of a thing is determined by our conception of it. If I look upon my ailment as the stroke of an offended God, I wear it like the chains of a slave. If I look upon it as the fire of the gracious Refiner, I can calmly await the beneficent issue. It is my Lord, engaged in chastening His jewels!

And so our Master first of all relieves the blind man of the false interpretation of his infirmity. "*Neither did this man sin, nor his parents.*" That lifts the sorrow out of the winter into the spring. It sets it in the warm, sweet light of grace. It becomes transfigured. It wears a new face, placed there in "the light of His countenance."

And then our Lord relieves the blind man of the infirmity itself. The ministry of blindness was accomplished, and sight was given. No man is kept in the darkness a moment longer than infinite love deems good. Our Lord does not overlook the prison-house, and leave us there forgotten. "He that keepeth Israel shall neither slumber nor sleep." So cheer thee, my soul! The Lord is on thy side! The Miracle-worker knows His time and "the dreariest path, the darkest way, shall issue out in heavenly day."

## BLINDED JUDGMENTS
### John ix. 13-25.

HERE is a ceremonialism which is blind to the humane. Its scrupulous ritualisms have dried up its philanthropy. It thinks more of etiquette than equity. It esteems genuflexions more than generosity. It values the husk more than the kernel. It is Sabbatarian but not humanitarian. My God, deliver me from all pious conventionalities which make me indifferent to the ailments and cries of my fellowmen!

And here is a dense prejudice which is blind to the evident. *"They did not believe that he had been blind."* A prejudice can deflect the judgment, as subtle magnetic currents can deflect the needle. The film of an ecclesiastical prejudice can be so opaque as to make us "blind to facts." We do not "see things as they are." Our perverted eyes give us a crooked world.

And here is a bitter violence which is blind to the glory of the Lord. "We know that this man is a sinner!" And so it comes to that. Our judgments can become so warped that when we look upon Him, "who is the chief among ten thousand and the altogether lovely," "there is no beauty that we should desire Him"! And therefore let this be my daily prayer, "Lord, that I might receive my sight!"

## THE ROCK OF EXPERIENCE
### John ix. 26-41.

THE Lord gains a witness, and a stalwart witness too! First, he stood upon his own inalienable experience. *"One thing I know, that whereas I was blind, now I see."* Second, he drew his own firm inferences from the beneficence of the work. And, in the third place, he reached his grand conclusion. *"If this man were not of God, He could do nothing."* A grand testimony, and given by one who "dared to stand alone!"

And the witness gained a Friend. "Jesus heard that they had cast him out, and when He had found him . . ." Our Lord is always seeking the outcasts. He never abandons the abandoned. When the faithful witness is driven into the wilderness he finds "a table spread" before him "in the presence of his enemies." The man who had recovered his sight was cast out, but on the threshold he met his Lord!

And further sight was given. By the first sight he could see his parents, by the second sight he saw the Son of God. The film was first removed from his eyes, and then from his soul, and he saw "the glory of the Lord." "And he said, Lord, I believe. And he worshipped Him."

## MAY The Twentieth

### THE LONE CRY IN THE BIG CROWD
MARK x. 46-52.

OUR Lord hears the cry of need even when it rises from the midst of the tumultuous crowd. A mother can hear the faint cry of her child in the chamber above, even when the room resounds with the talk and laughter of her guests. And our Lord heard the wail of poor Bartimæus! That lone, sorrowful cry pierced the clamour, "and Jesus stood still." My soul, cry to Him! "Jesus of Nazareth passeth by."

And Bartimæus knew what he wanted. He merged all his petitions in one. "Lord, that I might receive my sight!" And let me, too, come to my Saviour with some great, dominant, all-commanding request. I trifle with my Master. I ask Him for toys, for petty things, while all the time He is waiting to give me "unsearchable wealth," "sight, riches, healing of the mind." "The Lord is great"; and shall I add, "and greatly to be *prayed!*"

And how delicately gracious it is that our Lord should attribute the miracle to Bartimæus himself. "*Thy faith hath made thee whole!*" As though the Lord had had no share in the ministry! He makes so much of our faith, and our endeavour, and our obedience. "If ye had faith as a grain of mustard-seed!" That's all He wants, and miracles are accomplished.

## HUMAN FRAILTIES
### Isaiah xlii. 1-7.

WHAT a winsome revelation of the delicate gentleness of the Lord! "The bruised reed"—is it the impaired musical reed, that cannot now emit a musical sound, and can only be thrown away? He will not snap it and cast it to the void. The discordant life can be made tuneful again: He will put "a new song in my mouth."

"And the smoking flax"—the life that has lost its fire, and therefore its light, its enthusiasm, and therefore its ideals; the life that is smouldering into the cold ashes of moral and spiritual death! He will not stamp it out with His foot. The smouldering fire can be rekindled, a spent enthusiasm can be revived. "He shall baptize you . . . with fire!"

And so He comes to minister to the infirm. He comes to restore injured faculty; "*to open blind eyes.*" He comes to give vision to restored sight: "*to be a light of the Gentiles.*" And He comes to endow the restored life with a rich and gracious freedom: "*to bring out the prisoners from the prison.*" Sight, and light, and freedom! And my Lord is at the gate, and these gifts are in His hand.

## MAY The Twenty-second

### THE LIGHT AS DARKNESS
MATTHEW xiii. 10-17.

THE condition of the heart determines the quality of my discernment. If "the heart is waxed gross," the ears will be "dull of hearing," and the eyes will be "closed." My spiritual senses gain their acuteness or obtuseness from my affections. If my love is muddy my sight will be dim. If my love be "clear as crystal" the spiritual realm will be like a gloriously transparent air.

And the awful nemesis of sin-created blindness is this, that it interprets itself as sight. "The light that is in thee is darkness." We think we see, and all the time we are the children of the night. We think it is "the dawn of God's sweet morning," and behold! it is the perverse flare of the evil one. He has given us a will-o'-the-wisp, and we boastfully proclaim it to be "the morning star."

But there is hope for any man, however blind he be, who will humbly lay himself at Jesus' feet. Let this be my prayer, O Lord, "Cleanse Thou me from secret faults." Deliver me from self-deception, save me from confusing the fixed light of heaven with the wandering beacon-lights of hell. And again and again will I pray, "Lord, that I might receive my sight!"

## MAY The Twenty-third

### WIND AND FIRE
#### Acts ii. 1-21.

THE Holy Spirit will minister to me as a *wind*. He will create an atmosphere in my life which will quicken all sweet and beautiful growth. And this shall be my native air. Gracious seeds, which have never awaked, shall now unfold themselves, and "the desert shall rejoice and blossom as the rose." It was a saying of Huxley, that if our little island were to be invaded by tropical airs, tropical seeds which are now lying dormant in English gardens and fields would troop out of their graves in bewildering wealth and beauty! "Breathe on me, breath of God!"

And the Holy Spirit will minister to me as a *fire*. And fire is our supreme minister of cleansing. Fire can purify when water is impotent. The great fire burnt out the great plague. There are evil germs which cannot be dealt with except by the searching ministry of the flame. "He shall baptize you . . . *with fire*." He will create a holy enthusiasm in my soul, an intense and sacred love, which will burn up all evil intruders, but in which all beautiful things shall walk unhurt.

> "Kindle a flame of sacred love
> On these cold hearts of ours."

## MAY The Twenty-fourth

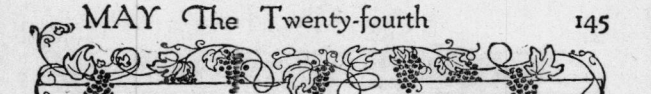

### CALVARY AND PENTECOST
#### Acts ii. 22-36.

THE Apostle Peter traces the stream of Pentecostal blessing to a tomb. This "river of water of life" has its "rise" in a death of transcendent sacrifice. And I must never forget these dark beginnings of my eternal hope. It is well that I should frequently visit the sources of my blessedness, and kneel on "the green hill far away."

It will save me from having a cheap religion. I shall never handle the gifts of grace as though they had cost nothing. There will always be the marks of blood upon them, the crimson stain of incomparable sacrifice.

And it will save me from all flippancy in my religious life. When I visit the cross and the tomb, life is transformed from a picnic into a crusade. For that is ever my peril, to picnic on the banks of the river and to spend my days in emotional loitering.

After all, my Pentecost is purposed to prepare me for my own Gethsemane and Calvary! Life is given me in order that I may spend it again in ready and fruitful sacrifice.

## MAY The Twenty-fifth

### VISIONS AND DREAMS
JOEL ii. 21-32.

AND this old-world promise is good for me to-day. It is like some weather-stained well, whose waters have continued flowing throughout the generations, right down to my own time. Let me drink!

Holy inspiration will give me insight into the mind of my God. *"Your sons and your daughters shall prophesy."* The breath of God creates an atmosphere in which spiritual realities are clearly seen. It is like the Sabbath air in some busy city, when the fumes and smoke of commerce have been blown away. "Thou shalt behold the land that is very far off."

And so in my younger days holy inspiration will give me visions. "Your young men shall see visions." I shall be an idealist, and I shall see things as they exist in God's idea, even though at present they be maimed and imperfect. I shall see them "according to the pattern on the Mount."

And in my later days holy inspiration will give me dreams. *"Your old men shall dream dreams."* And what shall they dream about? Not like the Chinese, of a golden age in a distant past, but of a golden age to be. Their dreams shall have a "forward-looking eye." They shall see "the new Jerusalem coming down out of heaven from God."

## MAY The Twenty-sixth

### THE UNITING OF SUNDERED PEOPLES

*"On the Gentiles also was poured out the gift of the Holy Ghost."*—ACTS x. 34-48.

AND this is ever the issue of a true outpouring of the Spirit: sundered peoples become one. At "low tide" there are multitudes of separated pools along the shore: at "high tide" they flow together, and the little distinctions are lost in a splendid union.

It is so racially. "Jew and Gentile!" Peter and Cornelius lose their prejudices in the emancipating ministry of the Spirit. And so shall it be with English and Irish, with French and German, with Asiatic and European: they shall be "all one" in Christ.

It is so socially. "Bond and free!" The master and the servant shall discover a glorious intimacy and union. And so shall rich and poor, the learned and the illiterate, the many-talented and the obscure. The pools shall flow together.

It is so ecclesiastically. Our sectarianisms are always most frowning and obtrusive when spiritually we are at "low tide." When the tide rises, it is amazing how the ramparts are submerged. It is not round-table conferences that we need, but seasons of communion when together we shall await the outpouring of the Holy Ghost.

## RECEIVING THE HOLY GHOST
### Acts ii. 37-47.

THE sacred process by which the Holy Spirit is received is the same throughout all the years.

First there is *repentance*. And repentance is not a flow of emotion, but a certain direction of mind. I may repent with dry eyes. It is not a matter of feeling, but of willing. It is to lay hold of the aimless, drifting thought, and *steer it toward God!* It is a change of mind.

Second, there is a definite and avowed choice of my new Goal, my new Lord and King. The Christian life cannot be a subterfuge. It cannot be lived incognito. I cannot be the Christ's and wear the livery of an alien power. There must be *confession,* a bold and clarion-like avowal that henceforth I am a soldier of the Lord.

And the spiritual experiences will be sure, as sure as the law-governed processes of the material world. There will be "*remission of sins.*" The old guilt will fall away from my soul as the chains fell from Peter's limbs when the angel touched them. And there will be "*the gift of the Holy Ghost.*" A new dynamic is mine! I enter into fellowship with the power of the ascended Lord.

## MAY The Twenty-eighth

### THE SONS OF GOD

*"For as many as are led by the Spirit of God they are the sons of God."*—ROMANS viii. 9-17.

AND how unspeakably wealthy are the implications of the great word!

If a son, then what holy freedom is mine! Mine is not "*the spirit of bondage.*" The son has "the run of the house." That is the great contrast between lodgings and home. And I am to be at home with the Lord.

And if a son, then heir! "All things are yours." Samuel Rutherford used to counsel his friends to "take a turn" round their estate. And truly it is an inspiring exercise! The Spirit shall lead me over my estate, and I will survey, with the sense of ownership, "the things which God hath prepared for them that love Him."

I wonder if I have the manner of a king's son? I wonder if there is anything in my very "walk" which indicates distinguished lineage and royal blood? Or am I like a vagrant who has no possessions and no heartening expectations?

"Lord, I would serve, and be a son!"

## MAY The Twenty-ninth

### MANY GIFTS—ONE SPIRIT
1 Corinthians xii. 1-13.

THERE is no monotony in the workmanship of my God. The multitude of His thoughts is like the sound of the sea, and every thought commands a new creation. When He thinks upon me, the result is a creative touch never again to be repeated on land or sea. And so, when the Holy Spirit is given to the people, the ministry does not work in the suppression of individualities, but rather in their refinement and enrichment.

Our gifts will be manifold, and we must not allow the difference to breed a spirit of suspicion. Because my brother's gift is not mine I must not suspect his calling. To one man is given a trumpet, to another a lamp, and to another a spade. And they are all the holy gifts of grace.

And thus the gifts are manifold in order that every man may find his completeness in his brother. One man is like an eye—he is a seer of visions! Another man is like a hand—he has the genius of practicality! He is "a handy man"! One is the architect, the other is the builder. And each requires the other, if either is to be perfected. And so, by God's gracious Spirit, the individual man is only a bit, a portion, and he is intended to fit into the other bits, and so make the complete man of the race.

## MAY The Thirtieth

### FINDING THE DEEP THINGS

"*The Spirit searcheth all things, yea, the deep things of God.*"—1 CORINTHIANS ii. 7-12.

THE deep things of God cannot be discovered by unaided reason. "*Eye hath not seen*": they are not to be apprehended by the artistic vision. "*Ear hath not heard*": they are not unveiled amid the discussion of the philosophic schools. "*Neither hath entered into the heart of man*": even poetic insight cannot discern them. All the common lights fail in this realm. We need another illumination, even that provided by the Holy Spirit. And the Spirit is offered unto us "that we might know the things that are freely given to us of God."

And here we have the reason why so many uncultured people are spiritually wiser than many who are learned. They lack talent, but they have grace. They lack accomplishments, but they have the Holy Ghost. They lack the telescope, but they have the sunlight. They are not scholars, but they are saints. They may not be theologians, but they have true religion. And so they have "the open vision." They "walk with God," and "the deep things of God" are made known to their souls.

We must put first things first. We may be busy polishing our lenses when our primary and fundamental need is light. It is not a gift that we require, but a Friend.

## MAY The Thirty-first

### CONNECTION AND CONCORD

"*By one Spirit are we all baptized into one body.*"—1 CORINTHIANS xii. 12-19.

IT is only in the spirit that real union is born. Every other kind of union is artificial, and mechanical, and dead. We can dovetail many pieces of wood together and make the unity of an article of furniture, but we cannot dovetail items together and make a tree. And it is the union of a tree that we require, a union born of indwelling life. We may join many people together in a fellowship by the bonds of a formal creed, but the result is only a piece of social furniture, it is not a vital communion. There is a vast difference between a connection and a concord.

Many members of a family may bear the same name, may share the same blood, may sit and eat at the same table, and yet may have no more vital union than a handful of marbles in a boy's pocket. But let the spirit of a common love dwell in all their hearts and there is a family bound together in glorious union.

And so it is in the spirit, and there alone, that vital union is to be found. And here is the secret of such spiritual union. "By one Spirit are we all baptized into one body." The Spirit of God, dwelling in all our spirits, attunes them into glorious harmony. Our lives blend with one another in the very music of the spheres.

## JUNE The First

### THE BEAUTY OF VARIETY
1 CORINTHIANS xii. 20-31.

GOD'S glory is expressed through the harmony of variety. We do not need sameness in order to gain union. I am now looking upon a scene of surpassing loveliness. There are mountains, and sea, and grassland, and trees, and a wide-stretching sky, and white pebbles at my feet. And a white bird has just flown across a little bank of dark cloud. What variety! And when I look closer the variety is infinitely multiplied. Everything blends into everything else. Nothing is out of place. Everything contributes to finished power and loveliness. And so it is in the grander sphere of human life. The glory of humanity is born of the glory of individuals, each one making his own distinctive contribution.

And thus we have need of one another. Every note in the organ is needed for the full expression of noble harmony. Every instrument in the orchestra is required unless the music is to be lame and broken. God has endowed no two souls alike, and every soul is needed to make the music of "the realm of the blest."

## OUR SPIRITUAL GUIDE

*"When He, the Spirit of truth, is come, He will guide you into all truth."*—JOHN xvi. 7-14.

HOW great is the difference between a guide-post and a guide! And what a difference between a guide-book and a companion! Mere instructions may be very uninspiring, and bare commandments may be very cold. Our Guide is an inseparable Friend.

And how will He guide us? He will give us insight. "He will guide you into all truth." He will refine our spirits so that we may be able to distinguish "things that differ," and that so we may know the difference between "the holy and the profane." Our moral judgment is often dull and imperceptive. And our spiritual judgment is often lacking in vigour and penetration. And so our great Spirit-guide puts our spirits to school, and more deeply sanctifies them, that in holiness we may have discernment.

And He will also give us foresight. He will enable us to interpret circumstances, to apprehend their drift and destiny. We shall see harvests while we are looking at seeds, whether the seeds be seeds of good or evil. All of which means that the Holy Spirit will deliver our lives from the governance of mere whim and caprice, and that He will make us wise with the wisdom of God.

# JUNE The Third

## THE SAFETY OF THE OCCUPIED HEART
### GALATIANS v. 16-25.

TWO friends were cycling through Worcestershire and Warwickshire to Birmingham. When they arrived in Birmingham I asked them, among other things, if they had seen Warwick Gaol along the road. "No," they said, "we hadn't a glimpse of it." "But it is only a field's length from the road!" "Well, we never saw it." Ah, but these two friends were lovers. They were so absorbed in each other that they had no spare attention for Warwick Gaol. Their glorious fellowship made them unresponsive to its calls. They were otherwise engaged.

"Walk in the Spirit, and ye shall not fulfil the lusts of the flesh." That great Companionship will make us negligent of carnal allurements. "The world, and the flesh, and the devil" may stand by the wayside, and hold their glittering wares before us, but we shall scarcely be aware of their presence. We are otherwise engaged. We are absorbed in the "Lover of our souls."

This is the only real and effective way to meet temptation  We must meet it with an occupied heart. We must have no loose and trailing affections. We must have no vagrant, wayward thoughts. Temptation must find us engaged with our Lover. We must "offer no occasion to the flesh." Walking with the Holy One, our elevation is our safety.

## LIFE'S REAL VALUES
### Proverbs viii. 10-19.

HERE is a man who knows the relative values of things. "*Instruction is better than silver*"; "*knowledge rather than choice gold*"; "*wisdom is better than rubies.*" He weighs the inherent worth of things, and puts his choice upon the best.

Let me remember that "all is not gold that glitters." The leaden casket is often the shrine of the priceless scroll. The glaring and the theatrical have often a ragged and seamy interior, and won't bear "looking into." A man may have much display and be very lonely; he may have piles of wealth and be destitute of joy. His libraries may cover an acre, and yet he may have no light. And a man may have only "a candle, and a table, and a bed," and he may be the companion of the eternal God.

I would seek these priceless things. And I would "*seek them early.*" I have so often been late in the search. I have given the early moments to seeking the world's silver and gold, and the later weary moments have been idly devoted to God. "They that seek Me early shall find Me." Let me put "first things first." "Seek ye first the kingdom of God and His righteousness."

## JUNE The Fifth

### THE SPEECH OF EVENTS
#### Acts xiii. 14-23.

DO I sufficiently remember the witness of history? Do I reverently listen to the "great voice behind me"? God has spoken in the speech of events. "Day unto day" has uttered speech. There has been a witness in national life, sometimes quiet as a fragrance, and sometimes "loud as a vale when storms are gone." Is it all to me as though it had never been, or is it part of the store of counsel by which I shape and guide my life?

And do I sufficiently remember my own providences, *"all the way my God has led me"*? When a day is over, do I carry its helpful lamp into the morrow? Do I "learn wisdom" from experience? That is surely God's purpose in the days; one is to lead on to another in the creation of an ever brightening radiance, that so at eventide it may be light.

And do I sufficiently remember that I, too, am making history for my fellows who shall succeed me? What kind of a witness will it be? Grim and full of warning, like the pillar of salt, or winsome and full of heartiness, like some "sweet Ebenezer" built by life's way? Let me pray and labour that my days may so shine with grace that all who remember me shall adore the goodness of my Lord.

## JUNE The Sixth

### LOVE'S EXPENDITURES
1 JOHN iii. 11-18.

"HEREBY perceive we the love of God, because *He laid down His life for us.*" And the real test of any love is what it is prepared to "lay down." How much is it ready to spend? How much will it bleed? There is much spurious love about. It lays nothing down; it only takes things up! It is self-seeking, using the speech and accents of love. It is a "work of the flesh," which has stolen the label of a "fruit of the Spirit." Love may always be known by its expenditures, its self-crucifixions, its Calvarys. Love is always laying down its life for others. Its pathway is always a red road. You may track its goings by the red "marks of the Lord Jesus."

And this is the life, the love-life, which the Lord Jesus came to create among the children of men. It is His gracious purpose to form a spiritual fellowship in which every member will be lovingly concerned about his fellows' good. A real family of God would be one in which all the members bleed for each, and each for all.

How can we gain this disposition of love? "God is love." "We love because He first loved us." At the fountain of eternal love we too may become lovers, becoming "partakers of the divine nature," and filled with all "the fulness of God."

## JUNE The Seventh

### MORAL SURGERY
#### Galatians vi. 1-8.

THIS is a surgical operation in the realm of the soul. A man has been *"overtaken in a fault,"* some evil passion has pounced upon him, and he is broken. Some holy relationship has been snapped, and he is crippled in his moral and spiritual goings. Perhaps his affections have been broken, or his conscience, or his will. Or perhaps he has lost his glorious hope or the confidence of his faith. Here he is, a broken man, the victim of his own broken vows, lame and halt in the pilgrim-way! And some surgeon is needed to re-set the dislocation, and to make him whole again.

And who is to be the surgeon? *"Ye which are spiritual restore such a one."* The men who live under the control of God's Spirit are to be the surgeons for broken hearts and souls. When a man has fallen by reason of sin, the Christian is to be a Good Samaritan, seeking to restore the cripple to health and strength again. We are to kneel and minister to him, binding up his wounds, giving him the balm and cordial of oil and wine.

And what is to be the spirit of the surgeon? "The spirit of meekness." We are not to be supercilious, for the "touch" of pride is never the minister of healing. We are to heal as though some day we may need to be healed.

## THE NEW BIRTH
### John iii. 1-21.

HERE is the Life in contact with the icy legalism of the day. Nicodemus was a Pharisee, and his piety was cold and mechanical. Religion had become a bloodless obedience to lifeless rules. Men cared more about being proper than about being holy. Modes were emphasized more than moods. An external pose was esteemed more highly than an internal disposition. The popular Saint lived on " the outsides of things."

Then came the Life. And what will He say to the externalist? " Ye must be born again." Nothing else could He have said. If the mechanical is to become the vital there is nothing for it but a new birth. To get from the outside into the inside of things, from the letter into the spirit, we need the miracle of renewal, the recreating ministry of grace.

And so it is to-day. The ritualistic is vitalized by the evangelistic. If the mechanical is to become the spontaneous, there is need of the " well of living water, springing up unto eternal life." When we are born again, ritual becomes helpful trellis for the spiritual flowers; the outward form becomes the helpmeet of redeeming grace.

## THE STORY OF A SORROWFUL SOUL
### Psalm iii.

THIS tearful little psalm tells me where a sorrowful soul found a place of help and consolation. He resorted to God.

"*Thou art a shield about me.*" He got the Lord between him and his circumstances. There is nothing else subtle enough to interpose. Our hurtful circumstances are so invasive and so immediate that only God can come between us and them. But when God gets in between we are immune. "Though an host should encamp against me, my heart shall not fear."

"*Thou art my glory.*" And that is an honour that need never be stained. My worldly glory can be besmirched. An evil man throws mud, and my poor reputation is gone. "There's always somebody ready to believe it!" But my glory with God, and in God—man's mud cannot touch that fair fame! Even Absalom cannot defile that resplendent robe.

"*Thou art the lifter-up of my head.*" The flower is "looking up" again! In the Lord's presence we recover our lost spirits. "He restoreth my soul." "And now shall mine head be lifted up above mine enemies round about me."

## PILLARS OF CLOUD AND FIRE

*"The Lord went before them by day in a pillar of cloud."*—EXODUS xiii. 17—xiv. 4.

I NEED His leadership in the daytime. Sometimes the daylight is my foe. It tempts me into carelessness. I become the victim of distraction. The "garish day" can entice me into ways of trespass, and I am robbed of my spiritual health. Many a man has been faithful in the twilight and night who has lost himself in the sunshine. He went astray in his prosperity: success was his ruin. And so in the daytime I need the shadow of God's presence, the cooling, subduing, calming influence of a friendly cloud.

"*And by night in a pillar of fire.*" And I need God's leadership in the night. Sometimes the night fills me with fears, and I am confused. The darkness chills me, sorrow and adversity make me cold, and I shiver along in uncertain going. But my God will lead me as a presence of fire. He will keep my heart warm even in the midnight, and He will guide me by the kindlings of His love. There shall be "nothing hid from the heat thereof." And my bewildering fears shall flee away, and I will sing "songs in the night."

## JUNE The Eleventh

### THE PATH ACROSS THE SEA
"*Thy way is in the sea.*"—Psalm lxxvii. 11-20.

AND the sea appears to be the most trackless of worlds! The sea is the very symbol of mystery, the grim dwelling-house of innumerable things that have been lost. But God's way moves here and there across this trackless wild. God is never lost among our mysteries. He knows his way about. When we are bewildered He sees the road, and He sees the end even from the beginning. Even the sea, in every part of it, is the Lord's highway. When His way is in the sea we cannot trace it. Mystery is part of our appointed discipline. Uncertainty is to prepare us for a deeper assurance. The spirit of questioning is one of the ordained means of growth. And so the bewildering sea is our friend, as some day we shall understand. We love to " lie down in green pastures," and to be led " beside the still waters," and God gives us our share of this nourishing rest. But we need the mysterious sea, the overwhelming experience, the floods of sorrows which we cannot explain. If we had no sea we should never become robust. We should remain weaklings to the end of our days.

God takes us out into the deeps. But His way is in the sea. He knows the haven, **He** knows the track, and we shall arrive!

## JUNE The Twelfth

### WAITING FOR THE SPECTACULAR

*"The waves covered their enemies. . . . Then believed they His words."*—PSALM cvi. 1-12.

THEIR faith was born in a great emergency. A spectacular deliverance was needed to implant their trust in the Lord. They found no witness in the quiet daily providence; the unobtrusive miracle of daily mercy did not awake their song. They dwelt upon the "special" blessing, when all the time the really special blessing was to be found in the sleepless care which watched over them in their ordinary and commonplace ways.

It is the old story. We are wanting God to appear in imperial glory; and He comes among us as a humble carpenter. We want great miracles, and we have the daily Providence. We see His dread goings in the earthquake; we do not feel His presence in the lilies of the field. We watch Him in the smoke and flames of Vesuvius; we do not recognize His footprints in the little turf-clad hill that is only a few yards from our own door.

It is a great day when we discover our God in the common bush. That day is marked with glory when our daily bread becomes a sacrament. When we enjoy a closer walk with God, common things will wear the hues of heaven.

## JUNE The Thirteenth

### CLOUDED BUT NOT LOST!

*"Clouds and darkness are round about Him."*
—Psalm xcvii.

WHEN Lincoln had been assassinated, and word of the tragedy came to New York, "the people were in a state of mind which urges to violence." A man appeared on the balcony of one of the newspaper offices, waving a small flag, and a clear voice rang through the air: "Fellow-citizens! Clouds and darkness are round about Him! His pavilion is dark waters, and thick clouds of the skies! Justice and judgment are the habitation of His throne! Fellow-citizens, God reigns!" It was the voice of General Garfield.

That voice proclaimed the divine sovereignty, even when the heavens were black with the menace of destruction. Lincoln had been assassinated, but God lived! Human confusion does not annihilate His throne. God liveth! "The firm foundation standeth sure." This is the only rock to stand upon when the clouds have gathered, and the waters are out, and the great deeps are broken up. God's sceptre does not fall from His grasp, nor is snatched by alien hands. The throne abideth. Joy will rise from the apparent chaos as springs are unsealed by the earthquake. He will bring fortune out of misfortune; the darkness shall be the hiding-place of His grace.

## THE LAW IN THE HEART

"*I will put My laws into their hearts.*"—
HEBREWS x. 16-22.

EVERYTHING depends on where we carry the law of the Lord. If it only rests in the memory, any vagrant care may snatch it away. The business of the day may wipe it out as a sponge erases a record from a slate. A thought is never secure until it has passed from the mind into the heart, and has become a desire, an aspiration, a passion. When the law of God is taken into the heart, it is no longer something merely remembered: it is something loved. Now things that are loved have a strong defence. They are in the "keep" of the castle, in the innermost custody of the stronghold. The strength of the heart is wrapped about them, and no passing vagrant can carry them away.

And this is where the good Lord is willing to put His laws. He is wishful to put them among our loves. And the wonderful thing is this: when laws are put among loves they change their form, and His statutes become our songs. Laws that are loved are no longer dreadful policemen, but compassionate friends. "O! how I love Thy law!" That man did not live in a prison, he lived in a garden, and God's will was unto him as gracious flowers and fruits. And so shall it be unto all of us when we love the law of the Lord.

## JUNE The Fifteenth

### THE KING'S GUESTS
*"Who shall ascend into the hill of the Lord?"*
—Psalm xxiv.

WHO shall be permitted to pass into the sanctuary of the cloud, and have communion with the Lord in the holy place? "He that hath clean hands." These hands of mine, the symbols of conduct, the expression of the outer life, what are they like? "Your hands are full of blood." Those hands had been busy murdering others, pillaging others, brutally ill-using their fellow-men. We may do it in business. We may do it in conversation. We may do it in a criminal silence. Our hands may be foul with a brother's blood. And men and women with hands like these cannot "ascend into the hill of the Lord." There must be no stain of an unfair and scandalous life.

"And a pure heart." We need not trouble about the hands if the heart be clean. If all the presences that move in the heart—desires, and motives, and sentiments, and ideals—are like white-robed angels, "without spot, or wrinkle, or any such thing," everything that emerges into outer life will share the same radiant purity. The heart expresses itself in the hands. Character blossoms in conduct. The quality of our current coin is determined by the quality of the metal in the mint. "As a man thinketh in his heart, so is he."

## SINAI AND CALVARY
### Hebrews xii. 18-28.

WE need not live at the foot of Mount Sinai. It is like living at the foot of Mount Pelee, the home of awful eruption, and therefore the realm of gloom and uncertainty and fear. We are not saved by law, neither indeed can we be. Neither can law heal us after our transgressions and defeats. The law has nothing for prodigal men but "blackness, and darkness, and tempest." It has no sound but dreaded decree, no message but menace, no look but a frown. Who will build his house at the foot of Mount Sinai?

"But ye are come unto Mount Zion." Our true home is not at Sinai, but at Calvary. There is no place for the sinner at the first mount; at the second mount there is a place for no one else. At Calvary we may find our way back to the holiness we lost at Sinai. Through grace we may drop the burden of our sin and begin to wear the garments of salvation. The way back to heaven is by "the green hill, without a city wall." It is a mount that can be reached by the most exhausted pilgrim; and the one who has "spent all" will assuredly find a full restoration of life at the gate of his Saviour's death. "Ye are come to Jesus, the mediator of the new covenant."

## JUNE The Seventeenth

### THE INVISIBLE PRESENCE
"*Show me Thy glory.*"—EXODUS xxxiii. 12-23.

MOSES wist not what he asked. His speech was beyond his knowledge. The answer to his request would have consumed him. He asked for the blazing noon when as yet he could only bear the quiet shining of the dawn. The good Lord lets in the light as our eyes are able to bear it. The revelation is tempered to our growth. The pilgrim could bear a brightness in Beulah land that he could not have borne at the wicket-gate; and the brilliance of the entry into the celebrated city throws the splendours of Beulah into the shade. Yes, the gracious Lord will unveil His glory as our "senses are exercised to receive it."

"My Presence shall go with thee." That is all the glory we need upon the immediate road. His companionship means everything. The real glory is to possess God; let Him show us His inheritance as it shall please Him. Life's glory is to "feel Him near." When the loving wife feels that the husband is in the house, and when the loving husband feels that the wife is in the house, that is everything! The joy of each other's presence is the crown of married bliss. And so it is with the soul that is married to the Lord: His presence is the soul's delight. "Thou, O Christ, art all I want." "O Master, let me walk with Thee."

## JUNE The Eighteenth

### THE BENEFITTED AS BENEFACTORS

*"Who comforteth us . . . that we may be able to comfort."*—2 CORINTHIANS i. 3-7.

AND how does the Lord comfort us? He has a thousand different ways, and no one can ever tell by what way the comfort will come to his soul. Sometimes it comes by the door of memory, and sometimes by the door of hope. Sometimes it is borne to us through the ministry of nature, and at other times through the ministry of human speech and kindness. But always, I think, it brings us the sense of a Presence, as though we had a great Friend in the room, and the troubled heart gains quietness and peace. The mist clears a little, and we have a restful assurance of our God.

Now comforted souls are to be comforters. They who have received benefits of grace are to be benefactors. They who have heard the sweet music of God's abiding love are to sing it again to others. They who have seen the glory are to become evangelists. We must not seek to hoard spiritual treasure. As soon as we lock it up we begin to lose it. A mysterious moth and rust take it away. If we do not comfort others, our own comfort will turn again to bitterness; the clouds will lower and we shall be imprisoned in the old woe. But the comfort which makes a comforter grows deeper and richer every day.

## JUNE The Nineteenth

### RECKONING UP THINGS
PSALM xc. 1-12.

NUMBERING things is one of the healthful exercises of the spiritual life. Unless we count, memory is apt to be very tricky and to snare us into strange forgetfulness. Unless we count what we have given away, we are very apt to exaggerate our bounty. We often think we have given when we have only listened to appeals; the mere audience has been mistaken for active beneficence. The remedy for all this is occasionally to count our benevolences and see how we stand in a balance-sheet which we could present to the Lord Himself.

And we must count our blessings. It is when our arithmetic fails in the task, and when counting God's blessings is like telling the number of the stars, that our souls bow low before the eternal goodness, and all murmuring dies away "like cloud-spots in the dawn."

And we must also "number our days." We are wasteful with them, and we throw them away as though they are ours in endless procession. And yet there are only seven days in a week! A day is of immeasurable preciousness, for what high accomplishment may it not witness? A day in health or in sickness, spent unto God, and applied unto wisdom, will gather treasures more precious than rubies and gold.

## JUNE The Twentieth

### THE REVEALING PRESENCE OF THE LORD

Ephesians vi. 1-10.

A STARLING never reveals the richness of its hues until we see it in the sunlight. A duty never discloses its beauties until we set it in the light of the Lord. It is amazing how a dull road is transfigured when the sunshine falls upon it! God's grace reveals the graces in all healthy things. Hidden lovelinesses troop out when we set them in the presence of the Lord.

And so the Apostle counsels an obedience which is "in the Lord." He wants us to know how beautiful common things can be when they are linked to Christ. And what he says about obedience he says about everything. One of the great secrets in the teaching of Paul is expressed in just this phrase, "in the Lord," "in Christ." It meant connection with a power-house whose energy would light up all the common lamps of life—the lamps of hope, of faith, of love, of daily labour, and of human service.

And this is the secret of the Christian life. We need no other; at least, all other secrets are involved in this. If we attend to this little preposition "in," we have entry into the infinite. If we are "in Christ," we are in the kingdom of everything that endures, and we are outside nothing but sin.

## JUNE The Twenty-first

### ROOM FOR THE SAPLINGS

*"Children crying in the temple, saying Hosanna!"*—MATTHEW xxi. 1-16.

CHILDREN'S voices mingling in the sounds of holy praise! A little child can share in the consecrated life. Young hearts can offer love pure as a limpid spring. Their sympathy is as responsive as the most sensitive harp, and yields to the touch of the tenderest joy and grief. No wonder the Lord "called little children unto Him"! They were unto Him as gracious streams, and as flowers of the field.

Let the loving Saviour have our children. Let there be no waiting for maturer years. Maturity may bring the impaired faculty and the embittered emotion. Let Him have things in their beginnings, the seeds and the saplings. Let Him have life before it is formed, before it is "set" in foolish moulds. Let us consecrate the cradle, and the good Lord will grow and nourish His saints.

## JUNE The Twenty-second

### CHILDLIKENESS
#### Mark ix. 33-41.

IT is the child-spirit that finds life's golden gates, and that finds them all ajar. The proudly aggressive spirit, contending for place and power, may force many a door, but they are not doors which open into enduring wealth and peace. Real inheritances become ours only through humility.

The proud are, therefore, self-deceived. They think they have succeeded when they have signally failed. They have the shadow, but they have missed the substance. They may have the applause of the world, but the angels sigh over their defeat. They pride themselves on having "got on"; the angels weep because they have "gone down."

When we grow away from childlikeness we are "in a decline." "God resisteth the proud; He giveth grace to the humble." The lowly make great discoveries; to them the earth is full of God's glory.

## JUNE The Twenty-third

### THE GREATEST BENEFACTORS
#### MATTHEW x. 29-42.

IT is a very wonderful thing that the finest services are within the power of the poorest people. The deepest ministries find their symbols in " cups of cold water," which it is in the power of everybody to give. The great benefactors are the great lovers, and their coin is not that of material money, but the wealth of the heart. A bit of affection is worth infinitely more than the gift of a necklace of pearls. To kindle hope in a fainting soul is far more precious than to adorn the weary pilgrim with dazzling gems. " He brought me heaps of presents, but I was hungering for love! " Such was the pathetic cry of one who was " clothed in purple and fine linen, and fared sumptuously every day."

" Cups of cold water," simple ministries of refreshment, the love-thought, the love-prayer, the love-word—these are the privileged services of all of us. And everybody needs these gentle and gracious services of refreshment, and often there is greatest need where there seems to be least.

## AT EASE IN ZION

*"Woe to them that are at ease in Zion."*— Amos vi. 1-7.

I WOULD be delivered from the folly of confusing ease and rest. There is an infinite difference between comforts and comfort. It is one thing to lie down on a luxurious couch: it is a very different thing to "lie down in green pastures" under the gracious shepherdliness of the Lord. The ease which men covet is so often a fruit of stupefaction, the dull product of sinful drugs, the wretched sluggishness of carnal gratification and excess. The rest which God giveth is alive and wakeful, abounding in tireless and fruitful service. "Oh, rest in the Lord."

But is it not a strange thing that men can be "at ease in Zion"? That they can play the beast in the holy place? Zion was full of holy memory, and abounded with suggestions of the Divine Presence. And yet here they could carouse, and lose themselves in swinish indulgence! A little while ago I saw a beautiful old church which had been turned into a common eating-house!

My soul, be on thy guard. Be watchful and diligent, and busy thyself in the practice of "self-knowledge, self-reverence, self-control."

## JUNE The Twenty-fifth

### DESOLATIONS WROUGHT BY SIN

"*The Lord hath spoken this word.*"—ISAIAH xxiv. 1-12.

"THE Lord hath spoken this word," and it is a word of judgment. It unveils some of the terrible issues of sin.

See the effects of sin upon the spirit of man. "*The merry-hearted do sigh.*" Life loses its wings and its song. The buoyancy and the optimism die out of the soul. The days move with heavy feet, and duty becomes very stale and unwelcome. If only our ears were keen enough we should hear many a place of hollow laughter moaning with troubled and restless sighs. The soul cannot sing when God is defied.

But see another effect of sin. "*The earth moaneth.*" That is a frequent note in Bible teaching. The forces of nature are mysteriously conditioned by the character of man. When man is degraded, nature is despoiled. The beauty of the garden is checked when man has lost his crown. "The whole creation groaneth in pain," waiting for the manifestation of the children of God.

Sin spreads desolation everywhere. When I sin, I become the centre of demoralizing forces which influence the universe. And so let me ever pray, "Deliver me from evil."

## CRUCIFYING THE FLESH

*"Arm yourselves likewise with the same mind."*—I PETER iv. 1-8.

LET not the body be dominant, but the soul. Let me study the example and counsel of the Apostle Paul.

*"I keep my body under."* Literally, I pummel it! If it is obtrusive and aggressive, its appetites clamouring for supremacy, I pummel it! Paul was not afraid of severe measures where carnality was concerned. He would fast a whole day in order to put the flesh in its place. And so should it be with all the Lord's children. We are too self-indulgent. It is well at times to put the body on the cross, and crucify its cravings.

*"Give no occasion to the flesh."* Do not give it a chance of mastery! And, therefore, do not feed it with illicit thought. Turn the mind away from the subjects in which the body will find exciting stimulant. It is thought which awakes passion, and thought can do much to destroy it. "Set your mind on things which are above." Keep the mind pure, and the swine will never enter the holy place.

## JUNE The Twenty-seventh

### GOD IS LIGHT!
*"In Him is no darkness at all."*—1 John i.

THAT wonderful mansion of God's Being is gloriously radiant in every room! In the house of my life there are dark chambers, and rooms which are only partially illumined, the other parts being in the possession of night. Some of my faculties and powers are dark ministers, and some of my moods are far from being "homes of light." But "God is light," and everything is glorious as the meridian sun! His holiness, His grace, His love, His mercy: there are no dark corners where uncleanness hides; everything shines with undimmed and speckless radiancy!

And if I "walk in the light," I, too, shall become illumined. "They looked unto Him and were lightened." We are fashioned by our highest companionships. We acquire the nature of those with whom we most constantly commune.

And the light He gives is also fire. It will burn away our sin. We may measure the reality and strength of our communion by the destruction of our sin. A great burning will be proceeding in our life, and one evil habit after another will be in the love-furnace of purification. The Lord still "purifies Jerusalem by the spirit of burning."

## JUNE The Twenty-eighth

### THE WAITING LIGHT
2 CORINTHIANS iv. 1-6.

I CAN shut out the sweet light of the morning. I can refuse to open the shutters and draw up the blinds. And I can shut out the Light of life.

I can draw the thick blinds of prejudice, and close the impenetrable shutters of sin. And the Light of the world cannot get into my soul.

And I can let in the waiting light of the morning, and flood my room with its glory. And the Light is "a gracious, willing guest." No fuss is needed, no shouting is required. Open thy casement, and the gracious guest is in! And my Lord has no reluctance in His coming; we have not to drag Him to our table. Open thy heart, and the Lord is in!

And when the light is within there will be radiance at the windows. And when the Lord is shining in our hearts there will be a witness in the life. Men will see that we are "with Jesus," because we are "light in the Lord."

Good Lord, deliver me from "the god of this world" lest I be blinded and become unable to see Thee! I open my heart to Thee! Shine in, Thou light of life, and make my soul the radiant witness of Thy grace.

## JUNE The Twenty-ninth

### EFFECTUAL PRAYERS
*"The effectual fervent prayer of a righteous man availeth much."*—JAMES v. 13-20.

OR, as Weymouth translates it, "The heartfelt supplication of a righteous man exerts a mighty influence." Prayer may be empty words, with no more power than those empty shells which have been foisted upon the Turks in their war with the Balkan States. Firing empty shells! That is what many professed prayers really are; they have nothing in them, and they accomplish nothing. They are just forged upon the lips, and they drop to the earth as soon as they are spoken. Effectual prayers are born in the heart; they are stocked with heart-treasure, with faith, and hope, and desire, and holy urgency, and they go forth with power to shake the world.

What are my prayers like? *If I were God, could I listen to them?* Are they mere pretences at prayer, full of nothing but sound? Is there any reasonable ground for assuming that they can accomplish anything? Or are my prayers weighted with sincere desire? Do they comprehend my brother's good as well as my own? Are they spoken in faith? Do they go forth in great expectancy? Then do they surely "exert a mighty influence," and they become fellow-labourers with all God's ministries of grace. The greatest thing I can do is greatly to pray.

## JUNE The Thirtieth

### GOD MY STRENGTH AND SONG

"*The Lord is my strength and my song.*"—
PSALM cxviii. 14-21.

YES, first of all "my strength" and then "my song"! For what song can there be where there is languor and fainting? What brave music can be born in an organ which is short of breath? There must first be strength if we would have fine harmonies. And so the good Lord comes to the songless, and with holy power He brings the gift of "saving health."

"And my song"! For when life is healthy it instinctively breaks into song. The happy, contented soul goes about the ways of life humming its satisfactions to itself, and is now and again heard by the passer-by. The Lord fills the life with instinctive music. When life is holy it becomes musical with His praise.

So here I see the appointed order in Christian service. It is futile to try to make people joyful unless we do it by seeking first to make them strong. First the good, and then the truly happy! First the holy, and then the musical. First God, and then the breath of His Holy Spirit, and then "the new song."

## JULY The First

### THE LIFE OR THE LIGHT OF MEN
"*In Him was life.*"—JOHN i. 1-18.

NOT merely a pool of life, but the well-spring. All rivers of enriching vitality have their source in Him. Nowhere is there a crystal stream which was not born at the Fountain. Let us make our claim for the Lord all-comprehensive and inclusive. Whatever energizes body, mind, or soul, has its origin in our Sovereign King. "All our springs are in Thee." "Thou of life the Fountain art."

"*And the life was the light of men.*" And what did He not light up? His amazing rays streamed down the darkest ways of men, and illumined the vast, sombre chambers of human circumstance. He lit up sin and showed its true colour! He lit up sorrow, and transfigured it! He lit up duty, and gave it a new face. He lit up common work, and glorified it. He lit up death, and we could see through it! But, above all, He lit up God, and "the people that sat in darkness saw a great light."

"*And the darkness apprehended it not.*" The darkness could not lay hold of it and quench it! It was not overwhelmed and eclipsed by the murkiest fog of prejudice, or by the dingiest antagonism of sinful pride. "The light showeth in the darkness," inviolable and invincible!

## LIGHT AND LIGHTNING

*"And the spirit of the Lord shall rest upon Him."*—ISAIAH xi. 1-10.

AND the spirit is one of light! All the doors and windows are open. His correspondences are perfect and unbroken. He is of "quick understanding," keen-scented to discern the essences of things, alert to perceive the reality behind the semblance, to "see things as they are." All the great primary senses are awake, and He has knowledge of every "secret place."

*"He shall smite . . . with the rod of His mouth, and with the breath of His lips shall He slay."* The spirit of light follows a crusade of holiness. The light becomes lightning! The "breathing," which cools the fever-stricken, can also become a hot breath, which wastes and destroys every plant of evil desire. It is an awful thing, and yet a gracious thing, that "our God is a consuming fire." It was foretold of our Lord that He should baptize "with fire."

And this crusade of holiness is in the ministry of peace. He will burn away all that defileth, in order that He may create a profound and permanent fellowship. When His work is done, there will be a mingling of apparent opposites, and antagonisms will melt into a gracious union. "The sucking child will play on the hole of the asp, and the weaned child shall put his hand on the adder's den."

## JULY The Third

### MY ELDER BROTHER
#### Hebrews ii. 9-18.

AND doth my Lord call me one of His brethren? Let me leisurely think upon it, until my very soul moves amid my affairs in noble and hallowed dignity. If I steadily remember "who I am," it will assuredly transfigure "what I am." I lose the sense of my high kinship, and then I am quite content to be "sent into the fields to feed swine."

And my elder Brother came to "destroy the works of the devil." That is the entire ministry of destruction. Nothing beautiful does He destroy, nothing winsome: only the insidious presences which are the foes of these things. He will destroy only the pestiferous microbes which ravage the vital peace of the soul. Our Lord is the enemy of the deadly, and therefore of "him that had the power of death—that is, the devil!"

And in this holy ministry of destruction He can defend my soul as "one who knows," Himself "having been tempted." He knows the subtlety of the devil, and where the soul is most perilously exposed, and He is therefore "able to succour them that are tempted."

## EMPTYING ONESELF

*" He emptied Himself."*—PHILIPPIANS ii. 1-11.

IN Mr. Silvester Horne's garden a very suggestive scene was one day to be witnessed. A cricketer of world-wide renown was playing a game with Mr. Horne's little four-year-old son! And the fierce bowler "emptied himself," and served such gentle, dainty little balls that the tiny man at the wickets was not in the least degree afraid! And the Lord of glory "emptied Himself," fashioning Himself to our "low estate," and in His unspeakably gentle approaches we find our peace.

And I, too, am to seek a corresponding lowliness of mind in order that I, too, may be of service to my weak and needy brother. It is for me to empty myself of the pride of strength, the brutal aggressiveness of success, the sometimes unfeeling obtrusiveness of health; I must empty myself, and "get down" by the side of weakness and infirmity, and in gentle fellowship humbly proffer my help.

And if the mind is to be in me "which was also in Christ Jesus," it is needful for me to commune with Him "without ceasing." His gentleness can make me great.

## THE DISCIPLESHIP THAT TELLS
"*He that followeth Me.*"—JOHN viii. 12-20.

YES, but I must make sure that I follow Him in Spirit and in truth. It is so easy to be self-deceived. I may follow a pleasant emotion, while all the time a bit of grim cross-bearing is being ignored. I may be satisfied to be "out on the ocean sailing," singing of "a home beyond the tide," while all the time there is a piece of perilous salvage work to be done beneath the waves. To "follow Jesus" is to face the hostility of scribes and Pharisees, to offer restoring friendship to publicans and sinners, to pray in blood-shedding in Gethsemane, to brave the derision of the brutal mob, and to be "ready" for the appalling happenings on Calvary! Therefore, following is not a light picnic; it is a possible martyrdom!

But if I set my face "to go," the Lord Himself will visit me with "*the light of life.*" And the resource shall not be broken and spasmodic: it shall be mine without ceasing. "Be thou faithful . . . and I will give thee . . . life." That life will flow into my soul, just as the oxygenating air flows down to the diver who is faithfully busy recovering wreckage from the wealth-strewn bed of the mighty sea. Let me be faithful, and every moment the Lord will crown me with His own vitalizing life!

## LIFE AS A VOICE
John i. 19-34.

THIS man humbly desires to be "*a voice*." He has no ambition to receive popular homage. He does not covet the power of the lordly purple. He does not crave to be a great person; he only wants to be a great voice! He wants to articulate the thought and purpose of God. He is quite content to be hidden, like a bird in a thick bush, if only his song may be heard.

And in order that he may be a voice he retires into the silent solitudes of the desert. He will listen before he speaks. Come thou, my soul, into his secret! The air is clamorous with speech behind which there has been no hearing. Men speak, and in their words there is no pulse of the Infinite. In their consolations there is no balm. In their reproaches there is no sword. Their words are empty vessels, full of sound! Let my voice be hushed until I have heard the voice of the Highest. "He that hath ears to hear, let him hear."

And when he spake, it was in clear and definite testimony, "Behold the Lamb of God!" The "voice" succeeded, for men began to look away from the herald to the herald's Lord. In forgetting John they found the King. They passed the *signpost,* and arrived at *home!*

## JULY The Seventh

### IN THE GOLDEN AGE
Isaiah xl. 1-10.

AND so these things are to happen when the Lord has come to His own, and His decrees are honoured in our midst.

Certain *inequalities* are to be ended. Valleys are to be exalted, and mountains are to be made low. There is to be a levelling! Men are to be equal in freedom and opportunity.

Certain *crookednesses* are to be ended. They are to be "made straight." Society has become warped with the heat of lust, and the fierce fever of competition, and the hot, devouring fires of greed. When the Lord is enthroned the fires will be put out, the heat will pass, and the twisted fellowships will be rectified.

Certain *roughnesses* are to be ended. Class works against class with jagged edge, like the teeth of a saw. They tear and rend one another, and the family of God is always bleeding. These "rough places" are to be "made plain." We are to "work in to one another," smoothly, congenially, in a frictionless peace.

And this Lord is coming, coming every day, and "His arm shall rule for Him." "Say unto the cities of Judah—Behold your God!"

## JULY The Eighth

### *WHAT MANNER OF MAN?*
#### MATTHEW xi. 7-15.

THERE are some men who are only as *desert reeds!* They move to the breath of the desert wind. They bend before it, no matter in what way it may be blowing. They never resist the wind. They never become "hiding places from the wind," stemming a popular drift. They are the victims of passing opinions, and are swayed by the current passions.

And some men are "*clothed in soft raiment*"! They shrink from the rough fustian, the labourer's cotton smock, the leather suit of George Fox. They are ultra-"finicky." They are afraid of the mire. They touch the sorrows of the world with a timid finger, not with the kindly, healing grasp of a surgeon.

And other men are "*prophets*"! They have a secret fellowship with the Infinite. When we listen to them it is like putting one's ear to the seashell: we catch the sound of the ocean roll. "The voice of the Great Eternal dwells in their mighty tones."

And others are "*children of the Kingdom.*" They are greater than the old prophets, because the mystic voice has become a Presence, and they have "seen the Lord." The veil has been rent, and they "walk in the light" as "children of light."

## JULY The Ninth

### SCHOLARS IN CHRIST'S SCHOOL
*"He taught His disciples."*—MARK ix. 30-37.

AND my Lord will teach me. He will lead me into "the deep things" of God. There is only one school for this sort of learning, and an old saint called it the Academy of Love, and it meets in Gethsemane and Calvary, and the Lord Himself is the teacher, and there is room in the school for thee and me.

But the disciples were not in the mood for learning. They were not ambitious for heavenly knowledge, but for carnal prizes, not for wisdom, but for place. "They disputed one with another who was the greatest." And that spirit is always fatal to advancement in the school of Christ. Our petty ambitions close the door and windows of our souls, and the heavenly light can find no entrance. We turn Gethsemane into "a place of strife," and we carry our clamour even to Calvary itself. From this, and all other sinful folly, good Lord, redeem us!

They who would be great scholars in this school must become "as little children." Through the childlike spirit we attain unto Godlike wisdom. By humility is honour and life.

## *THE GREAT RENUNCIATION*
### MATTHEW xvii. 1-13.

WHAT if the Transfiguration was the type of the purposed consummation of every life? If we had remained "without sin," it may be that we should have gradually ripened up to a moment when we should have become transfigured, and in the surpassing brilliance have been translated to higher planes of being. Perhaps our Lord had reached this material consummation, and was now on the wonderful borderland, and could by choice slip into "the glory!"

But He made another choice. And this was, of a truth, the "great renunciation!" He turned His back on the glory, and deliberately faced the darkening way which led to Calvary and the grave. I do not wonder that His mysterious visitors spake with Him "of the decease which He should accomplish at Jerusalem." He could talk about nothing else! He "set His face to go."

And in my Master's choice of death I find my hope of life. Through "the dark gate" I can find "the mount." My transfiguration is made possible in His humiliation. If my Lord had never descended I could never have ascended. If He had abode on the mount I should have remained in my sin. He has "opened to me the gates of righteousness."

## JULY The Eleventh

### THE FRIEND OF THE BRIDEGROOM

"*He that hath the bride is the bridegroom.*"—
JOHN iii. 23-36.

WE ministers sometimes speak of "my church." I occasionally read of Mr. So-and-So's church! I know that the phrase is colloquially used, but nevertheless, it is unfortunate. Words that are perversely used tend to pervert the spirit. And this phrase tends to displace the Bridegroom. It helps to make us obtrusive, unduly aggressive, when we ought to be reverently hiding our faces with our wings. The Bride is His!

"*But the friend of the bridegroom.*" That is my place, and that is my dignity. And what a title it is, making me a member of the finest and most select aristocracy in heaven or on earth! The "friend of the bridegroom" used to carry messages to the bride, to share in the wooing, and to help to bring the wedding about. And that, too, is my gracious office, to be a matchmaker for my Lord, to testify concerning Him, to speak His praises, until the soul "fall in love" with Him.

"*He must increase, but I must decrease.*" Yes, when the sun is rising the moon becomes dim! When the glory of the Bridegroom breaks upon the bride He becomes "all in all," "the chief among ten thousand, and the altogether lovely."

## JULY The Twelfth

### PREPARING HIS SERVANTS
John i. 35-51.

OUR Lord does not stumble upon His disciples by accident. His discoveries are not surprises. He knows where His nuggets lie. Before He calls to service He has been secretly preparing the servant. "I girded thee, though thou hast not known Me."

He knew all about Simon. "*Thou art Simon*"—just a *listener,* not yet a strong, bold doer: a man of many opinions not yet consolidated into the truth of experimental convictions. "*Thou shalt be called Peter.*" Simon become Peter! Loose gravel become hard rock! Hear-says become the "verilies" of unshakable experience! The Lord proclaims our glorious possibilities.

And He knew all about Nathanael. "*When thou wast under the fig-tree I saw thee.*" "In that secret meditation of thine, when thy wishes and desires were being born, 'I saw thee!'" "When others saw nothing, I had fellowship with thee in the secret place."

And He knows all about thee and me. "I know My sheep." We do not take Him by surprise. He does not come in late, and find the performance half over! He is in at our beginnings, when grave issues are being born. "I am Alpha."

## JULY The Thirteenth

### PLAIN GLASS

"*They were fishers.*"—MATTHEW iv. 12-22.

AND so our Lord went first to the fishing-boats and not to the schools. Learning is apt to be proud and aggressive, and hostile to the simplicities of the Spirit. There is nothing like plain glass for letting in the light! And our Lord wanted transparent media, and so He went to the simple fishermen on the beach. "God hath chosen the foolish things of the world."

And by choosing labouring men our Master glorified labour. He Himself had worn the workman's dress, and the garment which the King wears becomes regal attire. Yes, the workingman, if he only knew it, is wearing the imperial robe. He is one of the kinsmen of the Lord of Glory!

Our Lord took the fisherman's humble calling, and made it the symbol of spiritual service. "*I will make you fishers of men.*" And He will do the same for thee and me. He will turn our daily labour into an apocalypse, and through its ways and means He will make us wise in the ministry of the kingdom. He will make the material the hand-maid of the spiritual, and through the letter He will lead us into the secret places of the soul.

## JULY The Fourteenth

### *THE POSSIBILITIES OF THE UNLIKELY*

MATTHEW ix. 1-13.

A DISCIPLE from among the publicans! In what waste places our Lord Jesus finds His jewels! What exquisite possibilities Ruskin saw in a pinch of common dust! What radiant glory the lapidary can see in the rough, unpolished gem! The Lord loves to go into the unlikely place, and lead forth His saints. "In the wilderness shall waters break out!"

We must prayerfully cultivate this sacred confidence in the possibilities of the unlikely. We can never be successful helpers of the Lord unless we can see the diamond in the soot, and the radiant saint in the disregarded publican. It is a most gracious art to cultivate, this of discerning a man's possible excellencies even in the blackness of his present shame. To see the future best in the present worst, that is the true perception of a child of light.

"O give us eyes to see like Thee!" Well, this is the medium of vision:—"Blessed are the pure in heart, for *they shall see* God," and the godlike, even in the wilderness of sin. "Anoint thine eyes with eye-salve, that thou may'st see!"

## THE DAILY CROSS
### LUKE ix. 18-26.

OUR Lord never bribes His disciples by promising them ways of sunny ease. He does not buy them with illicit gold. He does not put the glittering crown upon the entrance-gate, and hide the cross behind the wall. No: on the very first stage of the sacred pilgrimage there falls "the shadow of the Cross." "*Let him take up his cross daily, and follow Me.*"

And yet, the Lord's blessing is hidden in the apparent curse. In the act of bearing the cross we increase our strength. That is the heartening paradox of grace. Virtuous energies pass from our very burdens into our spirits, and thus "out of the eater comes forth meat." We bravely shoulder our load, and lo! a mystic breath visits the heart, and a strange facility attends our goings! The dead cross becomes a tree of life, and a secret vitality renews our souls.

How foolish, then, O heart of mine, to avoid and evade Thy cross! Refuse the burden, and thou declinest the strength! Ignore the duty, and thou shalt feel no inspiration! Carefully husband thy blood, and thou shalt remain for ever anæmic! But lose thy life, and thou shalt find it!

## JULY The Sixteenth

### THE VINE AND THE BRANCH
#### John xv. 1-16.

I NEED the Lord. What can a branch do apart from the vine? It may retain a certain, momentary greenness, but death is advancing apace. And there are multitudes of professing Christians who are like detached branches; their spiritual life is ebbing away: they do not startle the beholder and cause him to exclaim, "How full of life!" They do not *strike* at all! They have no splendid "*force* of character," and they therefore exercise no arresting witness for the King. They are not "abiding" in the Eternal, and therefore there is no powerful pulse from the Infinite. "Apart from Me ye can do nothing!"

And my Lord needs me. For the vine has need of the branch! The vine expresses itself in the branch, and comes to manifestation in leaf, and flower, and fruit. And my Lord would manifest Himself in me, and cause my branch to be heavy with the glorious fruits of His grace. And if I deprive Him of the branch, and deny Him this means of expression, I am "limiting the Holy One of Israel." "My son, give Me thine heart!"

Lord, help me to abide in Thee! Save me from the follies of a fatal independence! Good Lord, "Abide in me."

## THE DYING OF SELF
JOHN xii. 12-36.

"EXCEPT a corn of wheat . . . die!" Yes, it is through death we pass to life. Discipleship in which there is no death can never be truly alive. The nipping winter is essential to the green and flowery spring. No tomb, no resurrection glory! In every life there must be a grave, and self must be buried within it.

We must die to self *in our prayers*. In many prayers self is obtrusive and aggressive from end to end. It is self, self, self! That self must be crucified. We must make more room for others in our supplications. On our knees the egotist must die, and the altruist be born. And "if it die, it bringeth forth much fruit"! There are multitudes of professing Christians who would experience a wonderful resurrection if they were more "given to hospitality" in their communion with the Lord.

And if self die in our prayers, nowhere else will it be seen. That which is truly slain when we are upon our knees will not reassert itself when we return to common ways of work and service. And, therefore, let the corn of wheat fall into the ground and die!

## JULY The Eighteenth

### THE MESMERISM OF THE WORLD
#### MATTHEW xix. 23-30.

MATERIAL possessions multiply our spiritual difficulties. It is hard for a rich man "*to enter into the kingdom of heaven.*" For what is the kingdom? It is "righteousness, and peace, and joy in the Holy Ghost." It is easy for a rich man to appear respectable, but how hard is it to be holy! He may surround himself with comforts, but how hard to get into peace! He may move in the cold gleam of a glittering happiness, but how hard to get into the rich, warm quietness of an abiding joy! Yes, our material possessions so easily range themselves as ramparts between us and our destined spiritual wealth.

And if we find that any material thing so mesmerizes us that we are held in fatal bondage, we are to sacrifice it. "If thine eye offend thee, pluck it out, and cast it from thee!" Whatever interposes itself between us and our Lord must go! It is a hard way, but it leads to a sound and boisterous health. We verily "receive an hundredfold!" We lose "a thing," and gain a grace. We lose fickle sensations and gain abounding inspiration. We lose the world, and gain the Lord!

## JULY The Nineteenth

### THE WRATH OF THE LAMB
JOHN ii. 13-22.

THE narrative of the cleansing follows the story of the wedding-feast. In the one the Lord has taken the spirit of the sanctuary into a worldly feast, and thereby illumined and glorified the feast. In the other, the spirit of the world has invaded the sanctuary, and thereby defiled and dishonoured it. The spirit of worldliness, like an unclean, insurgent flood, would enter and possess the entire realm of human life and service. And here it converted a legitimate convenience into an unhallowed business. It transformed a needful expedient into an unholy end. It fixed its tables in the very courts of the Temple, and exalted the quest of money above the worship of God.

"*And He made a scourge of cords.*" And is this "the Lamb of God"? Yes, "the Lamb of God" is also "the lion of Judah." The mild sunshine can become focussed into scorching flame! As soon as blessings touch sin they become curses. "For this was the Son of Man manifested, that He might destroy the works of the devil."

My soul, remember thou the scourge of thy Lord, and do not trifle in His holy place! Seek thou the clean hands and the pure heart, and the thunders of Sinai shall come to thee as beatific music from the hill.

## JULY The Twentieth

### DEFILING THE HOLY PLACE
#### Mark xi. 11-19.

IT was a teaching of the old Rabbis that no one should make a thoroughfare of the Temple, or enter it with the dust upon his feet. The teaching was full of sacred significance, however far their practice may have departed from its truth.

Let me not use the Temple as a mere passage to something else. Let me not use my religion as an expedient for more easily reaching "the chief seats" among men. Let me not put on the garments of worship in order that I may readily and quickly fill my purse. Let me not make the sanctuary "a short cut" to the bank!

And let me not carry the dust of the world on to the sacred floor. Let me "wipe my feet." Let me sternly shake off some things—all frivolity, easeful indifference, the spirit of haste and self-seeking. Let me not defile the courts of the Lord.

And let me remember that "the whole earth is full of His glory." Everywhere, therefore, I am treading the sacred floor! Lord, teach me this high secret! Then shall I not demean the Temple into a market, but I shall transform the market into a temple. "Lo, God is in this place, and I knew it not!"

## JULY The Twenty-first

### PURIFYING THE SANCTUARY
2 Chronicles xxix. 1-11, 15-19.

WORSHIP has vital connections with work. There are nerve-relationships between the heart and the hand. The condition of the sanctuary is reflected in the state of the empire. If there is uncleanness in "the holy place," there will be blight and degeneracy among the people. The fatal seeds of national instability and decay are not found in economics; they are found in the sanctuary. "Until I went into the sanctuary . . . then understood I!"

Hezekiah cleansed "the house of the Lord." He cast forth the filthiness out of the holy place. He ushered in his golden age with the reformation of worship. He recalled exiled and white-robed Piety to her appointed throne. He began the re-establishment of right by recognizing the rights of God. He gave the Lord His due! All our rights are born out of our "being right" with God! We begin to be rich when we cease to rob God!

"*And when the burnt offering began, the song of the Lord began also.*" That is ever so. Our real songs begin with our sacrifices. We enter the realm of music when we enter the realm of self-surrender. A willing offering, on a clean altar, introduces the soul into "the joy of the Lord."

## VISIONS AND TASKS

2 CHRONICLES xxxiv. 1-11.

JOSIAH *"began to seek after God."* The other day I saw a young art student copying one of Turner's pictures in the National Gallery. His eyes were being continually lifted from his canvas to his "master." He put nothing down which he had not first seen. He was "seeking after" Turner!

And thus it was with Josiah. His eyes were "ever toward the Lord!" He studied the "ways" of the Lord, in order that he might incarnate them in national life and practice. Wise doings always begin in clear seeing. We should be far more efficient in practice if we were more diligently assiduous in vision. It is never a waste of time to "look unto Him." Looking is a most needful part of our daily discipline. "What I say unto you, I say unto all, *Watch!*"

And because Josiah saw the holiness of the Lord he saw the uncleanness of the people. He had a vision of God's holy place, and he therefore saw the defilement of the material worship.

*"In the twelfth year he began to purge Judah."* Yes, that is the sequence. The reformer follows the seer. We shall begin to sweep the streets of our own city when we have gazed upon the glories of the holy city, the New Jerusalem.

## JULY The Twenty-third

### A GREAT SOUL AT PRAYER
2 CHRONICLES vi. 12-21.

LET me reverently study this great prayer in order that, when I go to the house of God, I may be able to enrich its ministry by the wealth of my own supplications.

Solomon prayed that the eyes of the Lord might be open toward the house "day and night." Like the eyes of a mother upon her child! Like the eyes of a lover upon his beloved! And therefore it is more than protective vision; shall we reverently say that it is *inventive* vision, devising gracious surprises, anticipating needs, preparing love-gifts; it is sight which is both insight and foresight, ever inspecting and prospecting for the loved one's good.

And Solomon prayed that God's ear might be open to the cry of His people's need. "*Hear Thou from Thy dwelling-place.*" He prayed that the house of God might be the place of open communion. That is ever the secret of peace, and therefore of power. If I know that I have correspondence with the Holy One, I shall walk and work as a child of light. If God hear me, then I can sing!

And Solomon prays for the grace of forgiveness. He prays for the sense of sweet emancipation which is the gift of grace. It is the miracle of renewal, and it ought to happen every time we open the doors of the sanctuary.

## LOVE OF THE SANCTUARY
### Psalm lxxxiv.

GRACIOUS is the strength of this man's desire for the holy place. He covets the privilege of the very sparrow which builds its nest beneath the sacred eaves! When he is away from the Temple its worship and music haunt his mind and soul. It wooes him in the market-place. Its insistent call is with him by the fireside. Yes, "in his heart are the highways to Zion!"

And the permanency of this devotional mood transfigures every place. It turns "*the valley of weeping*" into "*a place of springs.*" The colour of any place is largely determined by our moods. It is surprising what treasures we find when our soul is full of light. What discoveries old Scrooge made when the Christmas mood possessed his own heart! When we carry about the spirit of the sanctuary, we convert every spot into rich and hallowed ground.

"*I had rather be a door-keeper in the house of my God than to dwell in the tents of wickedness.*" Better to have the temple-spirit, even as a menial, than the unhallowed heart in the glittering high places of sin. "God's worst is better than the devil's best."

## JULY The Twenty-fifth

### NO TEMPLE THEREIN

"*And I saw no temple therein.*"—REVELATION xxi. 22-27.

AND that because it was all temple! "Every place was hallowed ground." There was no merely localized Presence, because the Presence was universal. God was realized everywhere, and therefore the little meeting-tent had vanished, and in place of the measurable tabernacle there were the immeasurable and God-filled heavens.

Even here on earth I can measure my spiritual growth by the corresponding enlargement of my temple. What is the size of my sanctuary? Am I moving toward the time when nothing shall be particularly hallowed because all will be sanctified? Are the six days of the week becoming increasingly like the seventh, until people can see no difference between my Monday manners and my Sunday mood? And how about places? Do I still speak of "religion being religion," and "business being business," or is something of the sanctuary getting into my shop, and is the exchange becoming a side-chapel of the Temple?

"*And the Lamb is the light thereof.*" When we have done with the local temple we can dispose of its candles. When we pass out of the twilight into the morning "the stars retire." The fore-gleams will change into the wondrous glory of the ineffable day.

## THE WELLS OF SALVATION
### JOHN iii. 1-21.

THE springs of our redemption are found in infinite love. "God is love!" Redemption was not inspired by anger, but by grace. We do not contemplate an angry God, demanding a victim, but a compassionate Father making a sacrifice. At one extreme of our golden text is eternal "love," and at the other extreme is "eternal life." What if the two are one? Etymologically, "love" and "life" are akin. What if they are only two names for the same thing?

To "believe" in the love is to receive the life. For when I believe in a person's love I open my doors to the lover. And to believe in the love of God is to let the heavenly Lover in. And with love comes a wonderful tropical air—light, and warmth, and air; and "all things become new!" It is the letting in of the spring, and things which have been in wintry bondage awake, and arise from their graves.

And so I "*enter into the kingdom of God.*" I become a native of a new and marvellous country. I begin to be acclimatized in the realm of the blest. And I "*see* the kingdom of God." Spiritual perceptions become mine, and I gaze upon the mystic glories of the home of God.

## THE WORK OF FAITH
### 1 John v. 1-13.

AND so by belief *I find life*. I do not obtain the vitalizing air through controversy, or clamour, or idle lamentation, but by opening the window! Faith opens the door and window of the soul to the Son of God. It can be done without tears, it can be done without sensationalism. "If any man will open the door, I will come in." "And he that hath the Son hath the life."

And by belief *I gain my victories*. "Who is he that overcometh . . . but he that believeth?" It is not by flashing armour that we beat the devil, but by an invincible life. On these battle-fields a mystic breath does more destruction than all our fine and costly expedients. To believe is to obtain the winning spirit, and every battle brings its trophies to our feet.

And by belief *I gain assurance*. "He that believeth . . . hath the witness in him." So many Christians fight in doubt and indecision, and their uncertainty impairs their strength and skill. It is the man who can quietly say "I know" who is terrible in battle and who drives his foes in confusion from the field.

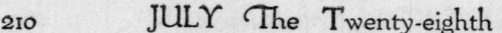

## ALL THINGS NEW!
### 2 Corinthians v. 14-21.

HERE is a new constraint! "The love of Christ constraineth me." The love of Christ *carries me along like a crowd.* I am taken up in its mighty movement and swept along the appointed road! Or it *arrests me,* and makes me its willing prisoner. It lays a strong hand upon me, and I have no option but to go. A gracious "necessity is laid upon me." *I must!*

And here is a new world. "*Old things are passed away.*" The man who is the prisoner of the Lord's love will find himself in new and wonderful scenery. Everything will wear a new face—God, man, self, the garden, the sky, the sea! We shall look at all things through love-eyes, and it is amazing in what new light a great love will set familiar things! Commonplaces become beautiful when looked at through the lens of Christian love. When we "walk in love" our eyes are anointed with "the eye-salve" of grace.

And here is a new service. "We are ambassadors . . . for Christ." When we see our Lord through love-eyes, and then our brother, we shall yearn to serve our brother in Christ. We shall intensely long to tell the love-story of the Lord our Saviour. What we have seen, with confidence we tell.

## JULY The Twenty-ninth

### NAMES AND NATURES
#### ROMANS viii. 1-10.

MEN will recognize my Christianity by the sign of the Spirit of Christ. And they will accept no other witness. I saw a plant-pot the other day, full of soil, bearing no flower, but flaunting a stick on which was printed the word "Mignonette." "Thou hast a name to live and art dead." The world will take no notice of our labels and our badges: it is only arrested by the flower and the perfume. "If any man hath not the Spirit of Christ he is none of His."

And in the Spirit of Christ I shall best deal with "*the things of the flesh.*" There are some things which are best overcome by neglecting them. To give them attention is to give them nourishment. Withdraw the attention, and they sicken and die. And so I must seek the fellowship of the Spirit. That friendship will destroy the other. "Ye cannot serve God and Mammon." If I am in communion with the Holy One the other will pine away, and cease to trouble me.

Lord, make my spirit a kinsman of Thine! Let the intimacy be ever deeper and dearer. "Draw me nearer, blessed Lord," until in nearness to Thee I find my peace, my joy, and my crown.

## SIN AS POISON

NUMBERS xxi. 4-9.

AND this is the familiar teaching, that sin is a serpent. It possesses a deadly poison. We may give it pleasant names, but we are only ornamenting death. A chemist might put a poison into a chaste and elegant flask, but he has in no wise changed its nature. And when we name sin by philosophic euphemisms, and by less exacting terminologies—such as "cleverness," "smartness," or "fault," or "misfortune," we are only changing the flask, and the diabolical essence remains the same.

And, then, sin is a serpent because it is so subtle. It creeps into my presence almost before I know it. Its approaches are so insidious, its expedients so full of guile. "Therefore, I say unto all, Watch!"

But in Christ the old serpent is dead! Christ "became sin," and in Him sin was crucified. The thing that bit is bitten, and its nefarious power destroyed. But out of Christ the serpent is still busy and malicious, claiming what he presumes to call his own.

Let me, then, dwell in Christ, where sin "has no more dominion." "Whosoever believeth shall not perish but have life."

## JULY The Thirty-first

### THE CLEAN FLAME OF LOVE
1 JOHN iv. 4-14.

THIS aged apostle cannot get away from the counsels of love. All his mental movements circle about this "greatest thing in the world." Once he would "call down fire upon men"; now the only fire he knows is the pure and genial flame of love. Beautiful is it when our fires become cleaner as we get older, when temper changes to compassion, when malice becomes goodwill, when an ill-controlled conflagration becomes a homely fireside.

And all the love we acquire we must get from the altars of God. "We love because He first loved us." We can find it nowhere else. "Love is of God." Why, then, not seek it in the right place? Why seek for palms in arctic regions, or for icebergs in the tropics? God is the country of love, and in His deep mines there are riches "unsearchable."

And the gracious law of life is this, that every acquisition of love increases our powers of discernment. "He that loveth knoweth . . . !" It is as though every jewel we find gives us an extra lens for the discovery of finer jewels still. And thus the love-life is a continual surprise, and the surprise will be eternal, for the object of the wonder is the infinite love of God.

## AUGUST The First

### GOD AS OUR ALLY!

ROMANS viii. 31-39.

"IF God is for us!" But we must make sure of that. Is God on the field, taking sides with us? Have we been so busy with our preparations, so concerned with many things, and everybody, that we have forgotten our greatest possible Ally? Is He on the field, and on which side! My soul, go on thy knees, and settle this in secret. That purpose of thine! That choice of thine! That work of thine! Is it hallowed with thy Lord's approval and seal?

And "if God is for us, who can be against us?" Nothing else counts. It is ever a foolish and futile thing to count the heads in the opposing ranks. "God is always on the side of the big battalions!" It is a black lie of the devil! We need not fear the big battalions if only we are securely in the right. We are not to count heads, but to weigh and estimate causes. Which of the causes provides a tent for the Lord of Hosts? Where has the truth its waving flag? Stand near that flag, my soul, and thou wilt be near thy Lord! And nothing shall separate thee from His love, and leave thee weak and isolated on the field. Thou shalt be "more than conqueror" in Him who loves thee, and will love thee for evermore.

## AUGUST The Second

### BY JACOB'S WELL
#### JOHN iv. 1-15.

A WEARY woman and a weary Lord! But the Lord was only weary in body; the woman was dry and exhausted in soul. Her heart was like some charred chamber after a destructive fire. All its furniture was injured, and some of it was almost burnt away. For sin had been blazing in the secret place, and had scorched the delicacies of the spirit, and the inward satisfaction was gone. And now she was very weary, and her daily walk had become a most tiresome march.

And the Lord, with sympathetic insight, discerned the inward dryness. There was no sound of holy contentment, no melody of joyful, spiritual desire. There was only the cold, clammy silence of death. "He knew what was in man." And there was no "river of water of life" making glad the streets of this woman's soul.

And so He would bring to her the waters of spiritual satisfaction, the holy well of eternal life. "In the wilderness shall waters break out, and springs in the desert." The Lord is about to work a miracle of grace, changing dull pang into healing peace, and suffocated desire into soaring fellowship with God. He is about to transform an outlawed woman into one of the "elect saints." How will He do it? Let us watch Him.

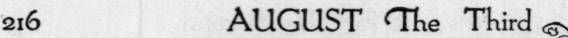

## CHANGING ASKING INTO THIRSTING

*" Go, call thy husband!"*—JOHN iv. 16-30.

I NEVER supposed that the transformation would begin here. I thought that there were some words which would remain unspoken. But here our Master speaks a word which only deepens the weariness of the woman, and irritates the sore of her galling yoke. What is He doing?

He is seeking to change the sense of wretchedness into the sense of sin! He is seeking to change weariness into desire! *He wants to make the woman thirst!* And so He puts His finger upon her sin. He cannot give the heavenly water to lips that merely ask for it. " Sir, give me this water!" No, it cannot be had for the asking, only for the thirsting! And so the gracious Lord turns the woman's eyes upon her own sinful life, in order that in the heat of a fierce shame she might cry out, " I thirst for God, for the living God!" And sure I am that, before the Lord had done with her, this quiet, lone cry leapt from her lips, and in immediate response to the cry she was given a deep draught from the eternal well.

And, good Lord, arouse my sense of my sin that I, too, may thirst for Thy water! Now, make me thirst for it, and in the thirst receive it!

## AUGUST The Fourth

### HIDDEN MANNA

*"I have meat to eat that ye know not of."*—
JOHN iv. 31-42.

AND what sort of meat is this? The Lord found secret refreshment in feeding other people. In vitalizing the woman of Samaria He restored His own soul. The disciples were amazed when they returned to find that the weariness had gone out of His face, and that He looked like one who had been at a feast!

And that is the law of life. "*My meat is to do the will.*" There is a secret nutriment in the bread we give away. The Lord gives us to eat of the "hidden manna" whenever we are seeking the refreshment of our fellows. Distributed bread has a sacramental efficacy for our own souls. The man who feeds the hungry shall himself be "satisfied as with marrow."

And these ways of service are open on every side. There are millions of weary people waiting, like the woman at the well. "*Lift up your eyes, and look on the fields: for they are white already to harvest!*" Be it mine to be a minister in the mighty service, and in the ways of obedience let me find delights and delicacies for my own soul.

"Bread of Heaven,
Feed me till I want no more!"

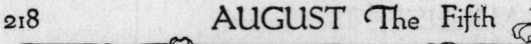

## BROOKS BY THE WAY
Isaiah xii.

THE wells of the Lord are to be found where most I need them. The Lord of the way knows the pilgrim life, and the wells have been unsealed just where the soul is prone to become dry and faint. At the foot of the hill Difficulty was found a spring! Yes, these health-springs are lifting their crystal flood in the cheerless wastes of evil antagonisms and exhausting grief.

Sometimes I am foolish, and in my need I assume that the well is far away. I knew a farmer who for a generation had carried every pail of water from a distant well to meet the needs of his homestead. And one day he sunk a shaft by his own house door, and to his great joy he found that the water was waiting at his own gate! My soul, thy well is near, even here! Go not in search of Him! Thy pilgrimage is ended, the waters are at thy feet!

But I must "*draw* the water out of the wells of salvation." The hand of faith must lift the gracious gift to the parched lips, and so refresh the panting soul. "I will *take* the cup of salvation." Stretch out thy "lame hand of faith," and take the holy, hallowing energy offered by the Lord.

## AUGUST The Sixth

### WATERS OF CONTENTMENT
#### Isaiah lv. 1-7.

THE refreshing waters are offered to "everyone" that is thirsty. The evangel is like some clear bugle peal, sounded on some commanding upland, and which is heard alike in palace and cottage, in school and at the mill, by the child of plenty and by the child of want. "Ho, everyone!" The appeal is to the common heart, whether the setting be squalor or splendour, whether the soul faints in the glare of the prosperous noon, or under the chill of the burdensome night. "Ho, everyone that thirsteth!"

And the waters may be ours "without money and without price." We have not to earn them by the sweat of body, mind, or soul. We have not to make a toilsome pilgrimage, on bleeding feet, to some distant Lourdes, where the sacred healer abides. No, we are asked to pay nothing, and for the simple reason that we "have nothing wherewith to pay." The reviving grace is given to us "freely," and all that we have to present is our thirst.

And yet we spend and spend, we labour and labour, but we buy no bread of contentment, and the waters of satisfaction are far away. The satisfying bread cannot be bought; it can only be begged. The water of life cannot be taken from a cistern; it must be drunk at the spring.

## AUGUST The Seventh

### RIVERS FROM THE SNOW
REVELATION xxii. 1-7, 17-21.

THE water of life flows out of the throne. Grace has its rise in sovereign holiness. This river is born amid the virgin snow. All true love springs out of spotless purity. "Love" from any other source is illegitimately wearing a stolen name. "Holy, holy, holy is the Lord!" That is the first note in the song of redemption. In that burning whiteness I discern the possibility of my own sanctification.

For the grace which flows out of sovereign holiness is a minister of the holy Lord to make me holy. If it were not perfectly pure it would itself be an agent of defilement. But it is "clear as crystal," and therefore it purifies and fertilizes wherever it flows. Rare trees grow upon its banks, and grace-fruits make every season beautiful. "Everything shall live whither the river cometh."

But without the river my soul shall be "as an unwatered garden." My life shall be a realm of perpetual drought. Things may begin to grow, but they shall speedily droop and die. The heavenly Husbandman shall find no fruit when He walks amid the garden in the cool of the day. And therefore, my soul, look to the river which flows from the throne! "There is a river, the streams whereof make glad the city of God," and that river is for thee!

## AUGUST The Eighth

### THE SCARLET SIN
Isaiah i. 10-20.

HOW can we deal with glaring sin, with sin that is "scarlet," that is "red like crimson"? And when the red stain has soaked into the very texture of the character, and every fibre is stupefied, what can we do then? Let me listen.

"*Wash you.*" But ordinary washings will not suffice. The ministry of education will fail. Art, and literature, and music will leave the internal stain undisturbed. They may impart a polish, but the polish shall be like the gloss on badly-washed linen. And the ministry of work will fail. Work never yet made a foul soul clean. There is "a fountain opened for all uncleanness." I must wash "in the blood of the Lamb." That red sacrifice can wash out the deep red stain.

"*Cease to do evil.*" Yes, I must turn my back on the roads of defilement. There must be a sharp decision, and an immediate reversal of my ways. "Halt!" "Right about turn!" "Quick march!"

"*Learn to do well!*" Yes, let me diligently learn, like a child at school, until the deliberative becomes the instructive, and "practice makes perfect."

## AUGUST The Ninth

### GOD'S REQUIREMENTS

"*What doth the Lord require of thee?*"—MICAH vi. 1-8.

"T O do justly." Then I must not be so eager about my rights as to forget my duties. For my duties are just the observance of my neighbour's rights. And to see my neighbour's rights I must cultivate his "point of view." I must look out of his windows! "Look not every man on his own things, but every man also on the things of others."

"*And to love mercy.*" And mercy is justice *plus!* And it is the "plus" which makes the Christian. His cup "runneth over." He gives, like his Lord, "good measure, pressed down, shaken together, running over." There is always "a little extra" for Christ's sake! And "blessed are the merciful."

"*And to walk humbly with thy God.*" And there I am at the root of the two graces which have been enjoined upon me. The lowly friend of the Lord will most surely be both just and merciful. He cannot help it. The fragrance will cling to him as the fragrance of the orange clings to him who labours in the fruitful groves of Spain.

## AUGUST The Tenth

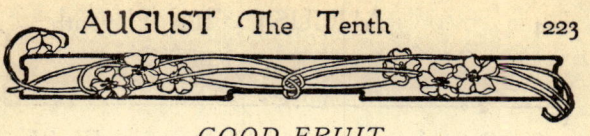

### GOOD FRUIT
Luke vi. 43-49.

MY Lord seeks "good fruit." It must be sound. No disease must lurk within it. My virtues are so often touched with defilement. There is a little untruth even in my truth. There is a little jealousy even in my praise. There is a little superciliousness even in my forbearance. There is a little pride even in my piety. It is not "whole," not holy. God demands sound fruit.

And "good fruit" demands "a good tree." We must not look for truth from an untrue soul. If the bullet-mould is deformed, all the bullets will share its deformity. First get the mould right, and every bullet will share its rectitude. When the soul is "true," all our words, and deeds, and gestures will be "of the truth," and will be true indeed. "Make the tree good."

And that is just what our Lord proclaims His willingness to do. He does not begin with effects, but with causes; not with fruit, but with trees. He does not begin with our speech, but with the speaker; not with conduct, but with character. And, blessed be His name, He can transform "corrupt trees" into "good trees," until it shall be said: "He that hath turned the world upside down has come hither also."

## THE CONSECRATION OF THE WILL
### JOHN v. 1-18.

MY Lord demands my will in the ministry of healing. "*Art thou willing to be made whole?*" He will not carry me as a log. When my schoolmaster put a belt around me, and held me over the water with a rope, and taught me to swim, I had to use my arms. The condition of help was endeavour. And so in my salvation. I have always will-power sufficient to pray and to try. In the effort of faith I open the door to the energies of God. Grace flows in the channels of the determined will. "O, God, my heart is set!"

And my Lord demands my will in the living of the consecrated life. "Sin no more!" I must "will" to be whole, and I must will to remain holy. And here is the gracious law of the kingdom, that every time I exercise my will I add to its power. Every difficulty overcome adds its strength to my resources. Every enemy conquered marches henceforth in my own ranks. I go "from strength to strength."

"God worketh in me to will!" The gracious Lord ever strengthens the will that is willing. He transforms the frail reed into an iron pillar, and makes trembling timidity bold as a lion.

> "Mighty Spirit, dwell with me,
> I myself would mighty be."

## AUGUST The Twelfth

### MY LIFE AND HOPE
JOHN v. 19-30.

HERE is my reservoir. "*The Son hath life in Himself.*" All vitality has its source in Him. He is the enemy of death and the deadly. I can paint the dead to look like life; I can use rouge for blood, and make the white lips red, but it all remains clammy and cold. I can galvanize, but I cannot vitalize. I can "break the ball of nard," and make perfume, "but still the sleeper sleeps." "In Him is life." "In Christ shall all be made alive!"

And here is my hope. "*The Son also quickeneth.*" He is not only a reservoir, He is a river. He is "the river of water of life." And His blessed purpose is to flow into desolate places, converting deserts into gardens, and making wildernesses to blossom as the rose.

And He will come my way if only I will "hear" and "believe." There is a flippant hearing which, while it listens, laughs Him to scorn. There is a cheap hearing which will venture nothing on His counsel. And there is the hearing of faith, which simply "takes Him at His word," and in the glorious venture experiences the unsealing of the fountain of eternal life. "Whosoever will, let him take of the water of life freely."

## THE INNER ROOMS
### JOHN v. 31-47.

WHAT should I think of a man who was contented to remain in the outer halls and passages of Windsor Castle, when he was invited into the royal precincts to have gracious communion with the King? And what shall I think of men who are contented to "search the Scriptures" and "will not come" to the Lord? They spend their life exploring the lobbies, when the Host and the feast are waiting in the upper room!

And some men spend their days in criticism and they never advance to worship. They are like unto one who should give his strength to the deciphering of some time-worn inscription on the outer wall of some grand cathedral, and who never treads the sacred floor in fruitful and enriching awe.

And some men live in the senses, and not in the conscience, in the awful presence of the great white throne. They are for ever seeking sensations, and avoid the fellowship of duty. They ride about in the channel, and they never come to the harbour. They have no settled moral home.

My Lord, help me to regard all good things as merely passages leading to Thee! Let all good things bring me into intimate fellowship with Thee.

## AUGUST The Fourteenth

### THE PARALYSIS OF THE SOUL
#### LUKE v. 17-26.

THE miracle done in the body is purposed to be a symbol of a grander miracle to be wrought in the soul. *"That ye may know that the Son of Man hath power on earth to forgive sins, then saith He . . . !"* He heals the paralyzed body that we may know what He can do with a paralyzed soul. He liberates the man who is bound by palsy that we may know what He can do for a man who is bound by guilt. We are to reason from the less to the greater, from the material type to the spiritual reality.

And so it is with all my Lord's doings in nature. They are a glorious symbolism of what He will do in the spirit. "That ye may know how beautiful the Son of Man can make the heart of man, then saith He to the seeds of the spring-time, Come forth!" And so nature becomes a literature, in which we see our possible inheritance in the Spirit.

But on our side it is all conditioned by faith. "There He could do no mighty works because of their unbelief." Even in the miracles of the Spirit our faith must co-operate. Divine grace and human faith can transfigure the race. "Lord, increase our faith!" And everywhere, let palsied souls be delivered, and attain to glorious freedom!

## WITHERED LIMBS
### Mark iii. 1-8.

THERE are withered limbs of the spirit as well as of the body. There are faculties and powers which are wasting away, sacred endowments which have lost their vital circulation. In some lives the will is a withered limb. In others it is the conscience. In others, again, it is the affections. These splendid moral and spiritual powers are being dried up, and they hang comparatively limp and useless in the life. They have been withered by sin and sinful negligence.

And the Lord is the healer of withered limbs. He can deal with imprisoned affections as the warm spring deals with the river which has been locked in ice. He can minister to a stricken will, and make it as a benumbed hand when the circulation has been restored. He can give it grip and tenacity. And so with all our powers. He, who is the Life, can vitalize all!

But here again the remnant of our withered endowment must be used in the healing. We must surrender to the Healer. We must obey. If the Lord says: " Stretch forth thy hand," we must attempt the impossible! In this region the impossible becomes possible in sanctified endeavour.

## AUGUST The Sixteenth

### THE CHURCH AS AN INFIRMARY
LUKE xiii. 10-17.

WHAT infirmities gather together in the synagogue! What moral and spiritual ailments are congregated in every place of worship! If the veil of the flesh could be removed, and the inward life revealed, how we should pity one another, and how we should pray! In how many lives should we behold a spirit "bound together," who "could in no wise lift herself up!" Wills like crushed reeds, consciences like broken vocal chords, hopes like birds with injured wings, and hearts like ruined homes!

But the blessed Lord still goes into the synagogue; nay, He anticipates our coming. And He is present "to heal the broken in heart," and to "bind up his wounds." His touch "has still its ancient power." Still does the gracious Master speak with authority. "Woman, thou art loosed from thine infirmity!" And immediately she is "made straight."

Then why do so many spiritual cripples leave the synagogue cripples still? Because they do not give the Healer a chance. No one can remain crooked and broken in conscience and will who grips the hand of the Lord of Life.

## THE PSALM OF PRAISE
### PSALM cvii. 1-15.

THE miracle of deliverance must be followed by the psalm of praise. There are multitudes who cry, "God be merciful!" who never cry, "God be praised!" "There were none that returned to give thanks save this Samaritan." Ten cleansed, and only one grateful! "Oh, that men would praise the Lord for His goodness!" Many a blessing becomes stale because it is not renewed by thanksgiving. Graces that are received ungratefully droop like flowers deprived of rain. Yes, gratitude gives sustenance to blessings already received. Therefore "in everything give thanks."

But emancipated lives are not only to break into praise before God, they must exercise in confession before men. "Let the redeemed of the Lord say so!" Unconfessed blessings become like the Dead Sea; refused an outlet they lose their freshness and vitality. I am found by the Lord in order that I, too, may be a seeker. I receive His peace in order that I may be a peacemaker. I am comforted in order that I "may comfort others with the comfort wherewith I am comforted of God." Have you ever received a blessing; "pass it on!" Tell the story of thy deliverance to the enslaved, that he, too, may find "the iron gate" swing open, and so attain his freedom.

## AUGUST The Eighteenth

### THE CHURCH OF THE FIRSTBORN
*"Pray for the peace of Jerusalem."*—PSALM cxxii.

AND my Jerusalem is "the church of the living God." Do I carry her on my heart? Do I praise God for her heritage, and for her endowment of spiritual glory? And do I remember her perils, especially those parts of her walls where the defences are very thin, and can be easily broken through? Yes, has my Church any place in my prayer, or am I robbing her of part of her intended possessions?

And is the *entire* Jerusalem the subject of my supplication? Or do I only think of a corner of it, just that part where my own little synagogue is placed? I am a Congregationalist; do I remember the Anglican? I am an Anglican; do I remember the Quaker. Am I thus concerned only with a small section of Jerusalem, or does my intercession sweep the entire city?

*"They shall prosper that love thee."* I cannot be healthy if I am bereft of fellowship. If I ignore the house of prayer I impoverish my home. The peaceful glow of the fireside is not unrelated to the coals upon the common altar. The sacrament is connected with my ordinary meal. To love the Church of Christ is to become enriched with "the fulness of Christ."

## AUGUST The Nineteenth

### IN GREEN PASTURES
Psalm xxiii.

THIS little psalm has been called the nightingale of the psalms. It sings "in the shade when all things rest." It makes music in the darkness; it gives me "songs in the night." And what does it sing about?

It sings of God's bounty in food and rest. *"Green pastures"; "still waters."* My Lord knows when my heart is faint, when it needs His reviving food. He knows when my heart is tired and needs His sweet rest. *"He restoreth my soul."*

And it sings of the God-appointed way across the hill. *"He leadeth me in paths of righteousness."* He makes the right way clear. He walks the path of duty with me. *"Yea, though I walk through the valley of the shadow I will fear no evil, for Thou art with me."*

And it sings of the feast which the Lord serves in the very midst of my foes. *"He spreadeth a table before me in the midst of mine enemies."* He gives me the fat things of grace in the very presence of frowning circumstances.

And it sings of the providence *which guards the rear*. "Goodness and mercy shall *follow* me!" God's grace comes between me and my yesterdays. It cuts off the heredity from the old Adam, and no far-off plague comes nigh my dwelling.

## AUGUST The Twentieth

### FEEDING THE FLOCK

ISAIAH xl. 1-11.

HERE is the gracious promise of provision. "*He shall feed His flock like a Shepherd.*" He knows the fields where my soul will be best nourished in holiness. I am sometimes amazed at His choice. He takes me into an apparent wilderness, but I find rich herbage on the unpromising plain. And so I would rest in His choice even when it seems adverse to my good.

And here is the gracious promise of gentle discrimination. "*He shall gather the lambs in His arm, and carry them in His bosom.*" Says old Trapp, "He hath a great care of His little ones, like as He had of the weaker tribes. In their march through the Wilderness He put a strong tribe to two weak tribes, lest they should faint or fail." Yes, "He knoweth our frame." He will not lay upon us more than we can bear. At the back of every commandment there is a promise of adequate resource. His askings are also His enablings. The big duty means that we shall have a big lift. And when we are tired He will lead on gently. Such is the grace and tenderness of the Lord.

## AUGUST The Twenty-first

### SATISFACTION

"*My people shall be satisfied with My goodness.*"—JEREMIAH xxxi. 10-14.

AND how unlike is all this to the feasts of the world! There is a great show, but no satisfaction. There is much decorative china, but no nutritious food or drink. "Every one that drinketh of this water shall thirst again." We rise from the table, and our deepest cravings are unappeased. "Why art thou cast down, O my soul?" We know. We have had a condiment, but no meat; a showy menu-card, but no reviving feast.

Nothing but the goodness of the Lord can satisfy the soul. Whatever else may be on the table of life, if this be absent we shall go away unfed. We may have money, and pleasure, and success, and fame, but they are all delusive husks if the grace of the Lord be absent.

This is the real furnishing of the feast. There are vast multitudes of things I can do without if only I have the holy bread of life in the gracious Presence of my Lord. In this sphere it is the Guest who makes the table! "Thou, O Christ, art all I want!" "Having Him we have all things." A glorious satisfaction possesses the soul, and though we may not increase our worldly possessions, we do something better, we "grow in grace and in the knowledge of our Lord and Saviour Jesus Christ."

## AUGUST The Twenty-second

### THE SICK AND THE LOST
Ezekiel xxxiv. 11-16.

SURELY everybody is included in this redemptive purpose of the Lord! He is looking for everybody, for everybody finds a place in His holy quest.

He is seeking the "*lost*" sheep. The one that has wandered far away, and now no longer hears the sound of the Shepherd's voice! The one that is carelessly nibbling the herbage on the very edge of perdition! He is looking for this one. Is He therefore looking for thee and me?

He is seeking "*that which was driven away.*" Some hireling, some enemy of the shepherd, drove it far away from the fold. "A thief and a robber," for his own purposes, hath done this. And the Lord's sheep are driven away by "principalities and powers," and by the violence of wicked men. Some impure and unworthy professor of religion can drive a whole household from the fellowship of the Church. And the Good Shepherd is seeking these. Is He therefore looking for thee or me?

And He is seeking "*that which was sick.*" And some of the Lord's sheep are sickly. The chill of disappointment, or failure, or bereavement has blown upon them, and they are "down." Or they have been feeding on illicit pleasure. And the Lord is seeking such. Is He therefore seeking thee or me?

## NOT LOST IN THE FLOCK

*"I know My sheep, and am known of mine."*—
JOHN x. 7-16.

THERE is mutual recognition, and in that recognition there is confidence and peace.

"*I know my sheep.*" He knows us one by one. My knowledge of the individual wanes in proportion as the multitude is increased. The teacher with the smaller class has the deepest intimacy with her scholars. The individual is lost in the crowd. But not so with our Lord. There are no "masses" in His sight. However big the crowd, even though it be "a multitude which no man can number," we still remain individuals, known to the Lord by name, and face, and personal need. If thou art away from the fold, thy face is missed, and the Shepherd is away in search of thee!

"*And I am known of mine.*" And the knowledge deepens with every day's experience. There are false shepherds who can subtly mimic the Good Shepherd, and in my early discipleship I am liable to be deceived. The devil himself can array himself like a shepherd, and imitate the very tones of the Lord. Therefore must I watch, and ever watch. But here is my hope and inspiration. Every day I spend with my Good Shepherd sharpens my discernments, enables me to see through the outer show of things, and to discriminate between the false and the true.

## OCTOBER The Twenty-seventh

### PAYING HOMAGE TO THE KING
Proverbs iii. 1-12.

"ACKNOWLEDGE Him." But not with a passing nod of recognition. I must not merely glance at Him now and again, admitting His existence on the field. To acknowledge Him is to acknowledge Him as King, with the right to control, and as predominant partner in all the affairs of my life, even the right to give the determining voice in all my decisions. No, it is not the recognition paid to an acquaintance, it is the homage paid to a King.

And if I thus acknowledge Him, He will direct my paths. Life shall always be moving on to its purposed end and glory. The path chosen will not always be the most alluring one, but it will be the right one, and therefore the safe one, and there will be wonderful discoveries on the uninviting track.

How will He let me know which path to take? I cannot say. We can never anticipate God's ways of dealing with us. But if my life is bent to the loving acknowledgment of His will, He will assuredly find a way to make His will known. The light will always reach the willing mind.

## OCTOBER The Twenty-eighth

### PLEASANTNESS AND PEACE

*"Her ways are ways of pleasantness, and all her paths are peace."*—PROVERBS iii. 13-26.

IN the ways of the Lord I shall have feasts of "pleasantness." But not always at the beginning of the ways. Sometimes my faith is called upon to take a very unattractive road, and nothing welcomes me of fascination and delight. But here is a law of the spiritual life. The exercised faith intensifies my spiritual senses, and hidden things become manifest to my soul—hidden beauties, hidden sounds, hidden scents! Faith adds a mysterious "plus" to my powers, and "all things become new."

And in the ways of the Lord I shall also find the gracious gift of peace. Not that the road will be always smooth, but that I may be always calm. I can be unperturbed when "all around tumultuous seems." I can journey in holy serenity, because the Lord of the road is with me. For peace consists, not in friendliness of circumstances, but in friendship with the Lord.

## OCTOBER The Twenty-ninth

### THE STORY OF THE PAST
DEUTERONOMY xxxi. 7-13.

AND no ears are more receptive to spiritual story than the ears of a little child. It is not needful to open the gate of interest; it is wide ajar already. And imagination also is there, ready to busy itself about the story. And so, too, is the spirit of homage and adoration. The children are ready for the King! "Suffer little children to come unto Me, for of such is the Kingdom of Heaven."

And, therefore, we have need of wise tellers of the story, who know the story themselves. And in these delicate regions I must ever remember how much my spirit shares in the story I tell. My spirit is a friend or a foe to my power. My words may be well chosen, but they may all be light as empty shells, devoid of all vitality. My words have just the power of their spiritual contents. "You cannot fight the French with 200,000 red uniforms," said Carlyle; "there must be men inside them." And we cannot engage in the evangelization with mere uniforms of words. There must be spirit inside them, even the spirit of pure and consecrated lives.

## OCTOBER The Thirtieth

### A TESTIMONY MEETING
PSALM xxxiv. 1-11.

THIS is a little testimony meeting, in which each of the witnesses tells the story of the Lord's gracious dealings with him. Let me listen to them.

"*He delivered me from all my fears.*" His fears held him in dungeons. Even the noontide was as darkness round about him, and there was no song in his soul. And the Lord broke open the prison-gate and let him out to light, and joy, and belief.

"*They looked to Him and were lightened.*" They looked upon the grace of the Lord, and were lit up, just as I have seen humble cottage windows ablaze with the glory of the rising sun. I must "set my face" towards the Lord, and I, too, shall catch the radiance of His glory.

"This poor man cried . . . *and the Lord saved him out of all his troubles.*" And these troubles were what I should call "tight corners," when the life is hemmed in by unfortunate circumstances, and there seems no way of escape. Disappointment shuts us in. Sorrow shuts us in. Lack of money shuts us in. Let me cry unto the Lord. He is a wonderful Friend in the tight corner, and He will bring my feet into "a large place."

## TWO GREAT MYSTERIES
### Psalm lxxxi.

THIS is an unutterable mystery, that a man can close his life against God. *"Israel would have none of Me."* We can shut out God as we can shut out the pure air. We can bar His entrance just as we can exclude the light from the chamber. And then the pity is, we can deceive ourselves into believing that the air is perfectly fresh and that the room is flooded with light. We lose our fine discernment, and we call evil good, and the darkness we call day. If we " refuse to have God " in our thoughts God gives us over to a " reprobate mind."

And it is an equally unutterable mystery that a man can open his life to the entertainment of Almighty God. " I will dwell with them!" That is my supreme honour, that the Lord will be my guest. I can " hearken " to Him, and " talk " to Him, and " walk " with Him. And He offers me protection. He will " subdue my enemies." And He offers me unfailing provision. The Guest becomes the Host! I put my little upon the table, and lo! I find that " the cruse of oil fails not, and the meal in the barrel is not consumed! "

## NOVEMBER The First

### IN THE DAYS OF YOUTH
ECCLESIASTES xii. 1-7.

IN my university days at Edinburgh there was a young medical student named Macfarlane. He was one of our finest athletes, and everybody liked him. One day he was stricken with typhoid, which proved fatal. Macfarlane in his days of boisterous health had neglected his Lord, and when one of his friends, visiting him in his sickness, led his thoughts to the Saviour, he turned and said, "But wouldn't it be a shabby thing to turn to Christ now?" "Yes," replied his friend, "it will be a shabby thing, but it will be shabbier not to turn to Him at all!" And I believe that poor Macfarlane turned his shame-filled soul to the Lord.

But it is shabby to offer our Lord the mere dregs in life's cup. It is shabby to offer Him the mere hull of the boat when the storms of passion have carried its serviceableness away. Let me offer Him my best, my finest equipment, my youth! Let me offer Him the best, and give Him the helm when I am just setting sail and life abounds in golden promise! "Remember now thy Creator in the days of thy youth."

## NOVEMBER The Second

### LEADING TO CHRIST

"*Suffer little children to come unto Me.*"—MARK x. 13-22.

"UNTO *Me!*" We must not keep them at any half-way house. We are so prone to be satisfied if only we bring them a little way along the road. If we get them to pray! If we get them to attend the Lord's house! If we get them to be truthful and gentle! All of which is unspeakably good. It is a blessed thing to be in "the ways of Zion"; it is a far more blessed thing to be in the palace with Zion's King and Lord. When we are dealing with little children, every road must lead to Jesus, and not until the road is trodden and we arrive at Him must we think our ministry accomplished.

And, therefore, if I am talking to the little ones about Samuel, or David, or Paul, I must always see the short lane which leads to the Lord. "Suffer the little children to come unto *Me!*" And once they really own Him, we may trust their instincts for the rest. The heart in the child will leap to the love of the Lord, "for of such is the Kingdom of Heaven." When a little one sees the Saviour, it is "love at first sight"!

## THE LORD'S OWN
### John xv. 11-25.

THE "Lord's own" possess the Lord's love. "*I have loved you.*" And love is not a beautiful sentiment, a passive rainbow stretched over the realm of human life. It is a glorious, active energy, infinitely more powerful than electricity, and always besieging the gates of the soul, or ministering to its manifold needs. Love is the greatest force in the world.

And the "Lord's own" are taken into the inner circle of intimacy, where the deepest secrets dwell. We are not kept on the door-step, or left standing in the hall, or limited to one or two "public rooms"; we are privileged to enter the King's privacy, and be nourished at the King's table, and listen to the King's table-talk concerning "all things" which He has heard of the Father. We have "the glorious liberty of *the children* of God."

And the "Lord's own" will experience the world's hatred. "*Therefore the world hateth you.*" Our very friendship with the Lord pronounces judgment on the world, and its hostility is aroused. If we are "partakers of the glory" we shall most assuredly be "partakers of the sufferings of Christ."

## NOVEMBER The Fourth

### THE HOLY SPIRIT AS WITNESS
#### JOHN xv. 26—xvi. 11.

THE Holy Spirit is to be a witness of Jesus. "*He shall testify of Me.*" He shall be "the Friend of the Bridegroom," and He shall sing the Bridegroom's grace, and goodness, and prowess, in the eager ear of the bride. And the early love of the bride shall become deeper and richer as more and more she enters into "the unsearchable riches of Christ."

And the Holy Spirit is thus to be a strengthener of the friends of the Lord. He will be my "*Comforter.*" By His gracious advocacy He will make my faith and hope invincible. The best service which can be rendered me is not to change my circumstances, but to make me superior to them; not to make a smooth road, but to enable me to "leap like an hart" over any road; not to remove the darkness, but to make me "sing songs in the night." And so I will not pray for less burdens, but for more strength! And this is the gracious ministry of "The Comforter."

Holy Spirit, strengthen me! Transform my frail opinions into firm convictions, and change my fleeting, dissolving views into abiding visions!

## NOVEMBER The Fifth

### THE TEMPLE OF THE BODY
ROMANS xii. 1-9.

THE Lord wants my body. He needs its members as ministers of righteousness. He would work in the world through my brain, and eyes, and ears, and lips, and hands, and feet.

And the Lord wants my body as "*a living sacrifice.*" He asks for it when it is thoroughly alive! We so often deny the Lord our bodies until they are infirm and sickly, and sometimes we do not offer them to Him until they are quite "worn out." It is infinitely better to offer them even then than never to offer them at all. But it is best of all to offer our bodies to our Lord when they are strong, and vigorous, and serviceable, and when they can be used in the strenuous places of the field.

And so let me appoint a daily consecration service, and let me every morning present my body "a living sacrifice" unto God. Let me regard it as a most holy possession, and let me keep it clean. Let me recoil from all abuse of it—from all gluttony, and intemperance, and "riotous living." Let me look upon my body as a church, and let the service of consecration continue all day long. "Know ye not that your bodies are the temples of the Holy Spirit?"

## NOVEMBER The Sixth

### PEACE IN TRIBULATION
JOHN xvi. 25-33.

HERE is a strange medley of experiences! I am to enjoy the gift of peace, and yet I am to be smarting under tribulation!

When the Holy Spirit is my guest I am to enjoy the gift of peace. "*These things I said unto you that ye might have peace.*" The life of the soul is to move without jar or discord. It shall be like a quiet engine-house, in which every wheel co-operates with every other wheel, and there is no waste or friction in the holy place. "All that is within me" blesses God's holy name.

And yet, while peace reigns within, there may be tribulation without! "*In the world ye shall have tribulation.*" Here is a peace which is not broken by the noise and assault of brutal circumstance. The most tempestuous wind cannot disturb the quiet serenity of the stars. When the world stones me, not one grain of its gritty dust need enter the delicate workings of my soul. That was the peace of my Lord, and it is my Lord who says to me: "My peace I give unto you!" So "*be of good cheer*," my soul! Thy Lord has "*overcome the world*," and thou shalt share His victory.

## NOVEMBER The Seventh

### REJECTED LOVE
#### Isaiah lxiii. 7-14.

IF I refuse the friendship of the Holy One I inevitably invite His hostility. *"But they rebelled, and vexed His holy Spirit: therefore He was turned to be their enemy, and He fought against them."*

And so, if I reject the forces of grace I do not turn them from my gate, I convert them into foes. Malachi teaches me that rejected sunshine becomes like a burning oven. The Epistle to the Hebrews teaches me that rejected love becomes "a consuming fire." Holiness nourishes virtue, it withers vice. If I offer my Lord a tender aspiration, His breath wooes it like the balmy air of the spring; if I come before Him with the weeds of ignoble dispositions, He blights them as with the nipping of the frost.

And is it not well, for thee and me, that our Lord is thus fiercely hostile to our sins? Is not this "consuming fire" the friend of my soul? May I not pray: Burn on, burn on, pure flame, until all the refuse and rubbish of my life are utterly consumed; burn on, burn on, until fierce flame becomes mild light, flinging its genial radiance over a transfigured desert?

## NOVEMBER The Eighth

### DOING THE IMPOSSIBLE
MATTHEW xxii. 1-14.

"STRETCH forth thine hand!" But that is just what he was unable to do. His hand was withered. His hand had hung there for years, a rebel to all the commands of the will. The Lord's imperative was the demand of the impossible! Yes, but the man obeyed. "He stretched it forth." What he had been unable to do he did at the bidding of the King.

Christ's commandments are always accompanied by adequate supplies of grace. His commandments are really inverted promises; every one is a true bond that the Lord will provide the needful power for its fulfilment. When we begin to obey we release the power, and we discover that the requisite ability has been given by the gracious Master who gave the call.

Let me, therefore, not fear the decree of the Lord. If "His commandments are exceeding broad," His love is exceeding deep. He will not mock our souls. He will not make us thirst, and then hold the water beyond our reach. He is faithful who called thee. Rise to obey, in all thy lameness, and thou shalt find that thy feet and ankle bones receive strength.

## NOVEMBER The Ninth

### THE HOLY SPIRIT AS EMANCIPATOR
2 CORINTHIANS iii. 4-18.

IN the Holy Spirit I experience a large emancipation. "*Where the Spirit of the Lord is, there is liberty.*" I am delivered from all enslaving bondage—from the bondage of literalism, and legalism, and ritualism. I am not hampered by excessive harness, by multitudinous rules. The harness is fitting and congenial, and I have freedom of movement, and "my yoke is easy and my burden is light."

And I am to use my emancipation of spirit in the ministry of contemplation. I am to "*behold, as in a glass, the glory of the Lord.*" My thought has been set free from the cramping distractions devised by men, and I am now to feast my gaze upon the holy splendours of my Lord. It is like coming out of a little and belittling tent, to feast upon the sunny amplitude of the open sky! I can "cease from man," and commune with God.

And the contemplation will effect a transformation. "*We are changed into the same image from glory to glory.*" The serene brightness of the sky gets into our faces. The Lord becomes "*the health of our countenance*," and we shine with borrowed glory.

## NOVEMBER The Tenth

### NEVERTHELESS!
#### Luke v. 1-11.

HERE is obedience in spite of the night of failure. "*Nevertheless, at Thy word I will let down the net.*" That word "nevertheless" has always made history. It has been spoken after scourgings, after "bonds and imprisonments." Ten thousand times has it been heard in the chamber of bereavement, the first sound to break the awful silence. "At evening my wife died. . . . In the morning I did as God commanded me." And may it be true of me! May my "nevertheless" of willing obedience rise like a lark above the storm.

And because there was obedience there came vision. In the wonderful answer to his faith Peter beheld the glory of his Lord. And so I never know where the unenticing road of obedience will lead me. At the end of the dull road there will be some gracious surprise! It is the rugged path which leads to the summit! The panorama comes as the reward of the toilsome climb! Always, in the realm of the Spirit, the dogged "nevertheless" will lead to the "shining tableland to which our God Himself is moon and sun."

## FOILING THE ENEMY'S PLOTS
### LUKE xxii. 24-34.

I DO not meet my tempter alone. The engagement has been foreseen by my Lord. *"Simon, Simon, Satan hath desired to have you!"* The tempter's plots, and wiles, and ambuscades are all clearly perceived. My Lord has got the enemy's maps, and his plan of campaign, for all things are open to the eyes of Him with whom we have to do. I do not fight a lonely warfare on a dark and unknown field. My Lord Himself both scouts and fights for those who are His own.

And one great means of His co-operation is the mighty ministry of intercession. *"But I have prayed for thee."* That "but" is the massing of the forces of heaven against the black and subtle hordes of hell. Let me ever remember that the Lord's prayers are always the conveyers of holy power to those for whom He prays. It is as when Christian met Apollyon in the Valley of Humiliation: there comes a sudden accession of strength to the bleeding warrior, and Apollyon retires wounded and beaten from the field.

And the only way to preserve the fruits of a triumph is by helping other warriors to gain a similar conquest. *"When thou art converted strengthen thy brethren."* I shall retain the hard, muscular limbs of a soldier if I am willing to share my blood with the entire army.

## SEPTEMBER The Ninth

### DEALING WITH SIN
Psalm xxxii.

HERE is the burden of unconfessed sin. *"When I kept silence my bones waxed old."* There is nothing brings on premature age like secret sin. It keeps the mind in perpetual unrest, and a troubled mind soon makes the body old. The real nourisher of the body is a quiet and radiant soul. But let the soul be in chaos, and the body will soon be a ruin.

And here, too, is the healthy act of confession. *"I acknowledged my sin unto Thee, and mine iniquity have I not hid."* He retained no single germ of the whole unclean brood. He brought them out into the light one by one, as though he were emptying a noisome kennel. He brought them out, and named them, in the awful Presence of the Lord.

And here is the ministry of forgiveness, and therefore the miracle of restored health. Let me mark the rich variety of the descriptive words. *"Forgiven!"* *"Covered!"* *"Imputed not!"* It is all removed and obliterated, and the place of defilement and profanity becomes the holy temple of the Lord.

## SEPTEMBER The Tenth

### CRITICISM AND PIETY

*"Thinkest thou, that judgest them that do such things, that thou shalt escape?"*—ROMANS ii. 1-11.

THAT is always my peril, to assume that by being severe with others I exculpate myself. I go on to the bench, and deliver sentence upon my brother, when my proper place is in the dock. And this is the subtlety of the snare, that I regard my criticisms and condemnations of other people as signs of my own innocence. This is the last refinement in temptation, and multitudes fall before its power.

The way to moral and spiritual health is to direct my criticisms upon myself. I must stand in the dock, and hear the grave indictment of my own soul. Unless I pass through the second chapter of Romans I can never enter the fifth and sixth, and still less the glorious forgiveness of the eighth. "There is therefore now no condemnation to them that are in Christ Jesus." I pass into that warm, cheery light through the cold road of acknowledged guilt and sin.

"If we confess our sins He is just to forgive us our sins, and to cleanse us from all unrighteousness."

## SEPTEMBER The Eleventh

### A FATAL DIVORCE

*"They feared the Lord, and served their own gods."*—2 KINGS xvii. 24-34.

AND that is an old-world record, but it is quite a modern experience. The kinsmen of these ancient people are found in our own time. Men still fear one God and serve another.

But something is vitally wrong when men can divorce their fear from their obedience. And the beginning of the wrong is in the fear itself. "Fear," as used in this passage, is a counterfeit coin, which does not ring true to the truth. It means only the payment of outward respect, a formal recognition, a passing nod which we give on the way to something better. It is a mere skin courtesy behind which there is no beating heart; a hollow convention in which there is no deep and sacred awe.

But the real " fear of God " is a spiritual mood in which virtue thrives, an atmosphere in which holy living is quite inevitable. " The fear of the Lord is *clean*." It is not lip-worship, but heart-homage, a reverence in which the soul is always found upon its knees. And so " the fear of the Lord is to hate evil "; it is an indignant repulsion from all that is hateful to God. It is the sharing of the Spirit of the Lord. There cannot be any true fear where the soul does not worship " in spirit and in truth."

## THE GARMENTS OF THE SOUL
### Joel ii. 12-19.

I AM so apt to think that the rending of an outer garment is a token of true penitence and amendment of life. But it is the inner garments I must deal with, the raiments and habits of the soul. Some of these robes—such as vanity and pride—are as gay and showy as a peacock; others are dirty and leprous, and we should not dare to bring them to the door, and display them in the light. But all need severe treatment; they must be torn, fibre from fibre, and reduced to rags.

But "rending" must be accompanied by "turning." *"Turn unto the Lord your God."* For the Lord our God is gracious, and His love will not only provide a new wardrobe, but a swift furnace in which to burn the remnants of the old. Yes, His "great kindness" will burn away the filth of my alienation, and will "bring forth the best robe" and put it on me. The good Lord will give me new habits. He will "cover me with the robe of righteousness, and the garment of salvation."

## SEPTEMBER The Thirteenth

### THE CLEAN HEART
Psalm li.

WHAT will the Lord do with my sin, if in true humility I come into His Presence? Let me hear the music of the evangel.

He will "*blot out my transgression.*" He will so erase it that even His own holy eyes can see no stain or shame. He will blot it out, as I have seen a gloomy cloudlet blotted out, and there has been nothing left but radiant sky.

And He will "*wash me throughly from mine iniquity.*" Yes, and that not like the washing of the hands, but like the washing of clothes, not like the washing of a surface, but the removal of uncleanness from a fabric, the ousting of every germ lurking in the innermost cells of the stuff. When the Lord washes a soul it is "throughly" done, and every strand is white in holiness.

So will He give me "*a clean heart*"; so will He "*renew a right spirit within me.*" The very atmosphere of my life shall be as the air after deluges of cleansing rain. It shall be sweet, and clean, and clear! I shall walk in a new inspiration, and I shall "behold the land that is **very far off.**"

## THE SENSE OF WANT

*"This man went down to his house justified rather than the other."*—LUKE xviii. 9-14.

THE Master sets the Pharisee and publican in contrast, and His judgment goes against the man who has made some progress in moral attainments, and favours the man who has no victories to show, but only a hunger for victory. The dissatisfied sinner is preferred to the self-satisfied saint. The Pharisee had gained an inch, but had lost his sense of the continent. The publican had not pegged out an inch of moral claim, but he had an overwhelming sense of the untrodden universe.

So this, I think, is the teaching for me. We are justified by the penitent sense of want and not by the boastful sense of possession. Our sense of lack is the measure of our hope, and our measure of hope determines the poverty or fulness of our communion with the Lord. The Pharisee had no "beyond," no realm of admiration, no hope! Aspiration was dead, and therefore inspiration had ceased. Our possibilities nestle in our cravings.

## SEPTEMBER The Fifteenth

### RESTORING A RUINED LIFE
Psalm ciii. 1-18.

COULD there be a sweeter chime than the opening music of this psalm?

"*Who forgiveth all thine iniquities.*" He receives me back home again, interrupts the broken story of my sin, and drowns my sobbings in His rejoicings.

"*Who healeth all thy diseases.*" He takes in hand the foul complaints which I acquired in "the far country," and with His powerful medicines, and His wonderful "bread of life," He drives the foul things from my soul.

"*Who redeemeth thy life from destruction.*" Yes, with His own blood He buys me back from a midnight servitude, strikes every chain and shackle from my limbs, and makes me dance in "the glorious liberty of the children of God."

"*Who crowneth thee with loving-kindness and tender mercy.*" He encircles me with the invulnerable army of His own love. Henceforth if the devil would get at me he must deal with God. "As the mountains are round about Jerusalem, so the Lord is round about His people."

"*Who satisfieth thy mouth with good things.*" He sets before me a glorious table, and enlivens my spirits with glorious fellowship. That so I can be no other than "satisfied," and my heart is at rest in the Lord. "Thou, O Christ, art all I want!"

## THE STEADFASTNESS OF THE LORD

"*My covenant shall stand fast.*"—PSALM lxxxix. 19-29.

SUCH a divine assurance ought to make me perfectly quiet in spirit. Restlessness in a Christian always spells disloyalty. The uncertainty is born of suspicion. There is a rift in the faith, and the disturbing breath of the devil blows through, and destroys my peace. If I am sure of my great Ally, my heart will not be troubled, neither will it be afraid.

And such a divine assurance ought to make me bold in will and majestic in labour. I ought to be inventive in chivalrous enterprise, and I ought to covet the hardest parts of the field. If the mighty Ally will never fail, I should never be afraid of the marshalled hosts of wickedness. "One with God is in a majority." "He always wins who sides with God." "The Lord is on my side, whom shall I fear?"

And such a divine assurance ought to give me a kingly demeanour. The members of the Court acquire a certain stateliness by their lofty fellowship. And, surely, one who walks with God should be characterized by something of the Divine glory, and men should know that his acquaintances are found in the courts of heaven.

## SEPTEMBER The Seventeenth

### THE NEVER-WITHERING LEAF
JEREMIAH xvii. 5-11.

LET me look at "the blessed man" in the interpreting symbol of this healthy and graceful tree.

The blessed life is a life of vast resource. *"As a tree planted by the waters, and that spreadeth out her roots by the river."* It is not watered by an occasional shower, it is unceasingly bathed by the vitalizing flood. Its rootlets are always drinking the nutritious waters of grace. The blessed life is planted on the banks of that wonderful river which takes its rise in the great white throne.

And just because of these boundless supplies, the blessed life is undisturbed in times of grave crisis and emergency. *"He shall not see when heat cometh."* He shall be cool when the unblessed are hot and fever-stricken. He shall "keep his head" in times of general panic. His powers of endurance shall make the world wonder! He shall "hold out" when everybody else is faint.

So shall there be nothing "sere and yellow" about him. *"His leaf shall be green."* His faith, and hope, and love shall remain fresh and beautiful even in "the dark and cloudy day."

## SEPTEMBER The Eighteenth

### THE ALL-ROUND DEFENCE

"*Thou hast beset me behind.*"—PSALM cxxxix. 1-12.

AND that is a defence against the enemies which would attack me in the rear. There is yesterday's sin, and the guilt which is the companion of yesterday's sin. They pursue my soul like fierce hounds, but my gracious Lord will come between my pursuers and me. His mighty grace intervenes, and my security is complete.

"Thou hast beset me . . . *before.*" And that is a defence against the enemies which would impede my advance and frighten me out of the heavenly way. There is fear—fear of the morrow, fear of consequences, fear of death! And my Lord will come between me and them, and their menace shall be destroyed. The fiery darts shall be quenched before they reach my soul.

"*And laid Thine hand upon me.*" And that is a defence against the enemies which may lie in ambush in present and immediate circumstances: the sudden temptation to passion, or the temptation to panic, or the temptation which would snare me to criminal ease. But my Lord's hand is all-sufficient! And so on every side my defence standeth; "the angel of the Lord encampeth round about them that fear Him."

## THE NEEDS OF THE BODY
### JOHN vi. 1-21.

THE Lord who came to save His people was sensitive to His people's hunger. In the presence of the supreme need the smaller need was not forgotten. He honoured the body as well as the soul. He ministered to the transient as well as the eternal. And that is ever the characteristic of true kingliness; it has a kingly way of doing the smaller things. I can measure my own progress toward the throne by my sovereign attention to scruples. "He that is faithful in that which is least, the same also is great."

The Lord is not oppressed by the multitude of His guests. "He Himself knew what He would do." We need not jostle one another for His bounty. We shall not crowd one another out. "There is bread enough and to spare." Even in the material realm this is true, and everybody would have his daily bread if the will of the Lord were done. There is no straitness in the gracious Host! It is the greed of the guests which mars the satisfaction of the feast.

And how careful the Lord of Glory was to "gather up the fragments"! Our infinitely wealthy Lord is not wealthy enough to "throw things away." He cannot afford to waste bread. Can He afford to lose a soul? "He goeth out after that which is lost until He find it"!

## SEPTEMBER The Twentieth

### THE PATHETIC MULTITUDE
MARK viii. 1-9.

My Lord has *"compassion upon the multitude."* And (shall I reverently say it?) His compassion was part of His passion. His pity was always costly. It culminated upon Calvary, but it was bleeding all along the road! It was a fellow-feeling with all the pangs and sorrows of the race. And a pity that bleeds is a pity that heals. "In His love and in His pity He redeemed us."

And the multitude is round about us still, and the people are in peril of fainting by the way. There is the multitude of misfortune, the children of disadvantage, who never seem to have come to their own. And there is the multitude of outcasts, the vast army of publicans and sinners. And there are the bewildering multitudes of Africa, and India, and China, and they have "nothing to eat"!

How do I regard them? Do I share the compassion of the Lord? Do I exercise a sensitive and sanctified imagination, and enter somewhat into the pangs of their cravings? My Lord calls for my help. "How many loaves have ye?" "Bring out all you have! Consecrate your entire resources! Put your all upon the altar of sacrifice!" And in reply to the call can I humbly and trustfully say. "O, Lamb of God, I come!"

## SEPTEMBER The Twenty-first

### LIFE AS BREAD
MARK viii. 10-21.

IT is gracious to know that my Lord is "the Bread of Life," and that I can feed on Him. It is fearful to know that I, too, am bread, and that others are feeding on me. Am I the nutriment of vice or the sustenance of virtue? Am I an evil leaven, like the Pharisees, or a holy leaven like the Lord? When little children feed on my presence do they grow in strength and beauty? Or do they become relaxed and demoralized? Who will feed upon me to-day, and what will be the end of it?

If I would have my life to be as hallowed and hallowing leaven I must regularly feed upon the Bread of Life. If I am sustained by the Lord, I too shall be a sustainer of all who aspire after a true and holy life. My very character will itself become heavenly bread, and men will be nourished by it even when I am unconscious of the ministry. When they have spent a brief hour in my company they will go away refreshed.

"Lord, evermore give us this bread!" So feed us with Thyself that we may share Thy nature. Let "virtue" go forth from us, and let it be as holy bread to all who are heavy-laden, and ready to faint.

## THE HANDFUL OF MEAL
1 KINGS xvii. 8-16.

WHAT marvellous "coincidences" are prepared by Providential grace! The poor widow is unconsciously ordained to entertain the prophet! The ravens will be guided to the brook Cherith! "I have commanded them to feed thee there." Our road is full of surprises. We see the frowning, precipitous hill, and we fear it, but when we arrive at its base we find a refreshing spring! The Lord of the way had gone before the pilgrim. "I go to prepare . . . for you."

But how strange that a widow with only "a handful of meal" should be "commanded" to offer hospitality! It is once again "the impossible" which is set before us. It would have been a dull commonplace to have fed the prophet from the overflowing larder of the rich man's palace. But to work from an almost empty cupboard! That is the surprising way of the Lord. He delights to hang great weights on apparently slender wires, to have great events turn on seeming trifles, and to make poverty the minister of "the indescribable riches of Christ."

The poor widow sacrificed her "handful of meal," and received an unfailing supply. And this, too, is the way of the Lord.

> "Whatever, Lord, we lend to Thee,
> Repaid a thousand fold will be."

## SEPTEMBER The Twenty-third

### THE DEDICATION OF SUBSTANCE
### 2 Kings iv. 38-44.

HERE is a man recognizing the sacredness of his substance. He saw the seal of the Lord upon his harvest, and he offered the first-fruits in token of its rightful Owner. Men go wrong when the only name upon their field is their own. "*My* power, and the strength of *my* hand hath gotten me this wealth." It matters nothing what the wealth may be—material substance, mental skill, or business sagacity. It becomes unhallowed power when we attach our own label to it, and erase the name of God.

This man dedicated his substance, and the hunger of his fellows was appeased. That is a great principle in human life. One man's satisfaction is dependent on another man's fidelity. His want is to be filled with my fulness. If I am selfish he remains hungry. If I acknowledge " the rights of God," and therefore " the rights of man," he has " enough and to spare." If I hoard my treasure I rob both God and man.

My gracious Lord, remove the scales from my eyes. Help me to be sensitive to the obligations of all wealth. Let my plenty call me to the children of need. Let me acknowledge my stewardship, and be Thy fellow minister in the service of man.

## AFTER THE TRIUMPH!
### MATTHEW xiv. 23-33.

AFTER the great miracle of feeding the multitude our Lord *"went up into a mountain to pray."* May we reverently wonder if it was a season of temptation? Did they want to make Him a King? Was our human Lord assailed by " the destruction that wasteth at noonday "? And did He shut Himself up with the Father?

I am so disposed to pray *up to* my successes, and to cease to pray *in* them! I remember God in my struggles, I forget Him in my attainments. I hold fellowship with Him on the road, I part company with Him when I arrive. I become a practical atheist in the midst of my successes. My only security is to go up into a mountain apart and pray. Unless I become closeted with God, and see all things in their true colours and proportion, I shall be lifted up in most unholy and destructive pride.

And let me notice that our Lord returned from His privacy with the Father to do even greater miracles still. He had appeased the pangs of hunger; now He appeases the passion of the sea. And so in my degree shall it be with me. If in all my triumphs I remain the humble companion of the Lord, my triumphs shall be repeated and enriched. " Greater works than these shall ye do."

## SEPTEMBER The Twenty-fifth

### THE SENSE OF GRACE
PSALM cvii. 21-32.

A VITAL part of all devotion is the remembrance of the goodness of God. Such a remembrance keeps my soul in the realm of grace. I am so inclined to proclaim my personal rights rather than glorify the favour of God, so inclined to exhibit my own prowess rather than God's most gracious bounty. And whenever I lose the sense of grace I become a usurper and take the throne. Our salvation is "not of works, lest any man should boast."

And such a remembrance would keep my soul in the mood of humility. "Nothing in my hands I bring." I can no more claim the glory of salvation than a child, who has cut a shallow trench on the sands, can claim the glory of initiating the roll of the ocean-tide. I owe all my desires and all my hopes and all my present attainments to the boundless goodness of God.

And such a remembrance would keep my soul in the dispensation of love. I cannot quietly and steadily contemplate the goodness of the Lord without my soul being kindled into loving response. Without high contemplations love smoulders, and will eventually die out. But God's goodness inflames the soul, and communicates its own most gracious heat. "We love because He first loved us!"

## SEPTEMBER The Twenty-sixth

### MY LORD AS MY BREAD
John vi. 26-35.

OUR life's bread is a Person. We may have much to do with Christianity and nothing to do with Christ. The other day I was in a great and wonderful bakery, but I never ate nor touched a morsel of bread. I touched the machinery. I was absorbingly interested in the processes, but I ate no bread! And I may be deeply interested in the means of grace, I may be familiar with all "the ins and outs" of ecclesiastical machinery, and I may never handle nor taste "the bread of God." Our religion is dead and burdensome until it becomes a personal relation, and we have vital communion with Christ.

"Thou, O Christ, art all I want." We find everything in Him. Everything else is preliminary, preparatory, subordinate, and to be in the long run dropped and forgotten. A ritual is only a way to "the bread," and by no means essential, and very often undesirable. The heart can find the Lord with a look, with a cry, and needs no obtrusion of ritual or priest. But how pathetic! To be contented to potter about among the ritual and never to find the Bread! To be in the house and never to see the Host! "Ye search the Scriptures . . . and ye will not come to Me."

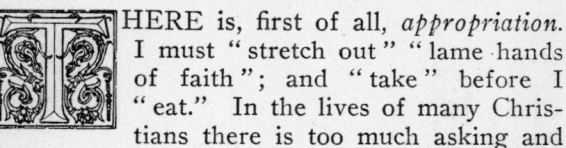

## TAKE AND EAT
### JOHN vi. 52-63.

THERE is, first of all, *appropriation*. I must "stretch out" "lame hands of faith"; and "take" before I "eat." In the lives of many Christians there is too much asking and too little taking. If it were only rightly regarded, prayer is companionship as well as petition, and companionship is literally significant of the sharing of bread. In every season of communion a part must be assigned to the taking of the things for which we have prayed. "*Receive ye the Holy Ghost.*"

And there is *assimilation*. We must "eat" as well as "take." It is in the exercises of obedience that we digest and incorporate the bread of life. Without our obedience the living Lord never becomes "part of ourselves." We never "become one in the bundle of life" with the Lord our God. And truth which is not assimilated becomes a drug. Instead of being a "savour of life unto life," it becomes a "savour of death unto death."

And there is *vitalization*. The assimilated bread of life makes everything alive. Every faculty in my being feels the touch of divine inspiration. It is native bread for native power, and everything is renewed.

## SEPTEMBER The Twenty-eighth

### THE DAILY MANNA

*"I will rain bread from heaven for you."*—
EXODUS xvi. 11-18.

AND this gracious provision is made for people who are complaining, and who are sighing for the flesh-pots of Egypt! Our Lord can be patient with the impatient: He can be "kind to the unthankful." If it were easy to drive the Lord away I should have succeeded long ago. I have murmured, I have sulked, I have turned Him out of my thoughts, and "He stands at the door and knocks!" I yearn for "the flesh-pots," "He sends me manna." "Was there ever kindest shepherd half so gentle, half so sweet?"

"*And they gathered it every morning.*" And that I think is the best time to gather the heavenly food. At night I am weary, my body is craving sleep, and I am not vitalized in the fields of grace. But in the morning I am refreshed, and I can go to the heavenly fields and gather "the things which God hath prepared for them that love Him." I can be fed as the day begins, and I can set out to my daily work with the taste of God in my mouth, and His mighty grace in my heart, and I shall delight to "walk in the paths of His commandments."

## SEPTEMBER The Twenty-ninth

### THE FOUNTAIN

1 JOHN v. 9-21.

MY Lord is "the fountain of life." "This life is in His Son." The springs are nowhere else—not in elaborate theologies, or in ethical ideals, or in literary masterpieces, or in music or art. "In Him was life." It is so easy to forget the medicinal spring amid the distractions of the fashionable spa. There are some healing waters at Scarborough, but they have been almost "crowded out" by bands and entertainments. It is possible that the secondary ministries of the Church may crowd out the Church's Lord. I do not object to the entertainment if only it opens out on to the Spring!

To have the Son is to have life. Nothing else is needed. "Thou, O Christ, art all I want." Ritualisms, and ecclesiasticisms, and formal theologies are not requisite. We can be saved without an academic knowledge of "the plan of salvation." Many a gamekeeper's little child knows all the roads on the estate, although she would be quite "at sea" in explaining "the plan of the estate" which hangs in the house of the steward. "This is life eternal, to know Thee and Jesus Christ whom Thou hast sent."

## WHITE ROBES IN THE STREETS
John xvii. 11-28.

THE man who has been fed with the "bread of life" must remain "in the world." The Lord gives no countenance to the life of the ascetic. Our sanctification is not to be gained by withdrawal and retreat. At the best, that would be a holiness sickly and anæmic, a coddled virtue devoid of firm muscle and iron nerve. Our Lord purposes a holiness which shall wear white robes in the streets, and shine like virgin snow in the market, and keep itself chivalrous and stately in the common fellowships of men.

"In the world," but *"not of the world."* The man who is fed on "the bread of life" is endowed with powers of resistance against "the noisome pestilence." The germs of worldly epidemics find no nutriment in him. "The prince of this world cometh, and hath nothing in Me." When an evil microbe finds no foothold it withers away. If I am not "of the world" I shall quite naturally and instinctively be able to resist "all the wiles of the devil."

And my Lord purposes me to have this positive, masculine holiness in order *"that the world may believe."* He wants disciples who will arrest the world by their glorious health, and by their invincible moral defences. He wants my purity to advertise His grace; He wants my faith to increase "the household of the faith."

## OCTOBER The First

### A WONDERFUL UNBELIEF
PSALM lxxviii. 15-25.

"THEY believed not in God . . . though He had——" Let everyone finish that sentence out of his own experience. How much grace can our unbelief withstand? The Lord had made the rock like unto a spring of water, and yet these people believed not! What has He done for thee and me? Let us retrace the pilgrimage of our own years. Let us recall the blessings by the way—the streams in the desert, the pillar of fire that led us in the night. And yet what is the quality of our faith? It is often weak and reluctant, riddled with timidities, or moth-eaten with worldly ease. It is not mighty and daring, riding forth every morning like a chivalrous knight to inevitable conquest. It creeps along, like Mr. Halting, and Miss Much-Afraid, and Mr. Little-Faith.

"He marvelled at their unbelief." The Lord Jesus wondered that men and women, seeing what they had seen, did not immediately spring to the life and service of faith. Perhaps we do not give time for faith to be born! Perhaps we do not see because we do not look. Perhaps we are blind to His mercies and are therefore dead to the faith. And therefore, perhaps, our first prayer should be, "Lord, that I might receive my sight," and then the prayer, "Lord, increase my faith."

## HUMBLING OUR PRIDE
### JOB xxxviii. 1-15.

"I WILL demand of thee, and answer thou Me." When our God begins to ask questions our pride is soon humbled, for the limits of our knowledge and power are speedily reached. The mist is very close to our doors, and in a very few steps we are lost on a trackless moor. Who can trace the real springs of a tear and lay his hand on the emotion that gave it birth? Who can lead us into the bright realm where smiles are born? Who knoweth the way of a frown, or who can uncover the secrets of fear? No living man can explain his own breathing, or can unravel the mysterious decree which moves his own finger!

And as there is so much mystery, it must be surely true that mystery is a very gracious thing. Uncertainty is the divine ministry of blessedness. If it were not so, He would have told us! "I have many things to say unto you, but ye cannot bear them now." If it were best for us that the mist should be removed, He would roll it up like a garment and give us the light of unclouded day. But the mist remains, the home of blessing. "He cometh in a thick cloud." "The clouds drop fatness."

## OCTOBER The Third

### WATCHING THE CREATOR
JEREMIAH x. 10-16.

"HE hath made the earth by His power." And He is making it still. Even in the material world " His mercies are new every morning." James Smetham used to speak of going into his garden " to see what the Lord is doing." He would stand on the top of Highgate Hill on a blustering night " to watch the goings of the Lord in the storm." And all this means that to James Smetham creation was not merely a single event, but a *process* whose countless events are still going on. He watched his Lord at work! Every sunset was a new creation from the Almighty Maker's hands.

To many of us the Creator is remote from His works. He is not immediately near. And so He no longer " walks in the garden in the cool of the day." The garden is no longer a holy place. Let us recover the sacredness of things. Let us " practise the presence of God." Let us link His love and power to every flower that blows. And so shall we be able to say, as we move amid the glories of the natural world, ' The Lord is in His holy temple."

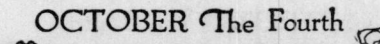

## CREATOR AND CREATURE
### Isaiah xl. 9-28.

LET me mark the range of this teaching. "Who hath measured the waters in the hollow of His hand. . . . He shall feed His flock like a shepherd." And let me mark it again. "The Creator of the ends of the earth . . . giveth power unto the faint." Almightiness offers itself to carry my burden! The Creator offers Himself to re-create me! I can engage the forces of the universe to help me on my journey. Emerson counselled us to hitch our wagon to a star. We can do better than that. We can hitch it to the Maker of the star! We have something better than an ideal; we have the Light of the world. We are not left to a radiant abstraction; we have a gracious God.

The water flows from the Welsh hills to every house in Birmingham. Rich and poor alike share the bounty of the mountains. The wealth of the mountains comes to the common thirst. And everybody, too, may have the water from the everlasting hills. "The water that I shall give him shall be in him." The river of life will flow to every soul of man.

## OCTOBER The Fifth

### THE SOUL AND NATURE
Psalm cxlviii.

"PRAISE ye the Lord." And the Psalmist calls upon the creation to join in the anthem. And that is the gracious purpose of our God, that the world should be filled with harmonious praise. It is His will that the character of man should harmonize with the flowers of the field, that the beauty of his habits should blend with the glories of the sunrise, and that his speech and laughter should mingle with the songs of birds and with the melody of flowing streams. But man is too often a discord in creation. The flowers put him to shame. The birds make him sound harsh and jarring. He is "out of tune."

What then? "Tune my heart to sing Thy praise." We must bring the broken strings, the rusted strings, the jarring strings to the Repairer and Tuner of the soul. It is the glad ministry of His grace to re-awaken silent chords, to restore broken harps, to "put new songs" in our mouths. He will make us the kinsfolk of all things bright and beautiful. We shall "go forth with joy," and "all the trees of the field shall clap their hands."

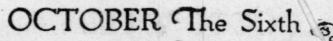

## HE KNOWETH OUR FRAME
### Psalm ciii. 13-22.

"HE knoweth our frame." The Bible abounds in such gracious and tender words. "He remembereth us in our low estate." "I have many things to say unto you, but ye cannot bear them now." "He will not permit you to be tempted above that ye are able." The burden is suited to our strength. The revelation is determined by our experience. The pace is regulated by our years. "He carrieth the lambs in His arms." He "leads on softly." Nothing is done in ignorance. "The Lord is mindful of His own. He remembereth His children."

And so I must practise the belief in God's compassionate nearness. In my childhood I used to sing "There's a Friend for little children, Above the bright blue sky." I know better now. He is nearer to me than I can dream. I used to sing "There is a happy land, Far, far away." Now I sing, "There is a happy land, *Not* far away." The good Father and His home are not in some remote realm. They are very, very near to me, and He knows all about me. "He knoweth our frame."

## OCTOBER The Seventh

### NEEDING AND WANTING
ACTS xvii. 22-31.

"AS though He needed anything." "He may not need us; but does He want us?" Such is the question I heard Dr. Parker ask as he preached upon these words. And he took up a handful of flowers which he had upon the pulpit, and said: "These flowers were gathered for me by little hands in a Devonshire lane. Did I need them? No. Did I want them? . . . Your little girl kissed you before you left for business this morning. Did you need it? . . . Did you want it?"

And so Almightiness may not need our weakness, but the loving Father wants His children. "We are His offspring." Our Father delights in the love of His children. The Saviour said to a Samaritan woman, "Give Me to drink." And perhaps it is within the scope of our holy privilege to refresh the heart of our Lord. Perhaps we can give Him to drink of the well of our affections, and He will see of "the travail of His soul and be satisfied."

## GOD'S GLORIOUS PURPOSE

*"I have created him for My glory, I have formed him; yea, I have made him."*—ISAIAH xliii. 1-7.

THAT is surely a superlative honour! "I have created him for My glory." I stood before one of Turner's paintings, and a man of fine judgment said to me, "That is Turner's glory!" He meant that in that picture the genius and the power and the grace of Turner were most abundantly expressed. And it is the will of God that man should express His glory, and by his righteousness and goodness witness to the great Creator's power and love. Amid all the wonders and sublimities of earth, and sky, and sea, man is to be the Almighty's "glory."

The contrast is pathetic when we turn from the Creator's purpose to our immediate life. There is so much that is shameful, crooked, and perverse. There is little or nothing of "glory." But, blessed be God! the purpose abides, and the Creator's work goes on. In His redemptive grace He has made provision for marred work, for spoilt and perverted life. "The crooked shall be made straight." "I will bring again that which is out of the way." "Where sin abounds grace doth much more abound."

## OCTOBER The Ninth

### *THE LARGER WATERS*
1 Thessalonians iv. 13-18.

DEATH is not an end; it is only a new beginning. Death is not the master of the house; he is only the porter at the King's lodge, appointed to open the gate, and let in the King's guests into the realms of eternal day. "And so shall we be ever with the Lord."

And so the range of three score years and ten is not the limit of our life. Our life is not a landlocked lake enclosed within the shore-lines of seventy years. It is an arm of the sea, and where the shore-lines seem to meet in old age they open out into the infinite. And so we must build for those larger waters. We must lay our life plans on the scale of the infinite, not as though we were only pilgrims of time, but as children of eternity! We are immortal! How, then, shall we live to-day in prospect of the eternal morrow?

## OUR REFUGE AND STRENGTH
### Psalm xlvi.

"GOD is our refuge and strength." And in the varied conflicts and perils of life we need both these resources. We need the "refuge." There are times when our mightiest warfare is to lie passive, to shelter quietly in the strong defences of our God. Our finest strategy is sometimes to "rest in the Lord and wait." We can slay some of our enemies by leaving them alone. We can "starve them out." They can be weakened and beaten by sheer neglect. We feed their strength, and give them favoured chances, if we go out and face them actively, "marching as to war." The best way is to hide, and keep quiet; and "God is our refuge."

But we also need the "strength." This is positive equipment for active service. The defensive is changed to the offensive, and in the "strength" of the Lord we advance against the foe. We "ride abroad, redressing human wrongs." We "tread upon the lion and the adder, the young lion and the dragon we trample under foot." We meet our enemy on the open field, and we slay him in his pride!

And so our God is our resource in the double warfare of active and passive crusade. In Him we can take refuge, and the enemy withers. In Him we can find fighting strength, and the enemy is overthrown.

## OCTOBER The Eleventh

### THE OLD COMPANION ON THE NEW ROAD

*"Get thee out . . . and I will show thee."*
*"So Abram departed . . . and the Lord appeared."*—GENESIS xii. 1-9.

WE must bring these separated passages together if we would appreciate the graciousness of the Lord's call. They are like the two sides of the same shield. They answer each other as voice and echo. When I move in obedience the Lord moves in inspiration. He never lets me go on my own charges. "All things are now ready." Before He makes me hunger the bread is prepared. Before I thirst the water is at hand. Before He calls me He has opened springs in difficult places and arbours of rest along the road. When Abram set out from his own country the Lord went before him.

And so I need not fear the arduous call. The very measure of its difficulty is also the measure of the riches of the divine provisions. "As thy day so shall thy strength be." At every turning of the winding way the Lord will appear unto us. At every new demand we shall discover new bounty, and everywhere in the unfamiliar road we shall gaze upon the familiar and friendly face of the Lord.

## OCTOBER The Twelfth

### ROUND-ABOUT WAYS
Acts vii. 1-7.

"UNTO a land that I will show thee." But what mysterious windings there often are before that land is reached! But God's windings are never wasteful and purposeless. The apparent deviations are always gracious preparations. We are taken out of the way in order that we may the more richly reach our end. George Pilkington yearned to go to the foreign field, and God sent him to a dairy farm in Ireland. But the Irish dairy farm proved to be on the way to Uganda; and all the experience and knowledge which Pilkington picked up in this strange business proved invaluable when he reached his appointed field. "He bringeth the blind by a way that they know not."

So I will remember that the "short cut" is not always the finest road. God's round-about ways are filled with heavenly treasure. Every winding is purposed for the discovery of new wealth. What riches we gather on the way to God's goal!

> "The hill of Zion yields
> A thousand sacred sweets
> Before we reach the heavenly fields
> Or walk the golden streets."

## OCTOBER The Thirteenth

### THE ROYAL AIR
Galatians iii. 6-14.

EMERSON says somewhere that he has noticed that men whose duties are performed beneath great domes acquire a stately and appropriate manner. The vergers in our great cathedrals have a dignified stride. It is not otherwise with men who consciously live under the power of vast relationships. Princes of royal blood have a certain great "air" about them. The consciousness of noble kinships has an expansive influence upon the soul. The Jews felt its influence when they called to mind "our Father Abraham."

So is it with men and women of glorious kinships in the realm of faith. Their souls expand in the vast and exalted relations. "The children of faith" have vital communion with all the spiritual princes and princesses of countless years. They have blood-relationship with the patriarchs, and psalmists, and prophets, and they dwell "in heavenly places" with Paul, and Augustine, and Luther, and Wesley.

Surely, such exalted kinship should influence our very stride, and set its mark upon our "daily walk and conversation." It ought to make us so big that we can never speak a mean word, or do a petty and peevish thing.

## COMMONPLACE PEOPLE
### John i. 35-47.

OUR Lord delights to glorify the commonplace. He loves to fill the common water-pots with His mysterious wine. He chooses the earthen vessels into which to put His treasure. He calls obscure fishermen to be the ambassadors of His grace. He proclaims His great Gospel through provincial dialects, and He fills uncultured mouths with mighty arguments. He turns common meals into sacraments, and while He breaks ordinary bread He relates it to the blessing of heaven.

And "this same Jesus" is among us to-day, with the same choices and delights. He will make a humdrum duty shine like the wayside bush that burned with fire and was not consumed. He will make our daily business the channel of His grace. He will take our disappointments, and, just as we sometimes put banknotes into black-edged envelopes, He will fill them with treasures of unspeakable consolation. He will use our poor, broken, stammering speech to convey the wonders of His grace to the weary sinful souls of men.

## OCTOBER The Fifteenth

### *THE CALL AND THE EQUIPMENT*
### LUKE v. 27-32.

MATTHEW was very weary, and the all-seeing Lord read the signs of his spiritual dissatisfaction and unrest. As Jesus "passed by" nothing escaped His watchful eye. He saw a look in Matthew's eye as of some caged creature longing for freedom. Matthew's office, the contempt of his fellows, and perhaps his own self-contempt held him in imprisoning disquietude. The Lord knew it all, and one word from Him and the iron gate was open, and the prisoner was free! "Follow Me! And he left all, rose up, and followed Him." With the Lord's command was conveyed the ability to obey, and Matthew stepped into "the glorious liberty of the children of God."

And this is the Master's way. His calls are always equipments. Every received commandment is also the vehicle of requisite grace. God's decrees are also promises, nay, they are immediate endowments. If we reverently open one of His callings we shall find it a store-house of needed strength.

And therefore we need not fear the calls of the Lord. They are not the harsh commandments of a tyrant, they are the loving invitations of a friend. If we obey them we shall taste the grace of them, and "His statutes will become our songs."

## OCTOBER The Sixteenth

### THE INSPIRATIONS OF THE PAST
Isaiah li. 1-6.

HERE is a sentence from Lord Morley: "If a man is despondent about his work the best remedy I can prescribe for him is to turn to a good biography." He counsels him to go into the yesterdays to find inspiration for the life of to-day. Other men's attainments are bugle-calls to me. "Look unto Abraham, your father." Look unto the blessings which waited upon his obedience! See how springs of refreshment broke out in the troubled way! God "called him and blessed him." Rekindle your hope at his radiant triumph. Strengthen your will in his glorious persistence.

Here do I see God's mercy in the gift of memory and in the witness of history. I can turn to the yesterdays for light and quickening. "Do ye not remember the miracle of the loaves?" Yes, I can recall the grace that met me in my need, the power that made the crooked straight and the rough places plain. And I am privileged to turn the pages of other men's testimonies and read the record of the Lord's dealings with them. And so do memory and history come as helpful angel-presences to my soul.

> "His love in time past
> Forbids me to think
> He'll leave me at last
> In trouble to sink."

## OCTOBER The Seventeenth

### NO QUEST OF GOD

"*He inquired not of the Lord.*"—1 Chronicles x. 6-14.

THAT was where Saul began to go wrong. When quest ceases, conquests cease. "He inquired not"; and this meant loss of light. God will be inquired after. He insists that we draw up the blinds if we would receive the light. If we board up our windows He will not drive the gentle rays through our hindrance. We must ask if we would have. The discipline of inquiry fits us for the counsel of the Lord.

"He inquired not"; and this meant loss of sight. When light fails, sight fails. The ponies in our pits become blind. When a spiritual power is not exercised in the heavenly, it is deprived of its appointed functions. And the tragedy is this, that the blind are deceived into thinking that they still retain their sight. "Ye say, we see!"

"He inquired not"; and this meant loss of might. For "the light of life" is not only illumination; it is inspiration too. It is both light and heat; it confers guidance and dynamic. When a man, therefore, refuses the light he becomes a weakling, and he will meet with disaster in the first tempestuous day.

## UNANIMITY IN THE SOUL

*"A double-minded man is unstable in all his ways."*—JAMES i. 1-8.

IF two men are at the wheel with opposing notions of direction and destiny, how will it fare with the boat? If an orchestra have two conductors both wielding their batons at the same time and with conflicting conceptions of the score, what will become of the band? And a man whose mind is like that of two men flirting with contrary ideals at the same time will live a life "all sixes and sevens," and nothing will move to purposeful and definite issues. If the mind flirt with Satan and Christ, life will be filled with disastrous instability and confusion.

The first thing we need, therefore, for influential and impressive living is unanimity. Unanimity in the mind is the primary factor in a forceful life. To bring "all that is within me" into concord, to make every instrument of the soul bow to one conductor, to lead all the powers into homage to the Lord—this is the unanimity which assures the perfection of holiness. "Unite my heart to fear Thy name." That is the mood which wins life's prize, "the prize of the high calling of God in Christ Jesus."

## OCTOBER The Nineteenth

### READY!
*"Let your loins be girded about."*—LUKE xii. 35-40.

LOOSE garments can be very troublesome. An Oriental robe, if left ungirdled, entangles the feet, or is caught by the wind and hinders one's goings. And therefore the wearer binds the loose attire together with a girdle, and makes it firm and compact about his body. And loose principles can be more dangerous than loose garments. Indefinite opinions, caught by the passing wind of popular caprice, are both a peril and a burden. Many people go through life with loose beliefs and purposes, and they never arrive at any glorious goal. "Let your loins be girded about." Bind your loose thinkings together with the girdle of truth into firm and saving conviction.

*"And your lights burning."*

Be ready for the emergency. When the darkness falls, don't have to hasten away to buy oil. Look after your resources, and be competent to meet the crisis when it comes. Let the light of conscience be burning with clear flame, like a brilliant lighthouse on a dangerous shore. Let the light of love be burning, like a lamp which sends its friendly, cheery beams to the pilgrims of the night. "Our sufficiency is of God," and the oil of grace will keep the lights burning through the longest night.

## OCTOBER The Twentieth

### THE LORD AS THE SERVANT

"*Jesus, knowing that the Father had given all things into His hands, and that He came forth from God, and goeth to God* . . ."—JOHN xiii. 1-20.

AND how shall we expect the sentence to finish? What shall be the issue of so vast a consciousness? "*He took a towel, and girded Himself . . . and began to wash the disciples' feet.*"

So a mighty consciousness expresses itself in lowly service. In our ignorance we should have assumed that divinity would have moved only in planetary orbits, and would have overlooked the petty streets and ways of men. But here the Lord of Glory girds Himself with the apron of the slave, and almightiness addresses itself to menial service.

And that is the test of an expanding consciousness. We may be sure that we are growing smaller when we begin to disparage humble services. We may be sure we are growing larger when we love the ministries that never cry or lift their voices in the streets. When a man begins to despise the "towel," he is losing his kingly dignity, and is resigning his place on the throne. "I have given you an example that ye also should do as I have done to you."

## OCTOBER The Twenty-first

### THE CONTRITE HEART
Isaiah lvii. 13-21.

LET us look at this description of the dwelling-place of the Eternal God. *"I dwell with him also that is of a contrite and humble spirit."*

And who are the contrite? In the original word there is the significance of pieces of rock or lumps of soil having been crumbled into the finest powder. Have I not sometimes heard the phrase—" He's just a lump of pride"? Well, that pride has to be broken down into the finest powder, until not a bit of stubborn self-conceit remains. And then the contrite become the humble! Our gracious Lord has sometimes to use heavy hammers in the destruction of this hard and stony pride: the shock of calamity, the battering of disappointment and defeat! Our pride *must* be ground to powder. Then He will come in and dwell with us!

And what then? He will *"revive the spirit of the humble, and revive the heart of the contrite ones."* Our broken pride shall be as broken soil in which our Lord will grow the flowers and fruits of the Spirit. The death of pride shall be followed by a revival of all things sweet and beautiful. When pride is laid low, it is a " day of resurrection." The wilderness shall " blossom as the rose."

## OCTOBER The Twenty-second

## THE TRUE STANDARD OF GREATNESS
### MATTHEW xviii. 1-7.

HERE is our Lord's estimate of true greatness. How infinite is the contrast between His standard and the standards of the world! The world measures greatness by money, or eloquence, or intellectual skill, or even by prowess on the field of battle. But here is the Lord's standard—"*Whosoever, therefore, shall humble himself as this little child, the same is the greatest in the kingdom of heaven.*"

Those people are greatest who are most like God. We become partakers of the Divine nature through a child-like relationship to God. The grace and power of God pour into our souls when we wait upon Him like a little child.

Child-likeness opens the doors and windows to the incoming of the Almighty. The child-like is the trustful, and no barriers of cynical suspicion block the channels of spiritual communion. And the child-like is the docile, and no boulders of arrogance or self-conceit block the channel of the invigorating waters of life. And so the child-like become the God-like, and, of course, they are the greatest among the sons of men. The little child enshrines the secret of the God-man, and we should be infinitely wise if we had the little child always in our midst.

## OCTOBER The Twenty-third

### *MASTERS AND SERVANTS*
MATTHEW xx. 20-28.

IT is always our peril that we hunger for place more than for character, for position more than for disposition, for a temporal sceptre more than for a majestic self-control.

These disciples coveted places on the right and left of the Lord, and they had little or no concern about their worthiness for the posts. Temporalities eclipsed spiritualities, fleeting fireworks hid the quiet stars. They wanted to be great and prominent, the Lord wanted them to be pure and good. They longed to be Prime Ministers, the Lord purposed that they should be glad to be ministers, working contentedly in an obscure place.

Now mark our Lord's response. "*Are ye able to drink of the cup that I drink of?*" They wanted to be the King's cup-bearers; He offers them to drink of His cup. They call for sovereignty: He asks for sacrifice. They crave sweetness: He offers them bitterness. They seek a life of "getting": He demands a life of "giving." Who has a cup of bitterness to drink? Go and share it with him! Where are the morally and spiritually anæmic? Go and give them thy blood! "Whoever shall lose his life shall find it." Through self-sacrifice we pass to our throne.

## OCTOBER The Twenty-fourth

### "PUSH" AND "PULL"
#### Luke xiv. 1-11.

THE world canonizes "push." It eulogizes the "man of push." It loves to see a man elbowing his way through the jostling crowd, and gaining for himself a "chief seat" at life's feast. He is proclaimed a "successful" man, and he rises in "the chief seat," and amid loud hurrahs he responds to the toast of his health.

Yes, "push" is the word of the world, but "pull" is the word of the Lord, and between the two there is the difference of darkness and light. "Push" is selfish and exclusive: "pull" is inclusive and neighbourly. "Push" takes as its motto, "The weakest to the wall!" "Pull" takes as its motto, "Bear ye one another's burdens, and so fulfil the law of Christ."

The final verdict upon life will be founded, not upon our own success in gaining a chief seat, but upon our success in encouraging the faint and the weakling, and in "helping lame dogs over stiles."

My gracious Lord, help me to put on "a heart of compassion" that by neighbourly feeling and ministry I may lead my fellows to the choice places of life's feast.

## OCTOBER The Twenty-fifth

### THE ROBE OF HUMILITY
#### 1 Peter v. 1-11.

LET me, therefore, learn this lesson, that if my Lord should give me prominence in His church it is not to feed my lust of dominion, but in order to strengthen and extend the influence of the church's life. *"Neither as lording it over the charge allotted to you, but making yourselves ensamples to the flock."*

The only truly imperial purple is the robe of humility. Any other sort of attire may appear to be kingly, but it has none of the glorious significance which belongs to our sovereign Lord. When a man puts on the robe of pride, he immediately belittles his manhood. When a man puts on the robe of humility, he becomes a greater man.

But humility is more than an imperial robe, it is a complete armour. It is fine for defence! The devil cannot get at the man who is "clothed in humility." There is no chink or crevice through which his deadly rapier can pierce. And it is equally fine for offence! Wearing this armour we can go out "redressing human wrongs." The stroke of pride is ever futile. When the humble man deals a blow, the power of the Almighty is in his right hand. **"Humble yourselves, therefore, under the mighty hand of God."**

## OCTOBER The Twenty-sixth

### THE LUST OF THE EXTERNAL
MATTHEW xxiii. 1-12.

PHARISAISM is the lust of externalities, and the utter negligence of the inward sanctities of the spirit. It thinks more of decorum than of holiness, more of etiquette than of equity, more of ritualism than of "the robe of righteousness and the garment of salvation." Pharisaism lives in the streets: it does not dwell in the inner chambers of our mystic life.

Pharisaism thirsts for the homage of men and not for the approbation of God. It is far more alert to the "Rabbi! Rabbi!" of the crowd than it is to the secret callings of the Lord. The path between itself and the highest is unfrequented and grass-grown; the path between itself and the multitude is a well-trodden and barren road.

My Lord, let me be warned! Let me not pervert the ministries of religion to the aggrandizement of self. Let me not, in appearing to worship Thee, be seeking the worship of men. Give me singleness of mind. Give me purity of heart. And may I discover true greatness in seeking greatness for others.

## OCTOBER The Twenty-seventh

### PAYING HOMAGE TO THE KING
PROVERBS iii. 1-12.

"ACKNOWLEDGE Him." But not with a passing nod of recognition. I must not merely glance at Him now and again, admitting His existence on the field. To acknowledge Him is to acknowledge Him as King, with the right to control, and as predominant partner in all the affairs of my life, even the right to give the determining voice in all my decisions. No, it is not the recognition paid to an acquaintance, it is the homage paid to a King.

And if I thus acknowledge Him, He will direct my paths. Life shall always be moving on to its purposed end and glory. The path chosen will not always be the most alluring one, but it will be the right one, and therefore the safe one, and there will be wonderful discoveries on the uninviting track.

How will He let me know which path to take? I cannot say. We can never anticipate God's ways of dealing with us. But if my life is bent to the loving acknowledgment of His will, He will assuredly find a way to make His will known. The light will always reach the willing mind.

## OCTOBER The Twenty-eighth

### PLEASANTNESS AND PEACE

"*Her ways are ways of pleasantness, and all her paths are peace.*"—PROVERBS iii. 13-26.

IN the ways of the Lord I shall have feasts of "pleasantness." But not always at the beginning of the ways. Sometimes my faith is called upon to take a very unattractive road, and nothing welcomes me of fascination and delight. But here is a law of the spiritual life. The exercised faith intensifies my spiritual senses, and hidden things become manifest to my soul—hidden beauties, hidden sounds, hidden scents! Faith adds a mysterious "plus" to my powers, and "all things become new."

And in the ways of the Lord I shall also find the gracious gift of peace. Not that the road will be always smooth, but that I may be always calm. I can be unperturbed when "all around tumultuous seems." I can journey in holy serenity, because the Lord of the road is with me. For peace consists, not in friendliness of circumstances, but in friendship with the Lord.

## OCTOBER The Twenty-ninth

### THE STORY OF THE PAST
Deuteronomy xxxi. 7-13.

AND no ears are more receptive to spiritual story than the ears of a little child. It is not needful to open the gate of interest; it is wide ajar already. And imagination also is there, ready to busy itself about the story. And so, too, is the spirit of homage and adoration. The children are ready for the King! "Suffer little children to come unto Me, for of such is the Kingdom of Heaven."

And, therefore, we have need of wise tellers of the story, who know the story themselves. And in these delicate regions I must ever remember how much my spirit shares in the story I tell. My spirit is a friend or a foe to my power. My words may be well chosen, but they may all be light as empty shells, devoid of all vitality. My words have just the power of their spiritual contents. "You cannot fight the French with 200,000 red uniforms," said Carlyle; "there must be men inside them." And we cannot engage in the evangelization with mere uniforms of words. There must be spirit inside them, even the spirit of pure and consecrated lives.

## OCTOBER The Thirtieth

### A TESTIMONY MEETING
PSALM xxxiv. 1-11.

THIS is a little testimony meeting, in which each of the witnesses tells the story of the Lord's gracious dealings with him. Let me listen to them.

"*He delivered me from all my fears.*" His fears held him in dungeons. Even the noontide was as darkness round about him, and there was no song in his soul. And the Lord broke open the prison-gate and let him out to light, and joy, and belief.

"*They looked to Him and were lightened.*" They looked upon the grace of the Lord, and were lit up, just as I have seen humble cottage windows ablaze with the glory of the rising sun. I must "set my face" towards the Lord, and I, too, shall catch the radiance of His glory.

"This poor man cried . . . *and the Lord saved him out of all his troubles.*" And these troubles were what I should call "tight corners," when the life is hemmed in by unfortunate circumstances, and there seems no way of escape. Disappointment shuts us in. Sorrow shuts us in. Lack of money shuts us in. Let me cry unto the Lord. He is a wonderful Friend in the tight corner, and He will bring my feet into "a large place."

## OCTOBER The Thirty-first

### TWO GREAT MYSTERIES
Psalm lxxxi.

THIS is an unutterable mystery, that a man can close his life against God. *"Israel would have none of Me."* We can shut out God as we can shut out the pure air. We can bar His entrance just as we can exclude the light from the chamber. And then the pity is, we can deceive ourselves into believing that the air is perfectly fresh and that the room is flooded with light. We lose our fine discernment, and we call evil good, and the darkness we call day. If we "refuse to have God" in our thoughts God gives us over to a "reprobate mind."

And it is an equally unutterable mystery that a man can open his life to the entertainment of Almighty God. "I will dwell with them!" That is my supreme honour, that the Lord will be my guest. I can "hearken" to Him, and "talk" to Him, and "walk" with Him. And He offers me protection. He will "subdue my enemies." And He offers me unfailing provision. The Guest becomes the Host! I put my little upon the table, and lo! I find that "the cruse of oil fails not, and the meal in the barrel is not consumed!"

## IN THE DAYS OF YOUTH
### ECCLESIASTES xii. 1-7.

IN my university days at Edinburgh there was a young medical student named Macfarlane. He was one of our finest athletes, and everybody liked him. One day he was stricken with typhoid, which proved fatal. Macfarlane in his days of boisterous health had neglected his Lord, and when one of his friends, visiting him in his sickness, led his thoughts to the Saviour, he turned and said, "But wouldn't it be a shabby thing to turn to Christ now?" "Yes," replied his friend, "it will be a shabby thing, but it will be shabbier not to turn to Him at all!" And I believe that poor Macfarlane turned his shame-filled soul to the Lord.

But it is shabby to offer our Lord the mere dregs in life's cup. It is shabby to offer Him the mere hull of the boat when the storms of passion have carried its serviceableness away. Let me offer Him my best, my finest equipment, my youth! Let me offer Him the best, and give Him the helm when I am just setting sail and life abounds in golden promise! "Remember now thy Creator in the days of thy youth."

## NOVEMBER The Second

### LEADING TO CHRIST

*"Suffer little children to come unto Me."*—MARK x. 13-22.

"UNTO *Me!*" We must not keep them at any half-way house. We are so prone to be satisfied if only we bring them a little way along the road. If we get them to pray! If we get them to attend the Lord's house! If we get them to be truthful and gentle! All of which is unspeakably good. It is a blessed thing to be in "the ways of Zion"; it is a far more blessed thing to be in the palace with Zion's King and Lord. When we are dealing with little children, every road must lead to Jesus, and not until the road is trodden and we arrive at Him must we think our ministry accomplished.

And, therefore, if I am talking to the little ones about Samuel, or David, or Paul, I must always see the short lane which leads to the Lord. "Suffer the little children to come unto *Me!*" And once they really own Him, we may trust their instincts for the rest. The heart in the child will leap to the love of the Lord, "for of such is the Kingdom of Heaven." When a little one sees the Saviour, it is "love at first sight"!

## NOVEMBER The Third

### THE LORD'S OWN
#### JOHN xv. 11-25.

THE "Lord's own" possess the Lord's love. *"I have loved you."* And love is not a beautiful sentiment, a passive rainbow stretched over the realm of human life. It is a glorious, active energy, infinitely more powerful than electricity, and always besieging the gates of the soul, or ministering to its manifold needs. Love is the greatest force in the world.

And the "Lord's own" are taken into the inner circle of intimacy, where the deepest secrets dwell. We are not kept on the door-step, or left standing in the hall, or limited to one or two "public rooms"; we are privileged to enter the King's privacy, and be nourished at the King's table, and listen to the King's table-talk concerning "all things" which He has heard of the Father. We have "the glorious liberty of *the children* of God."

And the "Lord's own" will experience the world's hatred. *"Therefore the world hateth you."* Our very friendship with the Lord pronounces judgment on the world, and its hostility is aroused. If we are "partakers of the glory" we shall most assuredly be "partakers of the sufferings of Christ."

## NOVEMBER The Fourth

### THE HOLY SPIRIT AS WITNESS
JOHN xv. 26—xvi. 11.

THE Holy Spirit is to be a witness of Jesus. "*He shall testify of Me.*" He shall be "the Friend of the Bridegroom," and He shall sing the Bridegroom's grace, and goodness, and prowess, in the eager ear of the bride. And the early love of the bride shall become deeper and richer as more and more she enters into "the unsearchable riches of Christ."

And the Holy Spirit is thus to be a strengthener of the friends of the Lord. He will be my "*Comforter.*" By His gracious advocacy He will make my faith and hope invincible. The best service which can be rendered me is not to change my circumstances, but to make me superior to them; not to make a smooth road, but to enable me to "leap like an hart" over any road; not to remove the darkness, but to make me "sing songs in the night." And so I will not pray for less burdens, but for more strength! And this is the gracious ministry of "The Comforter."

Holy Spirit, strengthen me! Transform my frail opinions into firm convictions, and change my fleeting, dissolving views into abiding visions!

## NOVEMBER The Fifth

### THE TEMPLE OF THE BODY
ROMANS xii. 1-9.

THE Lord wants my body. He needs its members as ministers of righteousness. He would work in the world through my brain, and eyes, and ears, and lips, and hands, and feet.

And the Lord wants my body as "*a living sacrifice.*" He asks for it when it is thoroughly alive! We so often deny the Lord our bodies until they are infirm and sickly, and sometimes we do not offer them to Him until they are quite "worn out." It is infinitely better to offer them even then than never to offer them at all. But it is best of all to offer our bodies to our Lord when they are strong, and vigorous, and serviceable, and when they can be used in the strenuous places of the field.

And so let me appoint a daily consecration service, and let me every morning present my body "a living sacrifice" unto God. Let me regard it as a most holy possession, and let me keep it clean. Let me recoil from all abuse of it—from all gluttony, and intemperance, and "riotous living." Let me look upon my body as a church, and let the service of consecration continue all day long. "Know ye not that your bodies are the temples of the Holy Spirit?"

## NOVEMBER The Sixth

### PEACE IN TRIBULATION
JOHN xvi. 25-33.

HERE is a strange medley of experiences! I am to enjoy the gift of peace, and yet I am to be smarting under tribulation!

When the Holy Spirit is my guest I am to enjoy the gift of peace. *"These things I said unto you that ye might have peace."* The life of the soul is to move without jar or discord. It shall be like a quiet engine-house, in which every wheel co-operates with every other wheel, and there is no waste or friction in the holy place. "All that is within me" blesses God's holy name.

And yet, while peace reigns within, there may be tribulation without! *"In the world ye shall have tribulation."* Here is a peace which is not broken by the noise and assault of brutal circumstance. The most tempestuous wind cannot disturb the quiet serenity of the stars. When the world stones me, not one grain of its gritty dust need enter the delicate workings of my soul. That was the peace of my Lord, and it is my Lord who says to me: "My peace I give unto you!" So *"be of good cheer,"* my soul! Thy Lord has *"overcome the world,"* and thou shalt share His victory.

## NOVEMBER The Seventh

### REJECTED LOVE
Isaiah lxiii. 7-14.

IF I refuse the friendship of the Holy One I inevitably invite His hostility. "*But they rebelled, and vexed His holy Spirit: therefore He was turned to be their enemy, and He fought against them.*"

And so, if I reject the forces of grace I do not turn them from my gate, I convert them into foes. Malachi teaches me that rejected sunshine becomes like a burning oven. The Epistle to the Hebrews teaches me that rejected love becomes "a consuming fire." Holiness nourishes virtue, it withers vice. If I offer my Lord a tender aspiration, His breath wooes it like the balmy air of the spring; if I come before Him with the weeds of ignoble dispositions, He blights them as with the nipping of the frost.

And is it not well, for thee and me, that our Lord is thus fiercely hostile to our sins? Is not this "consuming fire" the friend of my soul? May I not pray: Burn on, burn on, pure flame, until all the refuse and rubbish of my life are utterly consumed; burn on, burn on, until fierce flame becomes mild light, flinging its genial radiance over a transfigured desert?

## NOVEMBER The Eighth

### DOING THE IMPOSSIBLE
MATTHEW xxii. 1-14.

"*STRETCH forth thine hand!*" But that is just what he was unable to do. His hand was withered. His hand had hung there for years, a rebel to all the commands of the will. The Lord's imperative was the demand of the impossible! Yes, but the man obeyed. "He stretched it forth." What he had been unable to do he did at the bidding of the King.

Christ's commandments are always accompanied by adequate supplies of grace. His commandments are really inverted promises; every one is a true bond that the Lord will provide the needful power for its fulfilment. When we begin to obey we release the power, and we discover that the requisite ability has been given by the gracious Master who gave the call.

Let me, therefore, not fear the decree of the Lord. If "His commandments are exceeding broad," His love is exceeding deep. He will not mock our souls. He will not make us thirst, and then hold the water beyond our reach. He is faithful who called thee. Rise to obey, in all thy lameness, and thou shalt find that thy feet and ankle bones receive strength.

## THE HOLY SPIRIT AS EMANCIPATOR
### 2 Corinthians iii. 4-18.

IN the Holy Spirit I experience a large emancipation. "*Where the Spirit of the Lord is, there is liberty.*" I am delivered from all enslaving bondage—from the bondage of literalism, and legalism, and ritualism. I am not hampered by excessive harness, by multitudinous rules. The harness is fitting and congenial, and I have freedom of movement, and "my yoke is easy and my burden is light."

And I am to use my emancipation of spirit in the ministry of contemplation. I am to "*behold, as in a glass, the glory of the Lord.*" My thought has been set free from the cramping distractions devised by men, and I am now to feast my gaze upon the holy splendours of my Lord. It is like coming out of a little and belittling tent, to feast upon the sunny amplitude of the open sky! I can "cease from man," and commune with God.

And the contemplation will effect a transformation. "*We are changed into the same image from glory to glory.*" The serene brightness of the sky gets into our faces. The Lord becomes "*the health of our countenance,*" and we shine with borrowed glory.

## NOVEMBER The Tenth

### NEVERTHELESS!
#### LUKE v. 1-11.

HERE is obedience in spite of the night of failure. "*Nevertheless, at Thy word I will let down the net.*" That word "nevertheless" has always made history. It has been spoken after scourgings, after "bonds and imprisonments." Ten thousand times has it been heard in the chamber of bereavement, the first sound to break the awful silence. "At evening my wife died. . . . In the morning I did as God commanded me." And may it be true of me! May my "nevertheless" of willing obedience rise like a lark above the storm.

And because there was obedience there came vision. In the wonderful answer to his faith Peter beheld the glory of his Lord. And so I never know where the unenticing road of obedience will lead me. At the end of the dull road there will be some gracious surprise! It is the rugged path which leads to the summit! The panorama comes as the reward of the toilsome climb! Always, in the realm of the Spirit, the dogged "nevertheless" will lead to the "shining tableland to which our God Himself is moon and sun."

## NOVEMBER The Eleventh

### FOILING THE ENEMY'S PLOTS
LUKE xxii. 24-34.

DO not meet my tempter alone. The engagement has been foreseen by my Lord. *"Simon, Simon, Satan hath desired to have you!"* The tempter's plots, and wiles, and ambuscades are all clearly perceived. My Lord has got the enemy's maps, and his plan of campaign, for all things are open to the eyes of Him with whom we have to do. I do not fight a lonely warfare on a dark and unknown field. My Lord Himself both scouts and fights for those who are His own.

And one great means of His co-operation is the mighty ministry of intercession. *"But I have prayed for thee."* That "but" is the massing of the forces of heaven against the black and subtle hordes of hell. Let me ever remember that the Lord's prayers are always the conveyers of holy power to those for whom He prays. It is as when Christian met Apollyon in the Valley of Humiliation: there comes a sudden accession of strength to the bleeding warrior, and Apollyon retires wounded and beaten from the field.

And the only way to preserve the fruits of a triumph is by helping other warriors to gain a similar conquest. *"When thou art converted strengthen thy brethren."* I shall retain the hard, muscular limbs of a soldier if I am willing to share my blood with the entire army.

## NOVEMBER The Twelfth

### THE FASHIONING OF A DENIAL
Luke xxii. 54-62.

FROM Peter's denial I would learn the peril of the first cowardly surrender to sin. Surely Peter must have "trimmed" many times in the days which preceded his actual discipleship. Great crises do not make men, they reveal them. The men have been made in the smaller issues which go before. We march to our crises by a gradient, every step of which is a moral decision. The interior of the tree is secretly eaten away by white ants; the tempest reveals and completes the destruction.

And I would learn from Peter's denial the cumulative power of sins. One sin widens the road for a bigger one to follow. The second denial will be more vehement than the first. The third will add the element of blasphemy. Yes, every sin is a miner and sapper for a larger army in the rear. It not only does its own work, it prepares the way for its successor.

But I will connect this "dark betrayal night" with that sweet after-morning when the Lord and His denier met face to face by the lake. And that sweet morning of reconciliation is a possible experience for all the deniers of the Lord, and it is therefore possible for thee and me.

## NOVEMBER The Thirteenth

### A TRANSFORMED FISHERMAN

"*Simon Peter saith unto them, I go a fishing.*"
—John xxi. 1-14.

SIMON PETER had often gone a fishing, but never had he gone as he went in the twilight of that most wonderful evening. He handled the ropes in a new style, with a new dignity born of the bigger capacity of his own soul. He turned to the familiar task, but with a quite unfamiliar spirit. He went a fishing, but the power of the resurrection went with him.

This action of Simon Peter's is the only true test of the reality of any spiritual experience. How does it fit me for ordinary affairs? A spiritual festival should do for the soul what a day on the hills does for the body—equip it for the better doing of the duties in the vale.

This action is also a preparative to a renewal of the gracious experience. The road of common duty was just the way appointed for another meeting with his Lord, for in the morning-light there came a voice across the waters: "Children, have ye any meat?" "And that disciple whom Jesus loved saith unto Peter: 'It is the Lord.'"

## NOVEMBER The Fourteenth

### THE PURIFICATION OF LOVE
JOHN xxi. 15-25.

"LOVEST thou Me?" There was a day, only a little while back, when Simon Peter's love was not yet purified, and it indulged itself in loud and empty boasts. True love never blusters and brawls. It is like a stream of water flowing silently underground, and secretly bathing the roots of things, and keeping their heads fresh, and cool, and sweet. The boast has now dropped out of the love! It is now ashamed of words! "Lord, Thou knowest that I love Thee!"

Yes, true love expresses itself, not in clamorous boastfulness, but in quiet services. It ministers to the Lord's sheep and the Lord's lambs. It spends its strength on the mountains, "seeking that which is lost," and it does this in the darkness, where there is no applauding crowd. The true lover does not ask for some dramatic scene where he can die for the beloved; he delights in obscure services, the feeding and tending of the sheep of the flock.

But the love that does the humbler thing will be ready for the greater sacrifice whenever the day shall demand it. Some day the once boastful denier shall lay down his life for his Saviour, and through martyrdom he shall pass to his crown.

## NOVEMBER The Fifteenth

### THE MUSIC OF RECONCILIATION
Psalm lxxxv.

LET me listen to this psalm of reconciliation, as it makes music for my soul to-day.

It tells me of the Divine favour. "*Lord, Thou hast been favourable to Thy land.*" As I write these words, the sun has just slipped out from behind the cloud. It has been there all the time, but the ministry of the cloud was needed, and so it appeared as though there would be sun and spring no more. "Behind a frowning Providence He hides a smiling face."

And it tells me of the Divine forgiveness. "*Thou hast forgiven the iniquity of Thy people.*" Yes, when the sun appears, He loosens the frozen earth and streams, and turns the bondage into liberty. The soul that was imprisoned in freezing guilt attains a joyous freedom.

And it tells me of revival. "*Wilt Thou not revive us again?*" It is the next step in the returning spring. The sleeping, benumbed things will all awake! "The flowers appear on the earth." Where grace reigns, graces spring! Forgiveness is attended by renewal, and the wilderness begins to "blossom like the rose."

## NOVEMBER The Sixteenth

### THE MAKING OF A BRAVE MAN
#### ACTS iv. 13-22.

HERE is a marvellous transformation! I have been wondering at the littleness of the denier, and now this same denier is making the world wonder by his majestic boldness! His one resource is now the risen Christ, and his one moral standard is "whether it be right!" Once he quailed before an accusing maid; now he stands undaunted before the rulers of the earth. How has it all come about?

He has been to the empty tomb. The awe of the resurrection is upon his spirit. Through the once blind cul-de-sac of the grave he has seen the King and the great white throne.

And he has been by the lake on the morning of reconciliation. The live coal from the altar of his Lord's love has touched him and has purged away the uncleanness of his denial.

And he has been in the upper room at Pentecost, and the mighty Spirit has come upon him like wind and flame, endowing him with forceful and enthusiastic character. Now he can dare for God, now he can work for God, now he can burn for God! And this is how he has been transformed.

## NOVEMBER The Seventeenth

### IF GOD BE FOR US——!
#### ROMANS viii. 31-39.

WHO else is worth naming? How much does anybody count? If the sun be on my side, why should I be dismayed at any icy obstacle that may rear itself in my way? Sun *versus* ice! God *versus* my impediments! Why should I fear? If the atmosphere is on my side, then even the opposing strength of iron will rust away into powder. "The breath of the Lord bloweth upon it," and if the holy breath, God's Holy Spirit, is for us, then the apparently invincible obstacle will crumble away into dust.

But we are deceived by mass, and we are forgetful of spirit. Mere size affrights us. We are dismayed by numbers. We forget the quiet, pervasive, all-powerful ministry of the Spirit of God. We are overwhelmed by the phenomena of tempest and earthquake and fire, and we forget that almightiness hides in the "still, small voice," in "the sound of a gentle stillness." God's breath is more than the fierce threatenings of embattled hosts. "If God be for us, who can be against us?" I will hide myself in His holy fellowship, and "none shall make me afraid."

## NOVEMBER The Eighteenth

### EXHILARANT SPIRITS

"*He maketh my feet like hinds' feet.*"—PSALM xviii. 31-39.

THINK of Wordsworth's lines, in which he describes a natural lady, made by Nature herself:

"She shall be sportive as the fawn
That wild with glee across the lawn
Or up the mountain springs."

And it is this buoyancy, this elasticity, this springiness that the Lord is waiting to impart to the souls of His children, so that they may move along the ways of life with the light steps of the fawn.

Some of us move with very heavy feet. There is little of the fawn about us as we go along the road. There is reluctance in our obedience. There is a frown in our homage. Our benevolence is graceless, and there is no charm in our piety, and no rapture in our praise. We are the victims of "the spirit of heaviness." And yet here is the word which tells us that God will make our feet "like hinds' feet." He will give us exhilaration and spring, enabling us to leap over difficulties, and to have strength and buoyancy for the steepest hills. Let us seek the inspiration of the Lord. "It is God that girdeth me with strength, and maketh my way perfect."

## THE ARMOUR OF GOD
### Ephesians vi. 10-18.

THE Word describes the armour, and it directs us to the armoury. The description would oppress me if the directions were absent. If I have to forge the armour for myself I should be in despair. But I can go to the armoury of grace, where there is an ever-open door and abundant welcome for every person who fain would be a knight-errant of the Lord. The Lord will provide me with perfect equipment suitable for every kind of contest which may meet me along the road. There are no favourites among the pilgrims except, perhaps, the neediest, and to them is given " more abundant honour."

Sometimes one of the Lord's knights loses one piece of armour, and he must at once repair to the armoury. Perhaps he has lost his helmet, or his shield, or even his breastplate, and the enemy has discovered his vulnerable place. We must never continue our journey imperfectly armed. The evil one will ignore the pieces we have, and he will direct all his attack where there is no defence. Back to the armoury! Back to the armoury, that we may "put on the *whole* armour of God." The Lord is waiting; let us humbly and penitently ask for the missing piece.

## NOVEMBER The Twentieth

### THE REAL ARISTOCRACY
"*Abraham, my friend.*"—ISAIAH xli. 8-16.

I THINK that is the noblest title ever given to mortal man. It is the speech of the Lord God concerning one of His children. It is something to be coveted even to enjoy the friendship of a noble man; but to have the friendship of God, and to have the holy God name us as His friends, is surely the brightest jewel that can ever shine in a mortal's crown. And such recognition and such glory may be the wonderful lot of thee and me.

"Abraham, my friend." The Lord of hosts found delight in human friendships. He comes in to sup with us. He drinks of the cup of our delights. For, surely, it is one of the supreme characteristics of true friendship that it rejoices at the other's joy. And my heavenly Friend is glad in my gladness as well as sympathetic in the day of sadness and tears. Yes, He comes in to sup with me, and I may sup with Him.

"Abraham, my friend." And He shares His sweets with His friend, in inward counsels, and in tender revelations of His purposes and in the gifts of joy and peace. There is perfect openness between these friends; nothing is hid. They have the run of each other's hearts.

"I tell Him all my joys and fears,
And He reveals His love to me."

## THE EARLY BUILDERS
### 1 Kings viii. 1-21.

IT is always a healthy means of grace to link my own accomplishments with the fidelity and achievements of the past. Solomon traced his finished Temple to the holy purpose in the heart of David his father. I lay the coping-stone, but who turned the first sod? I lead the water into new ministries, but who first dug the well?

There is the temple of liberty. In our own day we are enriching it with most benignant legislation, but we must not forget our dauntless fathers, in whose blood the foundations were laid. When I am walking about in the finished structure, let me remember the daring architects who "did well" to have it in their hearts.

Such retrospect will make me humble. It will save me from the isolation and impotence of foolish pride. It will confirm me in human fellowship by showing me how many springs I have in my fellowmen.

And such retrospect will make me grateful to my God. Noble outlooks always engender the spirit of praise. The fine air of wide spaces quickens the soul to a song.

## NOVEMBER The Twenty-second

### RECOVERING LOST STRENGTH
1 KINGS viii. 22-36.

IN this portion of this great prayer I discern the unalterable mode in which nations and individuals recover their moral health and strength.

How do they lose it? Two words tell the story. They "*sin*" and are "*smitten*." It is an inevitable sequence. Every sin is the minister of disease. Sometimes we can see it, when the disease flaunts its flags in the flesh; lust and drunkenness have glaring placards, and we know what is going on within. But even when sin makes no visible mark the wasting process is at work. It is as true of falsehood as of drunkenness, of treachery as of lust. "Evil shall slay the wicked."

And how do we recover our lost estate? There are three words which tell the story. "*Turn!*" "*Confess!*" "*Make supplication!*" The words need no exposition. I must turn my face to my despised and neglected Lord; I must tell them all about my miserable revolt, and I must humbly crave for His restoring grace.

And the answer is sure. Such humble exercise sets the joy-bells ringing, and the rich forgiveness of the Lord fills the soul with peace. "O taste and see how gracious the Lord is."

## THE STRANGER
1 Kings viii. 37-53.

YES, indeed, what space has "the stranger" in my supplications? Has he any place at all? Are my intercessions private enclosures, intended only for the select among my friends? Do I ever open the door to anyone outside my family circle? Are my ecclesiastical sympathies large enough to include "outsiders" from afar? What do I do with "the stranger"?

There is nothing which keeps prayer sweet and fresh and wholesome like the letting in of "the stranger"! To let a new guest sit down at the feast of my intercession is to give my own soul a most nutritious surprise. It is a most healthy spiritual habit to see to it that we bring in a new "stranger" every time we pray. Let me be continually enlarging the circle of hospitality! Let some new and weary bird find a resting-place in the branches of my supplications every time I hold communication with God.

A prayer which has no room for "the stranger" can have little or no room for God.

## NOVEMBER The Twenty-fourth

### THE PRAYER WHICH ENDS IN SACRIFICE

1 KINGS viii. 54-66.

AND that is the healthy order of all true worship. It begins in spacious supplication in which "the stranger" finds a place. Then there is a lavish consecration of self and substance. And then the wedding-bells begin to ring, and "the joy of the Lord is our strength!" *"They went unto their tents joyful and glad of heart for all the goodness that the Lord had done."*

But so many suppliants miss the middle term, and therefore the gladness is wanting. Supplication is not followed by consecration, and therefore there is no exultation. It is a fatal omission. When we are asking for "the gift of God" our request must be accompanied by the gift of ourselves to God. If we want the water we must offer the vessel. No gift of self, no bounty of God! No losing, no finding! "When the burnt offering began, the song of the Lord began."

"Take my life, and let it be
Consecrated, Lord, to Thee."

## NOVEMBER The Twenty-fifth

### AFTER THE PRAYER THE FIRE!

*"When Solomon had made an end of praying the fire came down from heaven."*—2 CHRONICLES vii. 1-11.

AND the fire is the symbol of the Holy God. Pure flame is our imperfect mode of expressing the Incorruptible. This burning flame is heat and light in one. And when Solomon had prayed, the holy Flame was in their midst.

But not only is the flame the symbol of the Holy; it also typifies the power which can make me holy. We have no cleansing minister to compare with fire. Where water fails fire succeeds. After an epidemic water is comparatively impotent. We commit the infested garments to the flames. It was the great fire of London which delivered London from the tyranny of the plague. And so it is with my soul. God, who is holy flame, will burn out the germs of my sin. He will "purify Jerusalem with the spirit of burning." "Our God is a consuming fire."

Come to my soul, O holy Flame! Place Thy "burning bliss" against my wickedness, and consume it utterly away!

## NOVEMBER The Twenty-sixth

### UNCONSECRATED SOULS

*"This house which I have sanctified will I cast out of my sight, and will make it a proverb and a by-word among all nations."*—2 CHRONICLES vii. 12-22.

AND thus am I taught that consecrated houses are nothing without consecrated souls. It is not the mode of worship, but the spirit of the worshipper which forms the test of a consecrated people. If the worshipper is defiled his temple becomes an offence. When the kernel is rotten, and I offer the husk to God, the offering is a double insult to His most holy name.

And yet, how tempted I am to assume that God will be pleased with the mere outsides of things, with words instead of aspiration, with postures instead of dispositions, with the letter instead of the spirit, with an ornate and costly temple instead of a sweet and lowly life! Day by day I am tempted to treat the Almighty as though He were a child! Nay, the Bible uses a more awful word; it says men treat the Lord as though He were a fool!

From all such irreverence and frivolity, good Lord, deliver me! Let me ever remember that Thou "desirest truth in the *inward* man." "In the hidden parts" help me "to know wisdom."

## THE VALUE OF REVERENCE
### ROMANS xiii. 1-7.

WHEN I pay honour to honourable ministers I not only honour my God, but I enrich and refine my own soul. One of the great secrets of spiritual culture is to know how to revere. There is an uncouth spirit of self-aggression which, while it wounds and impoverishes others, destroys its finest spiritual furniture in its own ungodly heat. The man who never bows will never soar. To pay homage where homage is due is one of the exercises which will help to keep us near "the great white throne."

I know my peril, for I recognize one of the prevalent perils of our time. Some of the old courtesies are being discarded as though they belonged to a younger day. Some of the old tokens of respect have been banished to the limbo of rejected ritual. Dignitaries are jostled in the common crowd. "One man is as good as another!" And so there is a tendency to strip life of all its reverences, and venerable fanes become stables for unclean things.

My soul, come thou not into this shame! Move in the ways of life with softened tread, and pay thy respect at every shrine where dwells the grace and power of God.

## NOVEMBER The Twenty-eighth

### HOW TO FIGHT EVIL

*"Overcome evil with good."*—ROMANS xii. 9-21.

FOR how else can we cast out evil? Satan cannot cast out Satan. No one can clean a room with a filthy duster. The surgeon cannot cut out the disease if his instruments are defiled. While he removed one ill-growth he would sow the seed of another. It must be health which fights disease. It will demand a good temper to overcome the bad temper in my brother.

And therefore I must cultivate a virtue if I would eradicate a vice. That applies to the state of my own soul. If there be some immoral habit in my life, the best way to destroy it is by cultivating a good one. Take the mind away from the evil one. Deprive it of thought-food. Give the thought to the nobler mood, and the ignoble mood will die. And this also applies to the faults and vices of my brother. I must fight them with their opposites. If he is harsh and cruel, I must be considerate and gentle. If he is grasping, I must be generous. If he is loud and presumptuous, I must be soft-mannered and self-restrained. If he is devilish, I must be a Christian. This is the warfare which tells upon the empire of sin. I can overcome evil with good.

## NOVEMBER The Twenty-ninth

### TRANSFORMING OUR FOES
MATTHEW v. 38-48.

"LOVE your enemies."

It must be the aim of a Christian to make his enemy lovely. It is not my supreme business to secure my safety, but to remove his ugliness. He may only annoy me, but he is destroying himself. He may injure my reputation; but far worse, he is blighting his own character. Therefore must I seek to remove the greater thing, the corrosive malady in his own soul. I must make it my purpose to recover his loveliness, and restore the lost likeness of the Lord.

And only love can make things lovely. Revenge can never do it. Even duty will fail in the gracious work. There is a final touch, a consummate bloom, to which duty can never attain, and which is only attainable by love. All love's ministries are creative of loveliness. Wherever her finger rests, something exquisite is born. Love is a great magician; she transforms the desert into a garden, and she makes the wilderness blossom like the rose.

But where shall we get the love wherewith to make our enemy lovely? From the great Lover Himself. "We love, because He first loved us." The great Lover will love love into us! And we, too, shall become fountains of love, for our Lord will open "rivers in the high places, and fountains in the midst of the valleys."

## NOVEMBER The Thirtieth

### THE SPRING AND THE RIVER
"*With the Lord there is mercy.*"—Psalm cxxx.

THAT is the ultimate spring. All the pilgrims of the night may meet at that fountain. We have no other common meeting-place. If we make any other appointment we shall lose one another on the way. But we can meet one another at the fountain, men of all colours, and of all denominations, and of all creeds. "By Thy mercy, O deliver us, good Lord!"

"*There is forgiveness with Thee.*" That is the quickening river. Sin and guilt scorch the fair garden of the soul as the lightning withers and destroys the strong and beautiful things in woodland and field. The graces are stricken, holy qualities are smitten, and the soul languishes like a blasted heath. But from the fountain of God's mercy there flows the vitalizing stream of His forgiveness. "There is a river the streams whereof shall make glad the city of God." It is the mystic "river of life, clear as crystal." "Everything shall live whither the river cometh."

"*With Him is plenteous redemption.*" Salvation is not merely a recovered flower, it is a recovered garden. It is not the restoring merely of a withered hand; "He restoreth my soul." God does not make an oasis in a surrounding desert; He makes the entire wilderness to "rejoice and blossom as the rose."

## DECEMBER The First

### A FAITHFUL FRIEND
PROVERBS xxvii. 1-10.

"A FAITHFUL *friend is a strong defence.*"

He is a gift of God, and therefore a "means of grace." The Lord's seal is upon his ministry. How we impoverish ourselves by separating these precious gifts from their Giver? We desecrate many a fair shrine by emptying it of God. We turn many a temple into just a common house. When we think of our friend let us link him to our Father, and fall upon our knees in grateful praise.

He is God's minister in his encouragements. When he cheers me, it is "the Sun of righteousness who rises with healing in His wings." All radiant words are just lamps for "the light of life." All genial speech carries flame from the altar fire of heaven.

And he is God's minister in his reproofs. He uses a clean knife: there is no poison on the blade. And when he does surgeon's work upon me, it is clean work, healthy work, the relentless enemy of disease. Some men cut me, and the wound festers. There is malice in the deed. My friend wounds me in order that he may give me a larger, sweeter life.

## DECEMBER The Second

### THE LORD AS A FRIEND
#### JOHN xv. 8-17.

"YE are my friends!"

In my Lord's friendship there is *the ministry of sacrifice.* "Greater love hath no man than this, that a man lay down his life for his friends." This great Friend is always giving His blood. It is a lasting shame when professed Christians are afflicted with spiritual anæmia. And yet we are often so fearful, so white-faced, so chicken-hearted, so averse from battle, that no one would think us to be "the soldiers of the Lord." We need blood. "Except ye drink my blood ye have no life."

And in my Lord's friendship there is the *privilege of most intimate communion.*

"All things that I have heard of my Father I have made known unto you." He takes us into His confidence, and tells us His secrets. It is His delight to lift the veil, and give us constant surprises of love and grace. He discovers flowers in desert places, and in the gloom He unbosoms "the treasures of darkness." He is a Friend of inexhaustible resource, and His companionship makes the pilgrim's way teem with interest, and abound in the wonders of redeeming grace.

## DECEMBER The Third

### ARMS AND THE MAN!
#### 1 Thessalonians v. 4-10.

WHAT wonderful armour is offered to me in which to meet the insidious assaults of the devil!

There is *"the armour of light."* Sunlight is the most sanative energy we know. It is the foe of many a deadly microbe which seeks a lodging in our bodies. Light is a splendid armour, even in the realm of the flesh. And so it is in the soul. If the soul is a home of light, the eternal light, evil germs will die as soon as they approach us. They will find nothing to breed on. "The prince of this world cometh, and hath nothing in me."

And there is the armour of *"faith and love."* The opposite to faith is uncertainty, and the opposite to love is cynicism, and who does not know that uncertainty and cynicism are the very hotbeds for the machinations of the evil one? When faith is enthroned the soul is open to the reception of grace, and when love shares the throne the sovereignty is invincible.

And there is the armour of *"hope."* Even in a physical ailment a man has a mighty ally who wrestles in hope. And when a man's hope is in the Lord his God all the powers in the heavenly places are his allies, and by his hope he shall be saved.

## DECEMBER The Fourth

### CHILDREN OF LIGHT
1 Thessalonians v. 5-11.

CAN we think of a more beautiful figure than this—"*children of light*"? As I write these words I look out upon a building every window of which is ablaze with light, every room the home of attractive brightness. And my life is to be like that! And I look again and I see a lighthouse sending out its strong, pure, friendly beams to guide the mariner as he seeks his "desired haven." And my life is to be like that! And I look once more, and I see a common road lamp, sending its useful light upon the busy street, helping the wayfarer as he goes from place to place. And my life is to be like that!

And if my soul is all lit up in friendly radiance for others, the light will be my own defence. Light always scares away the vermin. Lift up a stone in the meadow, let in the light, and see how a hundred secret things will scurry away. And light in the soul scares away "the unfruitful works of darkness"; they cannot dwell with the light. Light repels the evil one; it acts upon him like burning flame. Yes, we are well protected when we are clothed in "the armour of light."

But how can we become "children of light," holy homes of protective and saving radiance? Happily, it is not our lot to provide the light, it is ours to provide the lamp. If we offer the lamp the Lord will give the flame.

## THE SECOND-BEST FOR GOD
### 1 Chronicles xvii. 1-15.

SO the best was for man, and the second-best for God! The cedar for self-indulgence, and the curtains for the home of worship! It is a marked sign of spiritual awakening when a man begins to contrast his own indulgences with the rights of God. There are so many of us who are lavish in our home and miserly in the sanctuary. We multiply treasures which bring us little profit, and we are niggardly where treasure would be of most gracious service.

"I dwell in a house of cedar," and yet I am thoughtless about God's poor! For I must remember that the poor are the arks of the Lord. "I was naked, and ye clothed Me not."

"I dwell in a house of cedar"; my liberties are many and spacious; and yet there are tribes of God's people held in the tyranny of dark and hopeless servitude. I dwell in England, but what about the folk on the Congo? I dwell in a land of ample religious freedom, but what about Armenia? Do my sympathies remain confined within my cedar walls, or do they go out to God's neglected ones in every land and clime?

## DECEMBER The Sixth

### THE GRACE OF LOWLINESS
1 CHRONICLES xvii. 16-27.

IT is by such lowliness that we arrive at our true sovereignty. All spiritual treasures are hidden along the ways of humility, and it is meekness which discovers them. The uplifted head of pride overlooks them, and its "finds" are only pleasure of the passing day.

Lowliness is the secret of spiritual perceptiveness. I find my sight in lowly places. The Sacred Word speaks of "the *valley* of vision." I usually associate vision and outlook with mountain summits, but in spiritual realms the very capacity to use the heights is acquired in the vale.

Lowliness is the secret of spiritual roominess. It is only the humble man who has any room for the Lord. All the chambers in the proud man's soul are thronged with self-conceits, and God is crowded out. Our Lord always finds ample room for Himself wherever the heart bows in humility and says: "I am not worthy that Thou shouldst come under my roof."

## CHOSEN AS BUILDERS

*"Take heed now, for the Lord hath chosen thee to build."*—1 CHRONICLES xxviii. 1-10.

AND how must he take heed? For it may be that the Lord hath also chosen me to build, and the counsel given to Solomon may serve me in this later day. Let me listen.

*"Serve Him with a perfect heart."* God's chosen builders must be characterized by singleness and simplicity. He can do nothing with "double" men, who do things only "by half," giving one part to Him and the other part to Mammon. It is like offering the stock of a gun to one man and the barrel to another; and the effect is nil. No, the entire gun! The "perfect heart"!

*"And with a willing mind."* For the willing mind is the ready mind, and God can do nothing with the unready. I never know just when He will call me to add another stone to the rising walls of the New Jerusalem, and if I am "otherwise engaged" I am a grievous hindrance to His gracious plans. He must be willing and ready who would be a builder of the walls of Zion. And to that man the Lord will entrust the privilege of responsibility.

## DECEMBER The Eighth

### JUDGED BY OUR ASPIRATIONS

*"Thou didst well, it was in thine heart."*—2 CHRONICLES vi. 1-15.

AND this was a purpose which the man was not permitted to realize. It was a temple built in the substance of dreams, but never established in wood and stone. And God took the shadowy structure and esteemed it as a perfected pile. The sacred intention was regarded as a finished work. The will to build a temple was regarded as a temple built. And hence I discern the preciousness of all hallowed purpose and desire, even though it never receive actual accomplishment. "Thou didst well, it was in thine heart."

And so the will to be, and the will to do, is acceptable sacrifice unto the Lord! "I wish I could be a missionary to the foreign field," but the duties of home forbid. But as a missionary she is accepted of our God, even though she never land on distant shore. Our purposes work, as well as the work itself. Desire is full of holy energy as well as fruition. The wish to do good is good itself; the very longing is a minister in the kingdom of our God. If, therefore, we are to be judged by our aspirations, there are multitudes of apparent failures who will one day be revealed as clothed in the radiance of spiritual victory.

## NATIONAL BLESSEDNESS

*"Blessed is the people that know the joyful sound."*—PSALM lxxxix. 1-18.

BLESSED is the people who love the sound of the silver trumpet which calls to holy convocation! Blessed is the people who are sacredly impatient for the hour of holy communion! Blessed is the people "in whose heart are the highways to Zion." And in what shall their blessedness consist?

In illumination. *"They shall walk, O Lord, in the light of Thy countenance."* The favour of the Lord shall shine upon them when they walk through rough and troublous places. There shall always be a sunny patch where the soul is in communion with its Lord.

In exultation. *"In Thy name shall they rejoice all the day."* There is nothing like sunshine for making the spirits dance! Light is a great emancipator, a great breaker-up of frozen bondages. It thaws "the genial currents of the soul," and the stream of life sings in its progress.

In exaltation. *"In Thy righteousness shall they be exalted."* They will be lifted up above their enemies. In elevation they will find their safety. God lifts us above our passions, above our cares, above our little fears and tempers, and we find our peace upon the heights.

## DECEMBER The Tenth

### THE ONLY WISE BEGINNING

*"The fear of the Lord is the beginning of wisdom."*—PSALM cxi.

IF I want to do anything wisely I must begin with God. That is the very alphabet of the matter. Every other beginning is a perverse beginning, and it will end in sure disaster. "I am Alpha." Everything must take its rise in Him, or it will plunge from folly into folly, and culminate in confusion.

If I would be wise in my daily business I must begin all my affairs in God. My career itself must be chosen in His presence, and in the illumination of His most holy Spirit. And in the subsequent days nothing must be done that is not rooted and grounded in Him.

If I would be wise as a teacher I must begin with God. I must not merely call Him in to bless my lesson when my labour is done. The very beginnings of my thinkings must be in Him. Our Lord will not write an appendix to a volume about which He has never been consulted. "They who seek Me *early* shall find Me." And so it is with the varied activities of our multitudinous life. If we would have them shine with quiet wisdom we must light them at the Sun of glory.

## DECEMBER The Eleventh

### THE SPEECH OF THE INCARNATION

*"He hath spoken to us in His Son."*—
HEBREWS i.

AND that blessed Son spake my language. He came into my troubled conditions and expressed Himself out of my humble lot. My surroundings afforded Him a language in which He made known His good news. The carpenter's shop, the shepherd on the hill, the ladened vine, a wayside well, common bread, a friend's sickness, the desolation of a garden, the darkness of "the last things"— these all offered Him a mode of speech in which He unveiled to me the heart of God.

He came as the Son to make me a son. For I had made myself a slave, and called my bondage freedom. I wore my badge of servitude with unholy pride. But when He came and spake to me, my lost inheritance dawned upon my wondering eyes, and I knew myself to be enslaved. But His was the glorious mission not only to awake but to emancipate, not only to unveil lost splendour but to recover it. He came to set us free, "and if the Son shall make you free ye shall be free indeed."

"This my son was lost and is found." Has that great word been spoken concerning me in the Father's home of light? "Lord, I would serve, and be a son, Dismiss me not, I pray."

## DECEMBER The Twelfth

### RELATING EVERYTHING TO GOD

*"Whether therefore ye eat, or drink, or whatever ye do, do all to the glory of God."*—1 CORINTHIANS x. 23-33.

AND so all my days would constitute a vast temple, and life would be a constant worship. This is surely the science and art of holy living—to relate everything to the Infinite. When I take my common meal and relate it to "the glory of God," the common meal becomes a sacramental feast. When my labour is joined "unto the Lord," the sacred wedding turns my workshop into a church. When I link the country lane to the Saviour, I am walking in the Garden of Eden, and paradise is restored.

The fact of the matter is, we never see anything truly until we see it in the light of the glory of God. Set a dull duty in that light and it shines like a diamond. Set a bit of drudgery in that light and it becomes transfigured like the wing of a starling when the sunshine falls upon it. Everything is seen amiss until we see it in the glory! And, therefore, it is my wisdom to set everything in that light, and to do all to the glory of God.

## DECEMBER The Thirteenth

### THE HOLY AND THE PROFANE

*"Put difference between the holy and the unholy."*—LEVITICUS x. 1-10.

THE peril of our day is that so many of these differences are growing faint. The holy merges into the unholy, and we can scarcely see the dividing line. Black merges into white through manifold shades of grey. Falsehood slopes into truth through cunning expediences and white lies. Lust merges into purity through conviviality and geniality and good-fellowship. So is one thing losing itself in another, and vivid moral distinctions are being obscured and effaced.

There is only one way to keep these native contrasts in vivid relief, and that is by living in the unsullied light of God's holy presence. "In Thy light shall we see light." Things are seen in their true colours only when we bring them before the great white throne. Fabrics seen in the gas-light reveal quite other shades when we bring them into the light of day. We must not make our distinctions in the gas-light of worldly standard and expediency; we must take them into His presence before whose radiance even the angels veil their faces, and we shall see things as they are, and we shall know "the difference between the holy and the profane."

## DECEMBER The Fourteenth

### THE SACRED USE OF LIBERTY
*"Take heed lest this liberty of yours becomes a stumbling-block."*—1 CORINTHIANS viii. 8-13.

THAT is a very solemn warning. My liberty may trip someone into bondage. If life were an affair of one my liberty might be wholesome; but it is an affair of many, and my liberty may be destructive to my fellows. I am not only responsible for my life, but for its influence. When a thing has been lived there is still the example to deal with. If orange peel be thrown upon the pavement, that is not the end of the feast. The man who slips over the peel is a factor in the incident, and my responsibility covers him.

I am, therefore, to consider both my deeds and their influence. How does my life trend when it touches my brother? In what way does he move because of the impact of my example? Towards liberty or towards license? To the swamps of transgression or to the fields of holiness? These are determining questions, and I must not seek to escape or ignore them. My brother is a vital part of my life. I must never shut him out of my sight. How is he influenced by my example? "If meat make my brother to stumble, I will eat no flesh while the world standeth."

## WHAT IS MY TENDENCY?

*"Whether we live, we live unto . . ."*—
ROMANS xiv. 7-21.

UNTO what? In what direction are we living? Whither are we going? How do we complete the sentence? "We live unto *money!*" That is how many would be compelled to finish the record. Money is their goal, and their goal determines their tendency. "We live unto *pleasure!*" Such would be another popular company. "We live unto *fame!*" That would be the banner of another regiment. "We live unto *ease!*" Thus would men and women describe their quests. "Unto" what? That is the searching question which probes life to its innermost desire.

"For whether we live, we live *unto the Lord.*" That was the apostle's unfailing tendency, increasing in its momentum every day. He crashed through obstacles in his glorious quest. He sought the Lord through everything and in everything. When new circumstances confronted him, his first question was this— "Where is Christ in all this?" He found the right way across every trackless moor by simply seeking Christ.

## DECEMBER The Sixteenth

### THE GREATEST WONDERS
HEBREWS xi. 30-40.

THE greatest wonders are not in Nature but in grace. A regenerated soul is a greater marvel than the marvel of the spring-time. A transfigured face is a deeper mystery than a sun-lit garden. To rear graces in a life once scorched and blasted by sin is more wonderful than to grow flowers on a cinder-heap. If we want to see the realm of surpassing wonders we must look into a soul that has been born again and is now in vital union with the living Christ. Even the angels watch the sight with ever-deepening awe and praise.

As the spiritual is the home of wonders, so also is it the field of brightest exploits. It is not what men have done by the sword that counts in the esteem of heaven—such deeds mean little or nothing; it is what they have done " by faith." Weak, frail men and women have put their faith in God, and have done the impossible! Faith unites the weakling with almightiness! Faith makes a lonely soul one with " the spirits of just men made perfect," and with them he shares " the power and the glory " of the eternal God.

## GOD'S PRESENCE OUR DEFENCE
### Exodus xv. 11-18.

WHEN we invent little devices to protect us against the evil one, he laughs at our petty presumption. It is like unto a child erecting sand ramparts against an incoming sea. The only thing that makes the devil fear is the presence of God. Our money can do nothing. Our culture can do nothing. Our social status can do nothing. Only God can deal with devils. "By the greatness of Thine arm they shall be still as a stone." When Thou art with me "I will fear no evil"; the fear shall be with my foes.

It is, therefore, the divine in anything which endows it with a strong defence. If the holy God dwells in our culture, then our culture becomes like an invulnerable fort. If God abides in our recreations, then our very sports are armed against our foes. If "the joy of the Lord" is in our festivity, then our very merriment is proof against the invasion of the world. When the Lord is in us, fear dwells in the opposite camp. "Therefore will not we fear though the earth be removed, and though the mountains be shaken in the heart of the seas."

## DECEMBER The Eighteenth

### THE SINNER'S GUEST

"*He is gone to be guest with a man that is a sinner.*"—LUKE xix. 1-10.

IT was hurled as an accusation; it has been treasured as a garland. It was first said in contempt; it is repeated in adoration. It was thought to reveal His earthliness; it is now seen to unveil His glory. Our Saviour seeks the home of the sinner. The Best desires to be the guest of the worst. He spreads His kindnesses for the outcasts, and He offers His friendship to the exile on the loneliest road. He waits to befriend the defeated, the poor folk with aching consciences and broken wills. He loves to go to souls that have lost their power of flight, like birds with broken wings, which can only flutter in the unclean road. He went to Zacchæus.

Yes, the Lord went to be "guest with a man that is a sinner," and He changed the sinner into a saint. The worldling found wings. The stone became flesh. Gentle emotions began to stir in a heart hardened by heedlessness and sin. Restitution took the place of greed. The home of the sinner became the temple of the Lord. "To-day is salvation come to this house forasmuch as he also is a son of Abraham."

## DECEMBER The Nineteenth

### THE SUN OF RIGHTEOUSNESS
*"A light to lighten the Gentiles."*—LUKE ii. 25-40.

THAT was the wonder of wonders. Hitherto the light had been supposed to be for Israel alone; and now a heavenly splendour was to fall upon the Gentiles. Hitherto the light had been thought of as a lamp, illuming a single place; now it was to be a sun, shedding its glory upon a world. The "people that sat in darkness" are now to see "a great light." New regions are to be occupied; there is to be daybreak everywhere! "The Sun of Righteousness is arisen, with healing in His wings."

"To lighten the Gentiles!" And thus the heavenly beams have come to thee and me, to Europe and America, and to all the nations of the earth. The amazing privilege is our personal inheritance. We are born to glorious rights in Christ Jesus. But a wealthy heir may neglect this inheritance. We may have the light and neglect our garden. We may have all the favours of a blessed clime, and yet our life may be like a wilderness. The Gentiles may have the light, and may yet be children of the darkness. It is ours to believe in the light that our lives may become "light in the Lord."

## DECEMBER The Twentieth

### THE COMING OF THE LORD
#### JOHN i. 1-14.

MY Lord came as *"the word."* He came as the expression of the mind of the eternal God. Ordinary words could not have carried the " good news." Ordinary language was an altogether inadequate vessel for this new wine. And so the mighty news was spoken in the incarnation of the Lord.

My Lord came as " life." *"In Him was life."* But not a mere cupful of life, or even a cup running over. He came as " the fountain of life." Nay, if I had the requisite word I must get even behind and beyond this. For He was the Creator of fountains. " The water that I shall give him shall be *in him a well.*" Yes, He was the fountain of fountains!

The Lord came as " light." *"The life was the light."* True light is always the child of life. Our clearest light comes not from speech or doctrine, still less does it emerge from controversy. It is the fine, subtle issue of fine living. And my light is to " shine before men " by reason of the indwelling life of the Christ.

And my Lord came as " power." *"To them gave He power."* All the power I need for a full, holy, healthy life I can find in Him. Every obligation has its corresponding inspiration, and I am competent to do His will.

## DECEMBER The Twenty-first

### THE LORD OF WORKING MEN
LUKE ii. 8-20.

AND so the good news was told to shepherds, to working men who were toiling in the fields. The coming King would hallow the common work of man, and in His love and grace all the problems of labour would find a solution.

The Lord of the Christmas-tide throws a halo over common toil. Even Christian people have not all learnt the significance of the angels' visit to the lonely shepherds. Some of us can see the light resting upon a bishop's crosier, but we cannot see the radiance on the ordinary shepherd's staff. We can discern the hallowedness of a priest's vocation, but we see no sanctity in the calling of the grocer, or of the scavenger in the street. We can see the nimbus on the few, but not on the crowd; on the unusual, but not upon the commonplace. But the very birth-hour of Christianity irradiated the humble doings of humble people. When the angels went to the shepherds, common work was encircled with an immortal crown.

And it is in the Lord Jesus that all labour troubles are to be put to rest. If we work from any other centre we shall arrive at confusion confounded. "I have the keys."

## DECEMBER The Twenty-second

### THE LORD OF THE WORSHIPPER
LUKE ii. 25-35.

AND so the good news was taken to the worshipper bowing within the gates of the Temple. The soul of old Simeon was filled with holy satisfaction and peace. The cravings of the heart were quieted, and its desires found the coveted feast in the holy Child of God.

And thus the Lord Jesus was not only to dignify the body but to gratify the soul. He was to be most efficient where He was most needed. And this has been the unfailing experience of the years. There is a hunger in my soul for which I can find no satisfying bread. I have tried many breads; I have tried nature, and art, and music, and literature, and I have tried human fellowship and social service. But my soul is hungry still! And the Lord Jesus comes to me, as I reverently grope in the vast temple, and He " satisfies the hungry soul " with good things. His " bread of life " is very wonderful; it lifts the soul into the restfulness of strength, and gives me a strange buoyancy, and " the glorious liberty of the children of God."

" My soul, wait thou only on Him! " He is thy hope, thy strength, and thy salvation! **He is** " the desire of all the nations."

## THE LORD OF THE STUDENTS
### Matthew ii. 1-12.

AND so the good news came to "wise men," shall we say to students, busying themselves with the vast and intricate problems of the mind. And the evangel offered the students mental satisfaction, bringing the interpreting clue, beaming upon them with the guiding ray which would lead them into perfect noon.

Yes, our wise men must find the key of wisdom in the Lord. In a wider sense than the meaning of the original word it is true that "the fear of the Lord is the beginning of wisdom." To seek mental satisfactions and leave out Jesus is like trying to make a garden and leave out the sun. "Without Me ye can do nothing," not even in the unravelling of the problems which beset and besiege the mind.

If my mental pilgrimage is to be as "a shining light shining more and more even unto perfect day," I must begin with Jesus, and pay homage to His Kingly and incomparable glory. I must lay my treasures at His feet, "gold, and frankincense, and myrrh." Then will He lead me "into all truth," and "the truth shall make me free."

## DECEMBER The Twenty-fourth

### ENTERING IN AT LOWLY DOORS
*"Unto us a Child is born."*—ISAIAH ix. 1-7.

HOW gentle the coming! Who would have had sufficient daring of imagination to conceive that God Almighty would have appeared among men as a little child? We should have conceived something sensational, phenomenal, catastrophic, appalling! The most awful of the natural elements would have formed His retinue, and men would be chilled and frozen with fear. But He came as a little child. The great God "emptied Himself"; He let in the light as our eyes were able to bear it.

"*Unto us a Son is given.*" And that is the superlative gift! The love that bestows such gift is all-complete and gracious. And the Son is given in order that we may all be born into sonship. It is the Son's ministry to make sons. "Now are we the sons of God," and we are of His creation.

> "Lord, I would serve, and be a son;
> Dismiss me not, I pray."

## CHRISTMAS CHEER
*" Good will toward men."*—LUKE ii. 8-20.

THE heavens are not filled with hostility. The sky does not express a frown. When I look up I do not contemplate a face of brass, but the face of infinite good will. Yet when I was a child, many a picture has made me think of God as suspicious, inhumanly watchful, always looking round the corner to catch me at the fall. That " eye," placed in the sky of many a picture, and placed there to represent God, filled my heart with a chilling fear. That God was to me a magnified policeman, watching for wrong-doers, and ever ready for the infliction of punishment. It was all a frightful perversion of the gracious teaching of Jesus.

Heaven overflows with good will toward men! Our God not only wishes good, He wills it! " He gave His only begotten Son," as the sacred expression of His infinite good will. He has good will toward thee and me, and mine and thine. Let that holy thought make our Christmas cheer.

## DECEMBER The Twenty-sixth

### DAYBREAK IN THE SOUL
Isaiah ix. 1-7.

IT is a lonely and a chilling experience to sit in the darkness. And the gloom and the cold are all the more intense when there is death in the house. In such conditions we are in great need of light and fire.

And that is how the children of men were feeling before the Saviour came. They "*sat in darkness*" and in "*the shadow of death.*" The world was cold, and sin and death were in it, and they longed for light and cheer. And "the great Light came," and His wonderful Presence not only illumines the house but banishes the fear of sin and death. "*They that dwelt in the land of the shadow of death, upon them hath the light shined.*"

Where can we get this living light except in the Lord Jesus Christ? Everything else is candle-light! It fails us in the midnight. It flickers amid conflicting currents. It goes out in the rough blast. The light of art and of literature fails me when I need them most. When I sit in the darkness, with death in the house, these kindly ministers have no effective beams. I turn to the Master, and He shines upon me, and it is daybreak in the soul!

## DECEMBER The Twenty-seventh

### THE SUNNY SIDE OF THINGS
#### 1 John i. 1-7.

I HAVE just come out of a gloomy room into a sunny room to write these words. I had my choice. I could have stayed in the sombre room, but I choose to come into the sunlit room and the warm, cheering beams are even now falling upon my page. "Walk in the light!" And I make my choice, and how often I choose to walk without Christ in the unfertilizing and unfruitful gloom of self-will! In the light of the Lord I could have a garden of Eden; how often I choose the dingy wilderness where I can grow neither flowers nor fruits.

"Walk in the light." The Lord's companionship always makes the sunny side of the street. It may be that the way is rough and stony and difficult, but in His company there is light that never fails, compared with which the world's noontide is only as the gloomiest night. And the souls that "walk in the light" gather "sacred sweets" all along the way. Heavenly fruits grow for the children of light, fruits of love and joy and peace, and the favoured pilgrim plucks them as he goes along. "All I find in Jesus." The way of light is the way of delight, and "the joy of the Lord is our strength."

## DECEMBER The Twenty-eighth

### IN HIM WAS LIFE
#### John i. 1-18.

I HAVE heard men speak of "wanting to see a bit of life," and I found that what they meant was to see a bit of death. It is as if a man should go to the hospital to see a bit of health, or as if he should go to a gory battlefield to see the human frame. It is like going to a refuse-heap to see a bit of garden. Life is not found in fields of license; it is not found among the wild oats of a dissipated youth. Life is found only in Christ, and if we want to see a bit of life we must go to Him.

"In Him was life"; and that not merely to be looked at but to be shared. He is the well to which everybody can bring his pitcher, and take it away filled. And my pitcher is just my need. "All the fitness He requires is to feel our need of Him." The Life is all-sufficient for the needs of the race. This Life can vitalize all that is withered and dead; it can make decrepit wills muscular and mighty, and it can transfigure the leper with the glow and purity of perfect health.

"Thou of life the Fountain art,
　Freely let me take of Thee."

## THE LOVE OF GOD
1 JOHN iv. 7-14.

LET me more assiduously think of God's love. Let me sit down to it. In the National Gallery can be seen two sorts of people. There are the mere vagrants, who are always "on the move," passing from picture to picture, without seeing any. And there are the students, who sit down, and contemplate, and meditate, and appropriate, and saturate. And there are vagrants in respect to the love of the Lord. They have a passing glimpse, but the impression is not vital and vitalizing, and there are the students, who are always gazing, and who are continually crying, "O the depth of the riches of the love of God in Christ!" "His riches are unsearchable!"

And God's love is the creator of my love. "While I muse the fire burns." I am kindled into the same holy passion. That is to say, contemplation determines character. We acquire the hues of the things to which we cling. To hold fellowship with love is to become loveful and lovely. "We love because He first loved us."

And then, in the third place, it is through my love that I know my Lord. *"Everyone that loveth knoweth God."* Love is the lens through which I discern the secret things of God.

**WITHDRAWN**
from
Funderburg Library